T0090103

Acclaim for
GUNSHOTS IN MY COOK-UP

"An excellent storyteller, Hinds can write with equal intensity about his little brother's aspiration to be an MC, hiring an intern to go through 'the Wack Box,' or hurtling down the highway Raekwon and Ghostface. . . . [T]his is a fan's memoir first, and a journalist's chronicle second."
—*Publishers Weekly*

"[Hinds] brings literary sophistication to a culture usually associated with money, thugs, and hustling. Far from the usual suspects, Selwyn exemplifies a generation of kids who know the 'hood but refused to let the 'hood define them."
—Russell Simmons, founder, Def Jam Recordings

"An honest, poetic, and heartfelt memoir of a hip-hop head's love affair with the music. He succinctly captures the love-hate relationship that many people in the urban community have with rap, the often drama-filled industry, and the characters who thrive off of its multiplatinum pop success. His Caribbean upbringing and culture reminds us of hip-hop's roots and diversity while adding a fresh and enlightening perspective."

—Emil Wilbekin, editor-in-chief, *Vibe*

"Anyone who has used hip-hop as a guide to modern life will welcome this book by one of its most honest interpreters. Hinds's seasoned knowledge of the culture, combined with his insider portraits of the stars, allows him to show us why there is a thin line between love and hate in this music industry."

—Andrew Ross,
Director of American Studies at NYU
and author of *The Celebration Chronicles*
and *No-Collar*

GUNSHOTS IN MY COOK-UP

Bits and Bites from a
Hip-Hop Caribbean Life

SELWYN SEYFU HINDS

ATRIA BOOKS

NEW YORK LONDON TORONTO SYDNEY

ATRIA BOOKS
1230 Avenue of the Americas
New York, NY 10020

ISBN: 978-0-7434-5137-6
        0-7434-5137-6 (Pbk)

First Atria Books trade paperback edition January 2004

10 9 8 7 6 5 4 3 2 1

ATRIA BOOKS is a trademark of Simon & Schuster, Inc.

Manufactured in the United States of America

For information regarding special discounts for bulk purchases,
please contact Simon & Schuster Special Sales at 1-800-456-6798 or
business@simonandschuster.com

In loving memory of
Wesley Simon

contents

1. I Write This For . . . 1

2. My Brother the Rap Star 6

3. Starlite Nights 23

4. To Her 33

5. Young Black Teenagers 40

6. My Uzi Weighs a Ton 58

7. Ills of a Nation 78

8. The Source of It All 88

9. Bullets Over Tinseltown 143

10. Streets Is Watching 153

11. Return of Preacher Son 163

12. Coming Home 177

13. The Sweetest Thing [Observation] 188

14. Home of the Beast 196

15. The Maker 200

16. Me, Machine:
    The Curious Case of
    a Man Called Sean 215

Contents

17. Spirit Diary   236

18. The Sweetest Thing [Rationalization]   245

19. Rush Hour   256

20. Fathers and Daughters   283

21. Props Given   289

1

I WRITE THIS FOR...

I write this for you, lover of hip-hop. Because I once was, still am, and always shall be just like you. I, too, marvel at the growth of this music, this expression of style and being, from local phenomenon in the battered South Bronx streets of 1970s New York City to global economic and cultural force today. I, too, have embraced it as though it were all I had. And for much of my life it did seem like all I had.

I know you, lover of hip-hop. We may not worship the same names but I have also sat with ears fixed to nightly mix shows on the radio, listening to the likes of Marley Marl, DJ Red Alert, Stretch Armstrong and Bobbito, and Funkmaster Flex, DJ prophets all, administering mass to legions of the faithful. You exist for that moment, like I do, that span of three minutes when something new, something fantastic comes over the airwaves. A missive from artist through DJ, then, finally, to you.

I've felt it, lover of hip-hop. The rush of passion that seizes the heart. And I've seen you feel it right alongside me. A late night in a dark club, perhaps. Haze of smoke makes lazy swirls in the low light. And just visible through it, an MC onstage, clutching a microphone, delivering rhymes that arrest our attention and make us both empty spent lungs, leaving the very stuff of ourselves on that club floor.

I've been there with you, lover of hip-hop. Face clenched in anger, jaw tight with tension as authoritarian detractors took vicious whacks at this thing we so loved. And I, too, sat there, impotent, glued to a television screen or newspaper; helpless to counteract the media stage they strode with such command.

It crawls in my gut as it does in yours, lover of hip-hop. Idealism. Love. Total submission. No food is as filling, no liquor more potent.

I write this for you, as well, hater of hip-hop. Because as a member of the hip-hop generation, one who came of age to hip-hop's sounds and sights, ambivalence is my birthright. So at times disgust crawls across the trail, hot on the heels of the devoted love that has just passed by. Then the sight of one too many bikini-clad video vixens, or the latest model in a numbing procession of jewel-encrusted, poor-excuses-for-MCs makes me hurl the remote control away. Then the sound of yet another simulacrum of a rapper—another faceless drone rapping bullshit because bullshit is *easy*—makes me drift into a reactionary corner where I am visited only by hip-hop ghosts of yore, like Run-DMC, Rakim, and Big Daddy Kane.

I understand you, hater of hip-hop, because sometimes disgust has been the least of it. Like when the bullets in Los Angeles drilled into the Notorious B.I.G. It was a thing so stupid, so senseless, so painful, it made me want to throw hip-hop into an attic and slam the door shut; never mind the voice of logic shouting that hip-hop itself could not be held responsible. But Tupac's killing in the fall of 1996 was searing enough. Biggie's death six months later shredded what love I had left, leaving bit-terness in its wake. And undiluted bitterness brews hate. Hate for the miasma and violence that has far too often hung about hip-hop like a shroud. Hate for any perpetra-tor of such violence and the paths, chosen and otherwise, that brought them hence.

I struggle to reach you, hater of hip-hop. Because I scream in rage and frustration when you make blanket dismissals and gross generalizations. Because I, too, have made them and I know better. Because I want to pound one simple fact into your head: those whom you would wave away with a fling of the hand are your children, the inheritors of your labor. If you think we are wrong, talk to us. If you fear, speak to us. Know that we can give you the sophistication you need and the context you lack. Know that we can be more self-critical and discerning than you imagine. Know that this thing we love that you deem so burlesque, so vulgar, and so wrong is so *right* to us. And if we seem lulled into the mindless state of sheep, seek to engage those who would be shepherds. Do not toss the whole herd from the cliff.

I also write this for the indifferent among you. You who sit between love and hate. You who have ceased to care or never cared. Because those caught in the throes of love and hate are too enflamed with passion to be objec-tive. Because compromise and understanding is a game of halfway steps and you occupy the middle ground. Because hip-hop is that important—as a language spo-ken by young people around the world, as a source of economic power for many who have lived on society's margins, as a bridge spanning cultural, racial, and regional difference, as a tool for incredible good or incredible callousness—and you should care.

I know you well, indifferent you. I see your face every day. You are my friends, seventies babies now pushing or past thirty. The funky children of Public Enemy for whom adulthood means wary distance from nowadays hip-hop with its mercantile, empty focus, its seeming lack of depth and meaning. You ain't heard nothing like "Fight the Power" in quite a while. The revolution that you dreamed of as you once danced to Chuck D's booming voice and the Bomb Squad's wailing sirens didn't just die; it was still-born. Captured by the unyielding seduction of the market-place. The vagaries of trend. The power of the buck.

I also see your face in my family, indifferent you. And in many families around me. Older aunts and uncles, perhaps. Parents maintaining a cautious distance from this thing that captivates your children. You wonder if this, too, shall pass.

I write this for Guyana. Because it is the country my family calls home, as well as the place where hip-hop and I met many years ago. Because I am a child of the Caribbean as much as I am a child of hip-hop. Because hip-hop and Caribbean culture have had a long, fruitful relationship, stretching from Jamaican immigrant Clive Cambell, otherwise known as Kool Herc, who, in the late sixties and early seventies, birthed the open-air jam sessions in the Bronx from which hip-hop culture would spring, to contemporary artists like Wyclef Jean and Busta Rhymes, whose Caribbean heritage informs every note and inflection of their artistry.

I must write this for me. I have to. Hip-hop has been my companion for over twenty years now, my muse for half that time. I have loved it, raged at it, been consumed by it, and despaired with it. Yet it has never left my side. Across the span of childhood in Guyana, teenage years in New

York City, university, and life as writer, journalist, and media executive, hip-hop has been my North Star. A beacon to guide steps along. A lamp to shed light upon the trail.

I have followed that beacon around the world and seen the effect of its light on others. From youth in Parisian and London clubs dancing to Biggie, to bedraggled Haitian teens shining with fierce pride upon catching sight of Wyclef Jean, to kids in Guyana raising toasts as Jay-Z's voice crackles through sidewalk speakers, hip-hop can wrap young people up in a fashion that never ceases to spark awe in me.

I did not know how to define this book at first. It is not quite a memoir. Nor is it some didactic, academic overview of hip-hop. I began composing *Gunshots* in 1999, and after a year or so I realized that what I remain, at my core, is a storyteller. And that this book, simply enough, is a collection of stories. These stories tell a tale of hip-hop through its impact on my life and those around me, a scope that encompasses the personal and the public, family and friends, little brothers and Lauryn Hill, next-door neighbors and Russell Simmons, the streets of Brooklyn and a waterfront in Port-au-Prince, Haiti, college newspapers and *The Source* magazine. They are stories that frame the conflicts—love, family, triumph, loss—all of us tiptoe through on a daily basis.

I write this for me, because as a member of this inherently conflicted, irony-ridden hip-hop generation I understand that demons must be wrestled with in the light of day. Hip-hop has deposited as many demons as it has angels upon our shoulders. Open, honest grappling with such demons is what we have striven for at our best, and avoided at our worst.

Ultimately, I write this for hip-hop. Because I should.

2

MY BROTHER THE RAP STAR

My little brother Rahsaan is nineteen years old. He stands about five foot ten, just around my height. But he is lean and lanky, so he looks taller. He has a bright, flashing smile, a charismatic personality, and a surprisingly deep voice for his age and size. And like many nineteen year olds, he walks through life supremely secure in his own immortality and omniscience.

Nineteen breeds a particular arrogance. At that age I had absolutely no doubt that the world moved to my dictates, that events shaped themselves to my whim. Thus, I could get to them when I felt like. And if said event and me didn't hook up in time, hey, it was someone else's loss, not mine.

Rahsaan's got some of that, too. But the nineteen-year-old genie on his shoulder informs him in a way all too unique to his generation. My brother trusts in this genie. He will brook no debate. See, he feels he's destined to be a rap star. The next Nas. Or the next Jay-Z.

Of course, big brothers play a role in realizing their younger siblings' dreams. Particularly when the big brother in question has got juice in the hip-hop world: former editor in chief of *The Source*; first-name basis with

Puffy, Russell, and the like; able to land record deals in a single bound. There is no doubt in Rahsaan's mind that I can and will get him a record deal. The conviction burns in him, a flame as strong as his belief in himself. His confidence in me is humbling, and a tad scary. And it leaves me wracked with ambivalence at best, and cursing my own hypocrisy at worst. For how can I help him succeed in his quest when I hate this beast that hip-hop has become?

I did not always feel this way about hip-hop. We have had a long relationship, hip-hop and I. We met in Guyana in 1980. Guyana sits perched on the northern coast of South America. It is a small country, matched in size by its easternmost neighbor, Suriname, and dwarfed by its southern and western neighbors, Brazil and Venezuela. Guyana is a multiethnic land, peopled by the descendants of African slaves, indentured Indian, Chinese, and Portuguese laborers, and the country's native Amerindians. For the majority of the twentieth century, Guyana was a colony of the British Empire. As a result, it bears the distinction of being the only English-speaking country in South America. Indeed, historically Guyana has been much more aligned, culturally and politically, with the island nations of the Caribbean, the former British West Indies.

In 1980, Guyana, along with the rest of the Caribbean, thrust itself further and further into postcolonial development. Cultural information streamed down from diverse sources: British, Eastern European, the Indian subcontinent, and the great informer of them all, America. On weekend afternoons I could usually be found at my cousins', the Jones family, in Republic Park, a suburb of Georgetown, Guyana's capital city. My cousins possessed that marvel of marvels, a VCR. And we would spend umpteen hours gazing at recorded bites of American culture.

One afternoon I arrived in the midst of a commotion. My cousins were all huddled around the television, talking loudly and gesturing excitedly. The figures on the tube before them seemed hazy and indistinct, yet strangely compelling. My nine-year-old eyes squinted to better make out events and I nudged my way through the larger bodies to wiggle closer to the television.

"To the hip, the hop . . ."

I gazed openmouthed at a strange, unfolding scene: dancers in bright, swirling outfits; three guys vocalizing in a singsong, conversational manner over the familiar rhythm track of Chic's "Good Times."

"This is the newest thing from the States," my eldest cousin said knowingly. "It's called rap."

Thus, my introduction to hip-hop: "Rapper's Delight" by the Sugar Hill Gang, hip-hop's first commercial release. That song hit a zone of instant familiarity. It recalled both the dancehall style of reggae so popular in Guyana, and the high-energy dance tunes of black Americans that were steady party favorites.

In the early eighties, B-boying swept through the Caribbean, borne on the wings of films like *Beat Street* and *Breaking*. Emulating their American brethren, kids in Georgetown formed dance crews and battled each other in stylized rituals. I was down with a crew called the Wiz Kids. Most of us were students at Georgetown's top high school, Queens College, a bastion of stiff, British-style education complete with uniforms festooned with the school crest, forms one through upper six, shorts pants for us young lads, trousers for the older boys, and a daily assembly at which we stood in white, yellow, and khaki-clad rows to blare the school song and national anthem from youthful lungs after the headmaster read the day's announcements.

We'd break up that regimentation at lunchtime. B-boy manuals supplanted math textbooks. Limbs popped and locked in robotic and electric fashion. Bodies performed ground acrobatics with moves like the headspin, the windmill, and backspins, daring each other with precarious abandon.

I was not great. I sucked at popping and was barely decent at floorwork. But I tried to make up for it with energy. Nevertheless, when the Wiz Kids would perform—at school events, in street battles—I usually stood to the side, cheering the more polished efforts of guys like Don Fletcher, Andy Ninval, and Glen Hanoman, three of the best B-boys in Georgetown during those days.

My family and I moved to New York in 1985. Flatbush, Brooklyn, the melting pot of Caribbean and African-American culture, became my new stomping ground. For the first time in my life I had the chance to stare hip-hop full in the face and drink deeply. We arrived at the outset of hip-hop's Golden Age. DJ Red Alert and Mr. Magic, mix-show masters at KISS-FM and WBLS, waged war on radio airwaves, vying for sonic control of hip-hop's mind and soul. Boom boxes atop shoulders, sidewalks, and stoops belted out the sounds of Run-DMC, Doug E. Fresh and Slick Rick, and U.T.F.O. In short order the legendary club Union Square would be born, providing a temple for the faithful to pay homage to their own pantheon of urban gods. I was intoxicated.

And I would love hip-hop faithfully. When my family moved to Freeport, Long Island, during my ninth grade year I stayed committed. And when we moved yet again, this time to Miami, Florida, during my senior year of high school, the bond grew even stronger, for now I was an ambassador of the urgent, New York hip-hop I loved. Eventually, in 1989, I would come back east for college. And through every personal incarnation of the next few years—radio and party DJ, club dancer, campus journalist—hip-hop and I remained a pair.

In 1994 I became a professional journalist at the *Village Voice*. Although my interests were broad and varied, hip-hop remained central to my writing. And that was where we began our estrangement, though I would not realize it for some time. But as I covered youth culture through hip-hop's lens, romance and reality drifted apart. And reality was not always pretty. Indeed, the more entrenched in the business I became—leaving the *Village Voice* to become music editor then editor in chief of *The Source*—the uglier reality seemed. From the inside the flaws and foibles of one-time heroes become all too glaring. When hip-hop legend KRS-One put out *By All Means Necessary* in 1988, it seemed the stuff of genius, set way upon some musical Olympus. When hip-hop artist KRS-One stood on club stages across the country and blasted *The Source* and its staff as incompetent, white college kids ripping for his 1997 release, *I Got Next*, it seemed the stuff of lunacy, since he knew we were anything but.

From the inside it is easy to lose track of the sheer primal joy of hip-hop, the ecstasy it channels on dance floors at its sonic heights, the mental stimulation it can bring about at its lyrical best. Instead, what becomes uncomfortably clear is the inherently exploitative nature

of a business built on the cultural product of young people of color, and the excesses and abuses that swirl within
it. As hip-hop exploded commercially in the late nineties,
a cold machine supplanted the cultural form that I'd
fallen in love with as a child. Market share took prece-
dence over music. Business decisions were now as likely
to be influenced by the threat of violence as by the words
of the most honey-tongued negotiator. In American history, entertainment and gangsterism have long been
bosom buddies, particularly when the entertainment
industry in question is on the cusp of reaching its economic potential. Hip-hop is just the latest, greatest hustle
in a line that stretches back to Frank Sinatra and his
alleged mob cronies, and even further.

I made my choice to be in this business. But to see my
brother lose the innocence of the fan, to become a part of
an industry where a top artist's former crew blows up
the car of his manager as a warning to cut them in on a
potentially lucrative deal, to see him become a pawn in a
record label system where someone else will retain the
lion's share of any profits while milking him for all he's
worth, then cut him loose when there is no more milk left
to give, these prospects chill me.

My eyes and ears may be directed at my dinner compan-
ions, but I am really observing my brother. He is not
being disruptive by any means, a quiet fifth to this dining
foursome. But I know him. So I can see the smile he fights
to keep from breaking out, the excitement brimming
within. The fascination.

He has good reason. It is a cool February night in 2000
and I am having dinner with Mark Hines—my friend
and partner in 360hiphop.com, the Russell Simmons-

founded Internet company I then worked for—and two guests. Those are the individuals causing the rumblings of anxiety in my brother. Directly in front of me looms Lyor Cohen, president of Island/Def Jam Records, long-time partner of Russell Simmons, and one of the most powerful men in urban music. To his right sits Kevin Liles, president of Def Jam/Def Soul, Cohen's heir and the man heavily responsible for Def Jam's steady success in recent years. They make quite the contrasting pair. Cohen is a tall, lean man with a quiet, intense demeanor that can explode with passion or rage. He has steely blue eyes and hair that has gone completely to gray. His voice still retains the unmistakable lilt of his native Israel. Liles is a shorter, rotund, black man from Baltimore. He laughs quickly, easily. And his heaviness does nothing to mask the brimming, compulsive energy within him. Liles went from Def Jam intern to company president in eight years. That is the crux of what one needs to know of him.

Kevin and Lyor are investors in 360hiphop. They also wield considerable power in the company that has the largest market share in the music arena—Universal, Island/Def Jam's parent company. If 360hiphop is to succeed, these two will be critical. So we talk quietly. Mark and I draw little diagrams on napkins, confidently expressing our plans for 360hiphop. We sketch out the information architecture and rattle out some core creative concepts. Lyor and Kevin listen carefully, nodding in appreciation at several junctures, giving important feedback.

Rahsaan pays rapt attention the entire time. Like any hip-hop kid his age he is most taken by the colorful, artistic personalities who dominate the culture's landscape:

Jay-Z and the like. But my brother has always been an entrepreneur as well as an artist—he started his own fashion label in high school—so the opportunity to be an observer of this particular huddle, to hear these stars of hip-hop's business frontier impart lessons learned from their own success makes his eyes widen in astonished appreciation. And when Kevin includes him in the conversation, indicating that as my younger brother he, too, is a part of the family and of course an internship at Def Jam is no problem, the beam on Rahsaan's face becomes cheese-eating in its dimensions.

I look at him thoughtfully.

Rahsaan lives with me now. As does our middle brother, twenty-five-year old Simeon. The hip-hop bug also bit Simeon through and through. At sixteen he belonged to a group called the Last Strawz. The group's independently released full length, entirely produced by Simeon, caused quite a stir in the Miami hip-hop community. The Strawz were renowned in those circles for their high-energy shows and precocious New York rhyme aesthetic, a departure from the Miami hip-hop norm, the bass style made popular by the likes of 2 Live Crew.

That was ten years ago. Simeon still loves to rhyme, but he spends more time these days making beats on his worn SP-1200 drum machine, although neither activity is suffused by the palpable need to blow up that guides every step of Rahsaan's dance with hip-hop.

My brothers have not always lived with me. They both moved up from Florida early in 2000, albeit for different reasons. Rahsaan, a student at Florida A&M, decided to take a year off from school to see about making it in the hip-hop business, a choice that generated no small degree of consternation in our education-first family. But my brother was determined; his mind made up. And despite some unease I could not begrudge him his decision since I had taken two years off from school and been enriched by the experience. He just needed to make sure he stayed productive and had guidance, which I was elected to provide.

Simeon's journey north was of the less specific variety. For him Miami was becoming little more than an anchor around his future—derelict friends and dead-end prospects. New York offered new opportunity, a fresh start.

The once-quiet Brooklyn apartment that I inhabit is now a hotbed of hip-hop energy. My brothers often make me feel like an old crank, grumbling at them to turn their music down. The bedroom they share lies on the second floor of the duplex apartment, just a ways down the hall from my own room. Most days and nights the sounds of beats and rhymes pour through their splayed-open doorway. When they catch sight of me passing, Rahsaan always calls out for me to come check a rhyme, hear a song. Sometimes I demur, citing exhaustion from work. Sometimes I give in, drifting into their sanctum to listen. Then Rahsaan will launch into rhyme mode, hands flashing, voice dipping and flowing smoothly, self-assurance pouring from every pore. At times Simeon will join in, though it is usually Rahsaan who presses me to listen.

And when I do, I have to admit that he's good. Very good. But I know I am sparing in my praise. I know my response is usually gruff. Part of it is my professional training as a music critic, these jaded ears that need to hear something extraordinary to be jolted, my cutting tongue that can be stingy with commendation. I remember the first time Rahsaan regaled me with the full extent of his lyrical stylings. He must have been seventeen at the time. I was still at *The Source* and had been visiting Miami for a music conference. From the moment I'd arrived Rahsaan had been pestering me to listen to him rhyme; so one night I just nodded when he asked yet again. He flew into his lyrics eagerly, ran through a litany, finished and gazed at me expectantly. I told him his tone and delivery was good. As for his content, well, I said flatly, unless you've been holding guns, flipping cocaine, and pushing Benzes in secret, you'd best find something more clever and honest to rhyme about. He was crestfallen, but unbowed.

Two years later, as I listen in the bedroom of our Brooklyn apartment, it becomes clear that his writing abilities are starting to catch up to his natural vocal tone and flow; though I still wince at the occasional *bitch* that flies off his tongue, along with other words, terms, and scenarios that sound alien coming from my little brother. And therein lies the heart of my reluctance: it is difficult, near impossible, for me to separate the little brother from the MC. Because I know all too well what can happen to MCs. And I hate what can happen to MCs.

Herein the romance of the hip-hop MC: you cultivate your skills; you get "put on," landing some significant record deal because you are dope and your talent is obvious to the gatekeepers of the hip-hop record business; you put an album out and sell hundreds of thousands if not millions of records; you become a big star and reap your just rewards of money and adoration from a music public gorged on hip-hop.

Herein the reality of today's hip-hop MC: you cultivate your skills, usually by mimicking some already popular artist or style, or by completely rejecting the same and going in the opposite direction; both these approaches have their respective challenges and will likely take you years to get noticed among the thousands who think they are just as dope as you; if you do get signed to a record label, it will be because someone knows you, an artist, a producer, an executive, as long as someone with a rep and track record can validate you getting put on goes from wispy dream to far-off goal; then, if you are among the lucky few to be signed, the most likely fate awaiting you is the label's shelf for they often have other priorities, A-level artists, and you may wait years for any meaningful shot; finally, let's assume your record does come out, statistics say it will perform in marginal fashion, under 200,000 copies sold, and the label will summarily drop you from its roster; but perhaps the record does do decently, say 350,000 to 500,000 units sold, this may leave you with some presence in the market and the ability to make money doing shows. However, you will in all likelihood be in deep hock to your label—which needs to recoup its money before you see a dime—for the dough they would have needed to spend to create that presence of yours: two videos perhaps, tour support, radio and video promotion, advertising and marketing campaigns, once costs are recouped you then make a paltry 7 to 10 percent of the net profits; last, you could always be Jay-Z or Eminem and sell enough units that you defy the economics of the record business, of course you have about as much a shot at that as some other kid with a dream has of being Jordan or Shaq.

Granted there have been several artists of late, most

notably Master P and his No Limit Records and Jay-Z with Roc-A-Fella Records, who have circumvented the typical fate by selling records independently, usually in their own region, before inking a deal with a major for a fifty-fifty joint venture, thus drastically changing the balance of power. However, for the vast majority of kids for whom the promise of the microphone beckons with great allure—most seduced by the driving narratives of contemporary hip-hop and its mythlike, illusory portrayal of easy fame, easy money, and easy women—once they've run the gauntlet of reality there is little payback but the pursuit itself. I cannot count the number of artists I ran into during my tenure at *The Source* who had lost record deals after one or two poorly performing singles, or after one disappointing album. Never mind the ones who actually had decent shots at a career, who actually had a small hit or successful album, the ones whose cool clock simply ran out with the fickle hip-hop buying public, or who fell victim to one business shenanigan or another. The industry is full of these lost souls caught in a perpetual struggle to get back on.

Although I know it smacks of hypocrisy and double standard, I dread serving as the conduit for my little brother's entry to this world. I know that I should not impose my cynicism on his idealism. But I am hard pressed to avoid it.

By late spring things have developed well for Rahsaan. The promised internship at Def Jam has materialized, and he holds a part-time sales position at the Soho store of Russell Simmons's Phat Farm clothing label. Rahsaan now spends his days in the very heart of the hip-hop industry. He has made new friends, other like-minded young interns at Def Jam. A couple of the kids dream of becoming big-time managers and they eagerly latch onto Rahsaan's talent. One day the lot of them troops up to my Chelsea office to outline their plans. They stalk in, these three tall young men: Rahsaan, his friend Tyson, and another kid named Danny. Mark and I sit with them to hear their ideas. The producers they have. The studio time that waits. The hookups within the industry. Rahsaan could be their big signing. They believe in his talent.

I listen carefully, all the while taking in their earnest faces. They remind me so much of Mark and myself, not that many years ago. Back when we were twenty-year-old college students and nascent producers, Mark and I would sneak our lyrically talented friends into the school's recording studio during the dead of night, intent on creating the hip-hop music we so loved. Like us ten years ago, there is no possibility of failure in these young men's eyes, no thought of delay. Time is an anachronism to them. Struggle naught but outmoded technology.

I give them a few words of encouragement and promise to do whatever I can when and if they need me. Later that night I pull Rahsaan aside to tell him that his friends are cool. More importantly, they've got the time that big brother does not. Hanging with them might be good. Go to clubs. Sit in studio sessions. Get your own bit of grassroots hustling on. Just don't sign anything. He nods. Beaming confidently.

He has reason for the confidence. Seems he's made a bit of a name for himself among the young folk at Def Jam by spitting rhymes in the office at the drop of a hat. Most nights he comes home and eagerly recites the day's events and the compliments and encouragement that came his way: He and Lady Luck, a young artist on Def Jam, went rhyme for rhyme and she thinks he's the shit; young A&R staffers at the label keep giving him beats to write to; and DJ Enuff, an A&R exec and DJ, even asked him to do a promo for his show on Hot 97, New York City's most dominant urban radio station.

Reasons indeed. Listen, anyone can kick rhymes, I tell him; but if you want to be a recording artist you have to be able to make songs. Stop worrying about getting signed to a label. Spend some time working on your craft.

So for the next few months he and Simeon begin their studio odyssey. They use a small, preproduction setup owned by Mark, myself, and the rest of our producer/songwriter crew who've stuck together since college. The studio is housed in an apartment in Mark's Riverside Drive building. We've had most of this stuff since school—outboard gear, sound modules, drum machines, turntables, guitars, and the audio program-enhanced computer that links the entire setup together.

My brothers have no idea how to use this equipment. And neither Mark nor I have time to teach them, focused as we are on the June 2000 launch of 360hiphop.com. They do get the occasional assist from the other guys in our crew. But for the most part they teach themselves through trial and error, with Rahsaan driving much of the process. I'm slow to catch on. One day they're badgering me about the studio, the next they're excitedly playing their compositions.

"You guys did that, alone?"

"Uh-huh."

I marvel at their tenacity. Only took me a year to learn how to navigate a digital recording studio.

The fruit of this labor becomes clear one summer evening. The event is a fashion show and talent exhibition that features Rahsaan. He's been attending rehearsals for a while, although I've paid hazy attention at best.

The show takes place in a small restaurant on Eighth Avenue, down a ways from Penn Station on Manhattan's Thirty-fourth Street. It is a second-floor walk-up, a dimly lit room accessed after cramped steps up one flight of stairs. To the rear of the room sits a small stage from which juts a makeshift catwalk. Tables and chairs take up the rest of the real estate, most of it occupied by the time I get there. The crowd is small. Friends and family of the models and performers. Once the show gets under way they are enthusiastic and vocal in their appreciation.

Rahsaan is one of the male models. He struts up and down the stage, completely cool and at ease in this voiceless parade. I lean back in my chair. A mix of pride and apprehension fills my stomach.

The talent portion of the show arrives. Now Rahsaan gains a voice, causing me to sit up and take notice. He strolls casually back down the catwalk, a microphone in one hand. Smiling at the crowd, totally relaxed, his lanky limbs clad in Phat Farm clothing. Through the speakers come familiar sounds. It's one of the songs he's recorded recently with Simeon.

Then he starts to rhyme. And my grudging reluctance steps aside. The kid is a performer born. He holds the microphone near the bottom and several inches from his face, avoiding the rookie mistake of clasping a microphone by the head and practically swallowing it. Thus his voice remains clear and distinct. He makes eye contact with all within range, engaging the watchers. At one point he hops off the catwalk and bops his way through the now enthusiastically clapping crowd. To Rahsaan this may as well be Madison Square Garden; such is his focus, his concentration. He ends. Bows with deep satisfaction. Strides from the stage. Looking like a man who has been doing this forever. Like a man who can, just maybe, redeem big brother's faith.

He catches me off guard a couple months later. It is midsummer by this time. The July night heat floods the apartment with still, humid air. We both move slowly. Our passage calculated to disturb the air as little as possible, as if to prevent its steamy molecules from settling on our skin.

I sit on the couch in the living room and turn on the television. After a few minutes he joins me. We watch the dancing images in silence.

"So," he begins, "I've been thinking and I've decided to go back to school this fall."

I look at him with surprise.

"Why?"

"Well," he casts his eyes downward, "it's just that, if it takes a while for me to get signed, I'm going to have to work to support myself. And if I don't go back to school I'm not going to be able to get much better than this Phat Farm job. I can't live in New York on that kind of money."

"And that's how you really feel? Mom didn't tell you to go back, did she?"

"Nah."

Well. I'm astonished, but pleased nonetheless.

"I think you've made a good decision. Look, you have to follow your dreams but you never know what can happen, so take advantage of the opportunity you have. Finishing school can only help you and you'll still be young when you get out."

He nods, eyes still on the floor. I look at him cautiously. Want to make sure he feels good about this decision.

Rahsaan looks up and grins.

"But I'm gon' come up here next summer. Send me some beats so I can write."

I chuckle.

"Get some good grades first, kiddo."

3

STARLITE NIGHTS

I was sixteen years old when the Starlite Ballroom almost killed me.

Things were dangerous back in those days. This was 1987. Before Mayor Giuliani cleaned up the streets of New York and stopped young, black men from being shot. By that year my family had moved from Brooklyn to the relatively calmer environs of Freeport, Long Island. But I grasped any and every opportunity to catch the Long Island Rail Road into Brooklyn. I rode the Babylon line, which passed through the elevated, wind-swept platform at Jamaica, Queens, gritty East New York, Brooklyn, then, finally, onto the bustling Atlantic Avenue hub. From there it took a simple ride on the No. 2 subway to reach the familiar asphalt of Church Avenue.

Starlite Ballroom isn't there anymore. A few years ago it transformed into a neighborhood convention center. But if you strode the pavement of Church Avenue in Flatbush in 1987 you would notice that the ballroom is not an attractive place by day's light. You would see that the surface of the second story is a dull white, relieved only by six darkly tinted windows and a pole jutting out from the building with a black sign that reads FOR HIRE:

WEDDINGS, PARTIES, DANCES ETC. The lower level would have greater impact on your eye. A graffiti-covered, slate gray affair serves as the door. Walls, of the beatup stucco persuasion, extend forward from either side of it at a thirty-degree angle. Just above those walls sits a row of windows with newspaper taped behind so that the curious cannot peep in for free. The windows are broken here and there by little pockmarks. They look like high-velocity exit holes marking the passage of bullets.

Places of worship sat on either side of the Starlite. The Emmaus Christian Community Church held down the east. The New Life Church of God occupied the west. I always thought the placement ironic, as if the churches were reluctant sentries keeping a wary, uneasy eye on the happenings in between.

Starlite lived just off the corner of Albany and Church. There are many other streets in the Flatbush section of Brooklyn—the Caribbean capital of the world—but none quite match Church Avenue's insistent pulse. Back then, like now, you had to dance down Church Avenue; the liveliness of the street rushed the body the instant you stepped out of the No. 2 subway stop on Nostrand Avenue. In those days I'd never fail to spot Jesus Man standing a few feet from the subway entrance, muttering on about the coming of the Lord, handing flyers to any who'd pause. Sidewalk DJs, topless in the hot summer sun, would spin the sounds of dancehall demigods— Beenie Man, Buju Banton—or hot soca rhythms. With every step a different smell would intrude—the spicy tang of a beef pattie, the aroma of freshly baked bread, the burnt rubber of dollar cabs screeching to load and unload passerbys. Farther down the avenue, NYPD personnel drifted around like bemused occupiers. Guyanese and Trinny rude boys swaggered down the sidewalk while their elders argued fiercely about cricket scores, the tragedy of IMF loans, and politics in the Caribbean.

Starlite would come alive with the dark. On any given Friday or Saturday night the players of Caribbean-American social drama floated by in roles worn smooth by constant use. Young ladies strolled the Ave. dressed in the theme of the month: an intricate hairdo, silver heels and high-riding skirts, jewels adorning slim fingers and chocolate necks. Not to be outdone, the guys came with a varied style all their own. From baggy pants-wearing, head rag-rocking rude boys resting against walls, to jewelry-bedecked types leaning low in slow-cruising Lexus cars. And the predatory beings—male and female—would inevitably emerge to mingle with the good folk. Crooks, cons, connivers. Lord help whomever they swarmed. Through it all, a dull, persistent, bass throb would rattle the windows and make the door vibrate.

The ballroom is jumping.

In 1987 every Church Avenue summer evening seemed steamy hot with a feel of mischief so real you could taste it on your tongue. My small crew could usually be found lounging on stoops on our block, Forty-second Street, or at Angie's corner store. Angie was a tiny, wizened Trinidadian lady who'd owned her small establishment forever. She'd sit behind the counter, fanning herself, while we'd buy the tiny juice bottles that sold for a quarter in our determined effort to stay cool. Ron, the son of Haitian parents, was the eldest. Then me. Then Richard and his younger brother Sean. Those two were my next-door neighbors and the children of Trinidadian parents.

These were the kids I'd been tight with since my family

immigrated to Brooklyn two summers before. We'd done nearly everything together: cruised to Coney Island, hunted for summer block parties, and kept each other out of trouble. Like that time, a bit earlier in the summer, when I was fixing to get my ass kicked by a local crew, the Church Ave. Boys. I hadn't done much. Just peered a bit too curiously at the crew one evening as they walked parallel to us along the other side of Church Avenue.

"Fuck you looking at?" a voice called.

"Yo, just keep walking," Ron said. We quickened our steps slightly. We were only moments away from our block, halfway between Forty-second and Albany, just past Starlite.

Close proximity to home didn't help. The fifteen or so members of CAB crossed the street with dark oaths and threats, intercepting us right at the corner of Forty-second and Church.

"What the fuck was you looking at?" The foremost of the group spat in my face. He was a big guy, looming threateningly above me. I curled back from him. Richard, Ron, Sean, and I had our backs against Richard's fence, hemmed in quite effectively by the crew surrounding us.

"Yo, let's just pop this dude and be out," another character somewhere to my left screeched.

We just stood there. Sean, who must have been twelve years old at the time, was shifting from foot to foot, fury and frustration painted on his face. Richard stood quietly to one side of me, Ron on the other. Both of them carried on muttered negotiations with a couple of the guys whom they'd recognized. I didn't know any of the faces staring at me. So I was scared shitless. The kind of fear when your Adam's apple swells up and seems liable to burst out your throat. So I did what most recently arrived

Caribbean kids in that era would do in such a situation . . . I began talking with a Jamaican accent.

"Wha ya deal wit? Mi nah wan no trouble, seen?"

See, Jamaicans had a rep in those days. Still do. Jamaican kids in Brooklyn were thought of as fearsome, aggressive, not to be fucked with lightly. For the rest of us Caribbean folk, donning the trappings of that reputation when convenient was a welcome ability. Didn't work that night though. Fifteen-to-four odds is too stacked a deck. Besides, most of those kids facing us were probably of Caribbean descent anyway.

I could tell the accent wasn't getting me anywhere. But at least we were talking. Me, protesting my innocence in "looking hard" at their crew. Them, enjoying the threat of imminent violence they hung over my head. The longer I could keep them from employing that threat, the better chance I had at escaping unscathed. But some grew restless with the talk, especially the little dude to my left who'd been screaming about "popping" me. I had to do something to break the tension.

It happened fast. One of the Church Ave. Boys carried a boom box from which leaked hip-hop rhythms. Another moved almost absent-mindedly to the music. Sean, still with that hostile look on his young face, said something to the effect of me being a better dancer than that kid hopping around over there. Then the big guy, like a heavy in a bad movie, gave me an incredulous look and motioned to the dancing kid.

He approached me with a leer on his face, stepping up to the sidewalk from the street where he'd been toward the rear of his crew. The guy with the radio turned the volume up and everyone crowded closer. Without a word the dancer slid into motion, spinning, gyrating, locking his limbs. Suddenly, while he was in midmove, I jumped into his space forcing him back with my own spins. Surprised, he stumbled back and I finished a sequence of moves in the space he'd just vacated. Howls went up from the onlookers. His crew and mine.

"Oooh, he got you, he *got* you!!" Sean's voice rang out fiercely.

All at once, as if by silent summons, the Church Ave. Boys began to draw back slowly. They'd had their entertainment for the night. The dancer threw a last glare of fury. Big guy looked at me quizzically, ghost of a smile on his lips.

"I thought you was Jamaican. What you know 'bout hip-hop dancing?"

I shrugged. They left.

In Flatbush parties usually took place in halls like the Starlite. These were large, cavernous spaces where DJs could stack towers of speakers to emit punishing sounds. I'd only been to a handful of these parties over my first two summers in New York, '85 and '86. Mostly 'cause I hated worrying my faithful grandmother who, when the summer nights grew long, would poke her head out of an upper window of that Forty-second Street house and worriedly call my name.

"Selwyn?"

The call would relay its way down the block to whatever stoop I happened to be sitting on.

"Coming, Mama," my reply would return to her, followed by me an hour or so later.

My dad took me to my first Brooklyn hall party. Dad lived in Los Angeles. He'd been there since he and my mother divorced in the midseventies. Before that we'd all lived in Washington, D.C., where my brother Simeon and I were born: me in 1971, Simeon four years later. After the divorce my mother packed us back to Guyana. I'd only seen my dad a couple of times during the ten years spent in Guyana. Now that we were in New York he intended to see us a lot more.

Dad always came out to New York during the summer. He'd usually come during Labor Day weekend, when the Caribbean Day Parade and all its lead-up festivities filled Brooklyn with the sights and sounds of Carnival: colorfully clad revelers dancing along the road, soca and calypso music blaring from sound systems mounted on trucks and posted on street corners.

That first Labor Day in New York, 1985, I was glued to Dad's hip as he took me around. My dad's social philosophy as regards his son was pretty simple: I should see everything. Caribbean folk are notorious for hard partying, especially during Carnival, and my dad was a prince of his people in that regard. So we went everywhere, clubs, bars, backyard parties. Wherever the good times were happening you would find my father and his little shadow. Mom was none too pleased with our social calendar, even more so after Dad took me to the Tilden Ballroom.

Tilden Ballroom owned a rough reputation. Like the Starlite, it was a hall often rented out for parties. It stood not far from the intersection of Tilden Avenue and Flatbush Avenue. Parties there drew the full spectrum of the community. A doctor dancing alongside a drug dealer. A businessman next to a hoodlum. All united by the music and party spirit. Mom wouldn't be found dead in a place like that. Not Dad though.

"The only way you can get through life is if you can talk to everyone," he was fond of telling me, "from the highest to the lowest. You have to be comfortable in every circle."

When Dad and I arrived at the Tilden Ballroom it was almost dawn. We'd been to several parties already. He parked his car among the line of vehicles strewn haphazardly on the block. Then we walked toward the party, me tucked in behind my dad's long, lean shape. As we neared the entrance we saw New York City EMS personnel taking a man away in a stretcher. A dead man. My eyes widened and I stared at the body in morbid fascination. Dad gently grasped my shoulder and steered me through the entrance. He stopped just inside the door to talk with a friend. I turned my head and watched the EMS ambulance swallow the dead man.

Two summers later my friends and I made ready to go to Starlite. It was just one block over from Forty-second and we could hear the party in full swing. Eagerness gripped me. This was the first time I'd be going to the Starlite.

We left our block to walk the short distance to the ballroom, joining the tide of people drifting along Church Avenue, all headed to the same destination. Anticipation mounted as we drew closer and caught sight of the flood of girls waiting to go in. That was enough of a lure for teenage boys.

We reached the door in the midst of a crush, managed to struggle to the front, pay the entry fee, and go in. We dove right into the mix of flesh and sound. The DJ that night was good and the reggae music rang urgent, loud, and insistent.

I found myself pressed up against the wall by an attractive, aggressive young woman. We'd met earlier that night; she was a friend of one of the girls from Forty-second. We danced passionately, almost frantically, acting like the hormone-driven teens we were. Kissing. Touching. Grinding. I drifted in my own private heaven. Then, out of the corner of my eye, I noticed a slim fellow with a red Kangol hat pull something from his waistline and point it in the air. A series of sharp reports cut through the din.

Crack. Crack. Crack.

General bedlam erupted as people scrambled to get clear. Some ducked behind speakers. Others hugged the floor close to the wall.

It felt surreal. I screamed to my friends, "Them shits ain't real, it's not real!" But the panicked partygoers could give a damn about my observations. I was jostled from behind and stumbled right into the gunman. The slim hand holding that piece swung around and pointed dead at me. I remember little about that gunman besides the hat he wore, the gun he pointed in my direction, and the all too audible click of what I now assume was either the hammer falling on an empty chamber, or a misfire. The sound galvanized me. I brushed past him and sprinted out of the ballroom. Ron ran right beside me.

We hurtled up Church Avenue. Panic and fear must have mutated into a kind of hysteria because the two of us laughed like maniacs as we sped all the way down to Troy Avenue, some four blocks away. Eventually we stopped to catch our breath, still grinning. After several minutes we made our way back down to the ballroom to look for those we'd lost in the crushing exodus, and to witness the aftermath. Fear now supplanted by curiosity and the familiar sense of teenage immortality.

I miss Starlite. And only partly because it shoved my face into my own mortality, though the possibility of what

might have happened that night remained unacknowl-
edged for years. Not until 1994, when I did a Church
Avenue story for the *Village Voice,* did I honestly consider
that, but for a roll of the dice, I might have been the body
carted out of the party at dawn to disappear into the cav-
erns of an EMS truck.

I miss Starlite because it was a fixture in the landscape
of my teen years. A place of wonder and, for one terrible
moment, fear. But more than that, the Starlite was an
inextricable part of the ebb and flow of life's routine. The
inevitable parties on Friday and Saturday. Then Sunday,
when services in the adjoining churches would be in full
swing. The congregations screamed and sang with a fervor much the same as the pounding reggae of the two
nights prior. I'd always stroll by on my way to the subway. The voices of the worshipers tagged behind,
demanding attention, hollering their turn at dominion
over the spirit. I'd glance around to see Starlite sitting
there. Still. Implacable. It waits patiently for the clock to
come around yet again.

4

TO HER

Wassup, Mom. It's me. Selwyn. Just dropping you a line. Wanna see how you're doing. Haven't had much time to talk to you since your birthday a month ago. Still adjusting to the fact that you're now fifty. Like you old or something. Folk be saying, "Man, your mom is so young!" But I've only got one mom, so you reaching a half century is a major deal to me.

Guess I worry a little bit now. About your mortality. About not having you. Started up two years back, I reckon. When you had that cancerous lump. I never told you, but the fear of losing you would crawl up my throat and stick there, lodged like some awful, pulsing thing. My hands would grow clammy and my imagination would run dark. Sometimes I would shake with rage and rail against Heaven for the injustice against you. You who had borne so much. You who had buried a husband just a year ago. A husband lost to the very cancer's touch that now gripped you.

But I should have known better. I should have known that the God who infuses your small frame and huge spirit with His strength had work for you yet. Had happiness a bit further down the line. You must have known, though. How else could you have maintained that wide smile and infectious laugh? How else could you have driven my fear from me? I remember wheeling you into the examining room, the sudden tightening of your little, brown hand around mine the only sign of the anxiety that must have raged within. In that moment I wanted to pick you up and run. Out of the hospital. Away from white-clad doctors and arcane metal gadgetry. To a place where my love was enough to protect and heal you.

But look at you now. As energetic as you've ever been. Happier than I've ever seen you. Must be the new man in your life. I suppose that's why you're marrying him. Okay, I admit it. When you came out and showed the family the ring that night before the birthday party I was momentarily knocked for a loop. Part of it was just sheer possessiveness and jealousy—you're still my first girl, after all. But part of it was the very idea of a stepfather. Another one. I still don't know how you managed those tense years with my first stepfather. How you stood at the nexus of our emotions. His rage, regret, and confusion. My pain, anger, and confusion. Yet you held firm. A neutral space, a calming soul between the warring males in your life.

I didn't get it when I was younger. From age eight through eighteen I swallowed his every blow, buried every shout, hid every angry glare deep beneath my desire to protect you. I know he never turned that anger on you. But back then I sought to hide my pain from you because I didn't want to be the rock upon which your marriage might crack. Looking back it's tough for me to fathom how I came up with that thought process. I suppose children of divorce feel guilt, even if their parents' split had little to do with them, and do all they can to not be the cause of such again. I know I felt that way. It was easier for me to swallow all that happened. To keep things buried deep. I never wanted you to know the full scope of my pain. Never wanted to be a conduit of your despair.

But the nights I sobbed in my room I would wonder: Why did you bring this man into my life? How could a child deserve this? I remember when I was just eight years old. We had been in Guyana a couple years and were living in Nandy Park, a suburb of Georgetown. Our relatives from Canada were visiting. I played with the cousins. You and your sisters went out to the store. Then I broke a drinking glass. By accident, like children do. He looked at me with rage. Yanked me bodily from where I stood and beat me down the hallway, all the way to my bedroom. Every time his hand connected with my backside I would stumble to the floor, only to get up and be struck down yet again. When I finally reached the sanctum of my bedroom—sitting, shivering upon the bed—he left for a while before returning to gaze menacingly in my eyes and reach out, quite deliberately, to slam my head against the concrete wall. Then again.

Little wonder I wanted to see you reject him utterly, banishing him from us. I had no patience for the space you had to negotiate. I wanted that steely spirit of yours to rage in my defense—without compromise.

Age has taught me better. It has taught me to appreciate all the emotions in play—mine, yours, even his. But the lessons weren't easy. God, I remember the weekend of his funeral in 1995 and the agonized feelings that swirled through me. Sadness, yes. But also rage and the frustration of seeing the final resolution that I'd always dreamed of snatched from possibility. In that dream I would return home to stand before him, now a man fully accomplished, and ask a simple question: Why? I never desired angry confrontation. I just wanted a reason.

Remember when you handed me that letter on the day after the funeral; the one he wrote but never gave me? It was an eerie, chilling thing. I sat in our sunlit Miami living room, staring at the envelope. Slowly, with tremulous fingers, I peeled apart the pages, still fresh and crispy white after six years, and read the words of a man struggling to make sense. Struggling to find reason in the goal of near perfection he envisioned for me. Struggling to rationalize the rage that would uncork when I inevitably fell short.

That was all he could tell me. But it doesn't matter anymore, Mom. Because to move on I've had to forgive him. Though honesty wakes me up at times to ask if I haven't merely chosen not to think about him. The way I figure, I can now look at the pain pooled in my soul and not drown in it. And if that ain't close enough to forgiveness, fuck it.

You know, folk asked me if I was ever angry with you because of him. And I told them no. Confused, looking for answers, yes. But not angry. How could I be? You've been my best friend, Mom. And you've loved me so intently, so intensely. There could never be anger with you. There could never be anything to forgive.

I've forgiven myself though. Oh, I'm not talking about my relationship with him anymore; I'm talking about hip-hop and me. I thought I'd disappointed you. I mean, what mother wants to struggle to pay for an Ivy League education, with no help from a spouse who deems the opportunity too expensive, only to hear the child in question declare that a long-envisioned medical career was being supplanted by adventures in hip-hop. Unsure adventures at that. Forgoing the vast majority of study time to write, make beats, do a hell of a lot of DJing, and suffer sorry-ass, inconsistent grades as a result. How was I supposed to carve a life from that? No wonder you were pissed.

Yet I still harbored guilt even when I got out of college and hip-hop began to make sense in an adult way. Yeah, *The Source* magazine and music journalism gave structure to my earlier adventures, but the mere sense of letting a parent down can resonate deeply. Couple that with my own personal demon who delights in reducing accomplishment to a mere pitstop on a road whose end keeps receding into the horizon and, shit, well, ain't always been easy.

You know when I came to terms with it, Mom? When depression finally, briefly pulled me under. Man, it's painful for me to think about it even today. You remember though, it was fall of 1998. Good ol' demon had me real low. Did a great job of stoking the pressure inside to a boiling point, converting everything around me to a hollow shell. The job. My just-ended relationship. Life's direction. None of it made sense. None of it made me happy. The habits I developed as a child didn't help much, either. The way I bottle things up. Internalize them until they explode. Like so many others of my generation, dancing through our days with false humor and leaky stoicism. Flesh and blood Mt. Helenas on the verge.

The effects of depression and the emotional paralysis it causes can be hard to explain to those who've never felt its cool touch. Picture being sucked deep into a psychic black hole. Feeling like you're hurtling toward a crash. Unable, even unwilling, to act. That's where my demon brought me on that Saturday evening in November. I'd been arguing with my ex. Bitter, angry words flew. And she left in tears.

I stood alone in our apartment, cursing myself for the fool I'd been. I cursed everything around me, no longer able to contain the pent-up emotion. My eyes squeezed tight and my brow furrowed, as if trying to turn time about. Then the door would swing open and she would glide backward into the living room. Her tears would flow up and the lines in her face, the lines that shaped that crumpled, heart-stricken expression, would slowly ease. The shards of broken glasses would glide up from the kitchen counter, where I'd methodically smashed one after another, and re-form whole. The air would spit the ugly words back down my throat. Then we'd be there again. In the center of the room. Glaring at each other.

But time had no reversal for purchase or lease. So I began to drink, without thought, without reason, save for the cackling voice at the back of my head that screamed at me to harm myself. And oh, did I harm. With wracking sobs shaking my frame and reaching, trembling fingers, I poured glass after glass of poison. Then, to top it off, I threw in some real poison—window cleaner. Don't ask me why. It seemed to make sense at the time. Besides, I was running out of alcohol.

Things get hazy around this point. I remember cool fear touching me as remaining logic surmised that something was quite fucked up. I slid from the couch in the living room and fumbled for the phone.

I called Dad first. In California. But he wasn't home.

Not sure why I didn't call you. Didn't want to panic you. Didn't want to scare you.

Dialed my best friend, Mark, next. Could barely speak to him between the sobbing and the delirium.

Remember his voice rising in panic. His assurance that he was coming right over. That he'd soon be there.

Time struggled by. Buzzer rang. Only a miracle stopped me from breaking my neck as I opened the apartment door and tumbled down one flight of stairs to the entrance of the Brooklyn brownstone I called home.

Mark's here now. And his pregnant wife, Alicia. Dragging me back upstairs. Talking to me as I bawl my insides out. Stomach clenches with agony. Feel the ammonia searing within.

Mark called EMS. They came, along with the cops. Don't remember that. Alicia says I flew into a rage when the cops entered my apartment. Cussed them out with a Guyanese accent. They wanted to cuff me before taking me to the ambulance. Mark wouldn't let them.

Pumped my stomach at the ER. Don't remember that, either. Just remember waking up at 4:00 A.M. to the moans of my bedside neighbor. He'd been shot or something. All kinds of stuff stuck into me, poking, hurting.

Remember asking the nurse on duty, in a quavering voice, What happened? You tried to hurt yourself real good, answer comes, drank ammonia. I start to cry again.

Remember the calls to family members. Their steady strength. The bedside support from family, friends, my ex. Dad soon flew in. And you, Mom. When you came into that awful room where your son laid low. When your eyes fell on me. There was no recrimination in that gaze. No hurt. No "what the hell did you just do?" Just unadulterated love. Guilt may have brought tears yet again; but in that moment I forgave myself.

5

YOUNG BLACK TEENAGERS

From a perch in the second-floor balcony, the main floor of New York City's Hammerstein Ballroom seems sheathed in shadow. Every so often the house lights wink on and off and the shadow moves. Heaves like something alive. Then the lights flare brightly enough to break the undulating shadow into its discrete parts: hundreds of youth gathered below, awaiting the arrival of hip-hop gods, the Wu-Tang Clan.

It is winter. Those below are outfitted appropriately. They wear baggy, heavy jeans and boots. Voluminous jackets. Hats pulled low. Some huddle together, smaller packs within packs. Others lope slowly around the outskirts with that rhythmic bop so particular of hip-hop youth.

They are antsy. The night has already grown long in the tooth; and, quite in character, Wu-Tang Clan has not yet put in an appearance. Today, November 21, 2000, marked the release of the group's third album, *The W*, and the faithful are hungry with anticipation for this show. Restless, they make do with the selections offered by the DJ on stage. They are a critical bunch, roaring with approval to songs by the hardcore likes of Wu-Tang and M.O.P., grumbling with reluctant appreciation to Jay-Z's ghetto capitalist tales, hissing angrily when the DJ puts on the drawled, southern strains of Master P.

Finally, suddenly, Wu-Tang arrives. They glide out onstage, these men from Staten Island who revamped hip-hop seven long years ago in 1993. They have all come: the RZA, the GZA, [yes] Ol' Dirty Bastard, Inspectah Deck, Raekwon the Chef, U-God, Ghostface Killa, Masta Killa, and Method Man. They stalk the stage like the hungry wolves they remain; each man dressed in head-to-toe leather. RZA, the leader, slides to the front. A roar greets him. He puts his hands up.

"All my niggas! All my Wu-Tang niggas! Put your Ws up in the air!"

The entire crowd makes the sign: arms straight up, palms facing forward, thumbs touching. With splendid timing the house lights crash on full bore to reveal a spellbinding sight: hundreds of white arms making the Wu-Tang W; hundreds of white faces gazing adoringly at RZA; hundreds of white mouths screaming in approval as RZA exhorts his "Wu niggas" to show their love.

I met my first hip-hop white boy a long time ago—1985 to be exact. My family had just moved to Freeport, Long Island, from Flatbush, Brooklyn. I didn't know what to expect from Long Island aside from three facts. One, we would now have a house, a far cry from the cramped, two-bedroom Flatbush apartment in which we'd been living. Two, trees and grass would replace concrete and asphalt. Three, expect white folk.

I hadn't had too much experience with white folk. In Guyana, as in most of the Caribbean, there are people of European descent. But their numbers are relatively

small, and Caribbean culture is such an all-encompassing identity that the huge fault lines that separate white
and black in the American racial experience are compar-
atively tiny, despite the Caribbean's colonial history. The
fractures rest elsewhere: between black and Indian in
Guyana and Trinidad, between warring political parties
and their supporters in Jamaica, between rich and poor
in Haiti.

The white folk I'd encountered in Brooklyn were discrete, remote figures. Policemen, transit workers, the
teachers at my junior high school, and a couple of older
guys who lived on my aunt's block, Forty-second
Street. But there were no white children my own age in
the regions I roamed around Church Avenue. Even at
my junior high school, located in the more mixed neighborhood of Midwood, the nonblack faces seemed few
and far between; and we didn't mingle socially in any
event.

Freeport was different. The signs that marked the
town's border did not announce "suburban experiment
in progress." But from the moment we took Exit 21 off
New York's Southern State Parkway my family dove into
the swirling beaker that was Freeport, Long Island. It
was a town where diversity was as apt to collide as
blend, a body of contrasts beneath a quilt of suburban
similitude. In Freeport only five minutes of car time separated palatial dwellings along Seaman Avenue, with
their middle-class inhabitants, from a grim stretch of
road just steps from the town's Long Island Rail Road
station where serious young men plied their trade in
crack cocaine. Afternoons at Freeport High saw yellow
buses fetch young cargo to respective corners of the
town. There was the South bus, which would wend its

way down tree-lined Brookside Avenue to deposit kids in bucolic settings before ending up at grittier Buffalo Avenue, home to Freeport's best rendition of a New York City housing project, a place where the acrid scent of poverty clung with stubborn insistence. And then the various North buses, some traveling up Brookside to the spacious homes on Seaman, some venturing more east than north, closer to the enterprising young toughs standing vigil on cold corners.

We all came together in the hallways of Freeport High: middle-class and working-class kids; the children of families like my own, recently transplanted from New York City boroughs, and those with established Long Island credentials; long-haired, dark-clad white kids hanging in packs outside the school's front door, puffing away on cigarettes; clean-cut white kids intent on the football or lacrosse teams; nerdy, seemingly unsophisticated black kids with generically branded clothing, the social kiss of death in high school; cool, hip-hop-edged black kids rocking Spotbilt sneakers, bomber jackets, and large sheepskin coats; and Spanish kids, mostly Puerto Rican, a smaller minority in the hallways and cafeteria but growing every day. We were a rainbow mix. West Indian, African-American, Latino, Irish, Italian, Jewish.

Sometimes we butted heads, like the lunch period in tenth grade when one of my boys calmly mentioned that he was heading over to Dodd Junior High School because we were gonna "scrap with the Puerto Ricans" in that school's parking lot. Contused faces ambled about Freeport High the next day, including that of my soccer teammate Boris, a lanky, burly Spanish kid whose face looked liked he'd been stomped with cleated shoes. Then there were the legendary fights in the park on Freeport's south side. These took place before my family moved from Brooklyn. According to the story, older black guys—like big Darren Wise, who'd long graduated from Freeport High—slugged it out on occasion with their white peers, who were quite put out by these black kids strutting like they owned the south side. Still, for the most part the kids from different groups ignored each other outside of academics and sports. But not all.

Within a week of my midterm arrival at Freeport High my math class had to take a big test. The lot of us sat hunched over wooden desks with pens poised under the watchful, scowling eye of our bespectacled teacher.

"Psssst!" There came an insistent sound from my left. At first I ignored it.

"Psssssst!" It came again. With greater volume.

I looked over cautiously. Just to my left sat a small, compact white kid. He wore a baseball cap over his eyes. His feet rode blue-and-white Spotbilts. I'd met him during my first couple days in the class. His name was Ronnie Wingey. He was a crack-up. Full of jokes and off-color observations. Upon meeting me Ron had been intrigued to hear I was from Brooklyn. Though once he realized I wasn't some bad boy type I think some of the NYC luster wore off.

"Yo, what's the answer to number two?" he whispered.

I looked at him with bemusement. Then I whispered the answer at him.

"Thanks," he muttered, scribbling away at his paper, wicked grin on his face.

There were only a few kids like Ron in Freeport High. John Henry, a tall quiet kid who played on the basketball

team and slouched through the hall with his black team-
mates; Big Stan, who proudly wore his Rastafarian
emblems around his neck and probably knew more
about reggae than anyone else in the school; and Mike
Ippoliti, a cocky, crazy Italian kid whose couldn't-care-
less attitude and ready laugh endeared him to his black
schoolmates. But there weren't a whole lot in 1985. Not
too many white kids wearing the trappings of hip-hop
like aficionados born.

Ron was the truth though. Even if one were tempted to
snicker at the rolling bop in his walk, the hip-hop
cadence in his talk, and his baggy, brand-conscious clothing style, you couldn't front on his cultural attributes.
Ron was just about the best DJ in Freeport High. And we
had some good DJs. But Ron could make a pair of
Technics 1200 turntables, the techno tools at the center of
hip-hop, work delicious, sonic magic. I have many memories of late-night parties during those years, Ron bent
deep over the turntables, often the only white face in the
room. He would cut, mix, and scratch record after record,
like EPMD's "You're a Customer" or De La Soul's "Plug
Tunin." The room would erupt in shouts and cheers as
the excited partygoers danced with increased energy,
screaming their approval of Ron's guidance.

Toward the end of our high school years Ron began
working with local hip-hop heroes Public Enemy, the
firebrand group on Russell Simmons's Def Jam label
who'd ignited political consciousness in the hip-hop generation. Public Enemy hailed from Roosevelt, a town that
adjoined Freeport. Kids in Freeport and Roosevelt were
little different from their city peers when it came to the
objects of their hip-hop affection. Acts like LL Cool J, Big
Daddy Kane, and Run-DMC were huge faves; but we

regarded Public Enemy with fierce pride, for these were homegrown icons. They might be seen cruising down Main Street, the road that connected Freeport with Roosevelt, subject to shouted sidewalk greetings and firsthand viewings. We imagined that Chuck D and Flavor Flav—PE's front men—were just a few degrees of separation from any of us. Little wonder that Ron's hush-hush work with Public Enemy gave him major props.

Shortly after high school that work stood revealed: Ron and four other young, white guys—among them DJ Skribble of future MTV fame—had formed a rap group. Ron was an MC in the crew, not the DJ, as his Freeport chums might have assumed. He'd put down the turntables and picked up the microphone, adopting a new moniker in the process, Kamron. The group's Svengali was Hank Shocklee, member of the Bomb Squad, the production outfit behind Public Enemy's cacophonous assaults. Shocklee dreamed up a public persona for the group that drew from PE's sense of the controversial as well as Long Island's multiracial stew. Thus, these five white kids became the Young Black Teenagers.

The rest of the world wasn't ready. Although the group was decently talented and had one minor hit, "Tap the Bottle," they ended up spending a good deal of time defending their notion of blackness as beyond physical identity, blackness as a state of mind. It was met with derision. Race became an increasingly sticky subject in hip-hop during the early nineties. Nation consciousness, Afro-bohemianism, inner-city defiance, and the stridently militant narratives of groups like Public Enemy, X-Clan, N.W.A., and the Native Tongues marked the period. Even those of us who knew and respected Ron found YBT difficult to swallow.

YBT did release two albums, *Young Black Teenagers* in 1991 on Shocklee's MCA imprint Soul, and 1993's *Dead Enz Kidz Doin Lifetime Bidz* on MCA proper; but eventually, perhaps inevitably, they faded away. In retrospect Shocklee's error may have been in substituting *black* for *hip-hop* in defining the cultural mind-set of which Ron and his group were a part. Though Young Hip-Hop Teenagers may not have been the catchiest name around, either.

The next time I saw Ron he was on the big screen. He played the dreadlocked college roommate of Kid—one half of the popular rap group Kid 'N Play—in the Hudlin Brothers' *House Party 2*, the 1993 sequel to their successful teen/rap vehicle *House Party*. It was an ironic role—Kamron as the white but ultrahip, dipped-in-black foil to the straitlaced, suburban-ish Kid. Ron didn't have to act that part. That was his reality. By this time I'd been in college for a few years and several folk on campus were none too happy at the idea of this white kid running around in what seemed like a gross parody of hip-hop identity. I often found myself defending Ron, insisting that his motives were genuine, that he was the real deal.

But this was 1993. And the growing commercial and cultural consumption of hip-hop by the mainstream had rekindled long-simmering debates over cultural ownership. The backlash against Vanilla Ice and his invented gangsta past had created the specter of a hip-hop Elvis, the term *wigger* was newly coined, Dr. Dre and Snoop had pushed hardcore hip-hop to its greatest pop appeal yet with Dre's *Chronic* album, and white youth were coming in from the sidelines where they'd been carefully listening to the likes of Public Enemy, where they'd been appreciative spectators since the incipient days of hip-hop culture, coming deeper inside the party to try the food and drink on for size. Folk looked on askance. Was this the trade-off for hip-hop's mass appeal? Is this the moment where we fall prey to the age-old game and surrender our homegrown cultural product to white people? And how the fuck can you defend that Kamron kid when you don't like the shit any more than we do?

Kamron and his crew weren't the first white artists in hip-hop. Nor were high schoolers in 1985 the first white folk to be down with hip-hop. Far from it. In the mythmaking about hip-hop's origins its early racial makeup too often gets homogenized as solely African-American. Even hip-hop's adherents, including me, have often been guilty of that generalization. Hip-hop wasn't simply a by-product of disaffected black youth in the South Bronx during the seventies. There were incredible contributions by Latino youth, particularly in the formation and evolution of hip-hop's B-boy and graffiti subcultures. Legends like Rock Steady Crew's Crazy Legs, whose B-boy dance crew has achieved worldwide fame since its inception in the late seventies, DJ Charlie Chase and Whipper Whip are as seminal in their own right as Kool Herc, Afrika Bambaataa, and Grandmaster Flash, the black DJs widely credited as the founding fathers of hip-hop culture. And white folk were there, too. Perhaps not in the same cultural production mode—with the noteworthy exception of graffiti artists like Zephyr and Seen—but certainly as observers and participants of the burgeoning scene, particularly with the onset of the eighties when promoters like Russell Simmons began taking hip-hop parties downtown.

Once hip-hop moved into the commercial phase of its existence—post the 1979 release of "Rapper's Delight" by the Sugar Hill Gang, on Sylvia Robinson's Sugarhill Records—once it became something that had market value as well as cultural cool, the white presence expanded accordingly. The year 1981 witnessed the emergence of Tom Silverman's Tommy Boy Records, the label at which De La Soul and Queen Latifah would later reside, and Profile Records, founded by Cory Robbins and Steve Plotnicki. Profile would soon become the recording home of Joseph Simmons, younger brother of Russell, Darryl McDaniels, and Jason Mizell, collectively known as Run-DMC, perhaps the most significant hip-hop group of all time. Profile landed Run-DMC because Russell Simmons, who managed the group at the time, could not make headway with the black executives at the major labels. These executives, with their background in traditional R&B, simply refused to take a chance with Run-DMC's first single "Sucker MCs," a stark number full of angular, almost harsh, percussion and aggressive vocals. But Robbins and Plotnicki were willing to roll the dice. Hip-hop's symbiotic relationship between white, corporate backers with capital and distribution and black talent, whether artists or heads of boutique labels, has existed ever since.

As the eighties unfolded white hip-hoppers moved into the arena of cultural production, albeit in relatively small numbers. Lord Stotch, a Manhattanite who came on the scene in 1980, is acknowledged in some quarters as the first white rapper. Rick Rubin, who would partner with Russell Simmons at the Def Jam label, was a talented and prolific producer. In 1986 the Beastie Boys, three young white kids with a zany punk edge, released *License to Ill* on Def Jam to explosive success. Queens, New York, producer Paul C, whose 1989 murder remains unsolved, was a visionary in the crafting of percussive and textured hip-hop compositions, teaching and influencing black artists like Large Professor and Organized Konfusion.

A steady trickle of white MCs came after the Beasties: 3rd Bass, a well-received New York duo made up of a heavy-set Jewish kid, MC Serch, and his lean, cigar-smoking WASP counterpart, Prime Minister Pete Nice, made a few important records during the early nineties; Everlast, a smooth-faced kid who rapped alongside Ice-T in the late eighties, would later reinvent himself as the grizzled, buzzed-cut frontman of the Irish-influenced group House of Pain. That group's 1992 smash "Jump Around" remains a hit on college campuses and frat houses to this day. The list also includes Mark Wahlberg's younger incarnation, Marky Mark, along with his Funky Bunch, the aforementioned Vanilla Ice, Milkbone, a kid from Staten Island who made a temporary blip on the radar, and EL-P, erstwhile lead MC for underground hip-hop legends Company Flow. And last, though far from least, the exclamation point on the end of this particular genealogy, Eminem.

Hip-hop has certainly had its white artists but none of them have threatened the natural, assumed order of things. Indeed, for all the hand-wringing over Vanilla Ice's runaway success, more than seven million copies of 1990's *To the Extreme,* and the subsequent charges that he was a fake and a fraud, his commercial triumph could be hand-waved to some degree, ascribed to the long history of black music ending up more profitable once a white face becomes attached to it. Talent, in this case, was not a factor. Ice never threatened to seize any MC crown. Eminem represents a whole other kettle of fish. Picture a white sprinter emerging from some corner of the country to whup Maurice Green's ass. That's Eminem; easily one of the best MCs around. And for all the media focus on Eminem's commercial success, his offensive narratives, and the role his whiteness played in his early adoption by MTV, his critical chops and outstanding craftsmanship in the art of MCing gets underplayed.

MC judgments in hip-hop can be very subjective, yet there exist a core set of standards that we understand, even if they're not articulated at all, or get articulated differently in different places. There are three essential components to the craft. First, tone, the sound of an MC's voice. Great MCs have tones as distinct and varied as those of bebop's horn greats—the rumbling bass of a Notorious B.I.G., the urgent baritone of Tupac Shakur, the airy, melodic shuffle of a Snoop Dogg. All instantly recognizable. Second, delivery, the rhythmic pacing and flow of the MC's voice. Styles of delivery can range tremendously, from the rapid fire, staccato bursts often used by southern MCs like Dre of OutKast, to the more measured, cleverly syncopated patterns of a Jay-Z. Third, content, simply enough, the narrative and the structural devices the MC uses to communicate it. A good MC possesses all three elements. A great MC performs them all consistently, live atop a stage or on record. That's the territory in which Eminem strides.

But being white in hip-hop, no matter how good you are, is a complicated thing. Although hip-hop's purchasing public is some 70 percent white, the culture's modes, tones, and styles, its aesthetic heart, remains defined by its nonwhite core. Thus, any operation by a white hip-hopper within this heavily nonwhite space, a space where blacks hold a power at odds with the greater scheme of things and cling to it accordingly, is an operation fraught with the history of American cultural exchange. New languages must be learned, motives examined, and autonomy closely guarded. For white artists this operation can manifest in a curious balance between a sometimes unspoken deference where non-white artists are concerned, and a game of one-upmanship with other white folk as regards hip-hop cool. With Eminem it emerges both in his stated position of eschewing the word *nigger* in his songs—an interesting position given that the term is tossed about in rap like so much confetti, not to mention Eminem's protracted use of other offensive terms—and in his almost maniacal tirades against the likes of Everlast, Limp Bizkit, Insane Clown Posse, etc., white artists all. Yet Eminem has never uttered a disparaging word on record against black hip-hop artists—well, save for maybe Will Smith, and even that one was pretty light. He's tossed no disses, no challenges, no lyrical fuck-yous. And that sort of edgy competitiveness is such a de rigueur part of hip-hop that its absence in Eminem's work thus far is glaring.

If Eminem is exhibit one of the white presence in hip-hop, my old boss Dave Mays, owner and publisher of *The Source* magazine, is exhibit two. Mays was a walking, breathing avatar of the general, surface perception of hip-hop. The clothes, the jewelry, the cars. You name it; he rocked it. In fact, I'd sometimes joke that if we stood side by side, him in baggy hip-hop gear from head to toe, me in a suit, it might be challenging to tell, race-based presumption aside, who was the editor of a hip-hop magazine and who was the publisher. But Mays was like my high school friend Ron in many ways. He'd been down with hip-hop for a long time, a part and parcel of its fabric since high school in the eighties all the way through his college days at Harvard, where he started *The Source* as a newsletter. You couldn't question his sincerity and commitment lightly. Mays loved hip-hop; especially it's hardcore, rougher elements. And oh, did he look upon other white folk with deep suspicion. Mays would be quick to snort with scorn about "these white boys running around like they hip-hop," a comment that could encompass anyone, from writers, to fans, to music industry executives. His self-indoctrination in hip-hop's street ethos would, upon occasion, even cause him to cast that suspicious eye beyond white folk, nudging me to inquire if so-and-so writer wasn't, perhaps, a bit too "bourgie" to really understand hardcore hip-hop. That so-and-so editor was just too damn "corny" and altogether out of touch with hip-hop. I would always look at Mays with astonishment when he said something like that. Eventually, he would acquiesce and go along with any personnel decisions I made. But I never understood the ease with which he could say and think such things about young, black journalists who clearly were attuned to hip-hop, or I wouldn't have picked them in the first place. Yet they didn't register high enough on his personal meter. It demonstrated a remarkable sense of authority and presumption, not to mention a class-oriented bias that seemed ludicrous coming from a Harvard-educated white kid. Then, a year later, a very smart, young white writer I later worked with put it in context. Jon Caramanica—also a Harvard-educated hip-hop head, ironically enough—and I were sitting in the offices of 360hiphop.com the day after I attended the Wu-Tang show at the Hammerstein Ballroom, musing about the all-white hip-hop crowd and the attitudes of some white boys in hip-hop. Jon might have been talking about the kids at the show, but he made me understand Mays and his ilk a bit better.

"Look," he said, "it's like a sliding scale. As a white boy in hip-hop, you gotta have someone on the scale below you. First, it's all the corny white kids, then the ones new to hip-hop. The ones trying really hard. Clearly you're cooler than that. But then you start measuring yourself up to the black kids, thinking surely you're cooler, more hip-hop than the ones who don't seem to wear hip-hop on their sleeve, the ones who you perceive as corny. Then you start thinking you're more hip-hop than they are."

Life would lack a certain poetic balance if my narratives of Eminem and Dave Mays did not collide. Fortunately, they do. In the spring of 1999, one year after a young editor named Riggs Morales chose this amazing white MC as the feature for *The Source*'s Unsigned Hype column, a platform for undiscovered talent, that MC, Eminem, was riding the tremendous wave of his debut album's first single, "My Name Is." The editorial staff decided that we would put him on the cover and use the occasion to compose a package discussing the white presence in hip-hop. Dave seemed lukewarm to the cover idea but didn't raise significant protest.

We shot Eminem the following month in a Chelsea studio. He seemed very quiet and low key, nodding silently when introduced. He padded around the studio with his baggy clothes and blond hair, curiously flipping through the CD collection atop the stereo in one corner of the space. Once the shoot began he willingly followed the photographer's direction, becoming more animated as the shutter whirred, grinning brightly when an entourage member exclaimed that, shit, he, Eminem, was gonna be on the cover of *The Source*.

Later, the news trickled out that *Rolling Stone* also planned to feature Eminem on its cover. I pressed ahead anyway, convinced that the uniqueness of the moment and the strong editorial package was worth it. Mays, however, began to backpedal. Eventually, he decided against it, ostensibly because *Rolling Stone* was going to beat us to the newsstand, a very logical reason by our publishing orthodoxy. Truth be told, *Rolling Stone* just provided a decent excuse. The real reason we didn't do it was because Mays felt uncomfortable with the image on the cover. I'll never forget showing a mock-up to him and the incredulous look on his face as he muttered, "Jesus, a white boy on the cover of *The Source!*"

Ironically, Eminem would get his *Source* cover a year later and some months after my departure. Nevertheless, by that juncture, on the eve of Eminem's sophomore album, it was a safe, predictable choice. The white elephant that had been tromping by Eminem's side as he'd run through hip-hop's house the year prior had, for the most part, been reckoned with and accepted, and now occasioned few raised eyebrows. Unsurprisingly, *The Source* grabbed the expected roof-shattering sales for that issue. But the magazine had clearly missed a moment the year prior.

I don't go back to Freeport that often today. It is not a calculated thing. The town is only some thirty minutes from my Brooklyn neighborhood. And some of my good friends and their families still reside there. I simply don't go much. When I do tread its streets there is happiness kindled by fond memories. But there is sadness, as well, stoked by the reality of far too many old compatriots locked into a low-ceilinged existence. Far too many friends and acquaintances for whom a bigger, broader world never materialized. Freeport just seems so constricted now, so small.

But one thing seemed broader three years ago: the interplay of diversity at Freeport High. That spring, 1998, *The Source* came up with the idea for an issue on race and the hip-hop generation. For the main feature we decided that three staffers should go back to their former high schools and interview a group of students about race. I chose to go back to mine.

Now, some ten years after I'd made my last exit, I strode through Freeport High's wide double doors. As fate would pen it, the school was having a day-long celebration of ethnic diversity, a program that had been instituted a few years back. The hallways seemed both more colorful, and more homogenous than in my day. There were bodies of different types, faces of different shades. But all seemed to wear variants of the same uniform. Oversize jeans and khakis, bright-colored windbreakers, Nike sneakers. Almost to a person they possessed the rudimentary components of a late-nineties hip-hop outfit. They looked like multicolored copies shot from some machine duplicating the same document. Indeed, in this environment a Ronnie Wingey would not stand out in the stark relief of a decade earlier. He would simply be one of many.

I spoke to a group of these students in the school's auditorium. They rested on the edge of the stage, facing the sprawl of empty seats. I sat on a chair before them, peering into their eager eyes. They were white, black, and Latino. Boys and girls. All were bright. All full of candor and energy. Race and identity was still conflicted territory to them, but they drew hope and strength from what they held in common. And what they held in common was hip-hop.

"Hey," one young girl said softly, "now we have something to talk about. Something we all relate to. Something we all share."

"And what happens when the music goes off?" I asked them. "Does the conversation continue?"

They looked at each other. Most nodded enthusiastically. Some shook their heads. All looked thoughtful.

The music hasn't gone off for Ronnie Wingey. I have not spoken to him in at least three years but I know he still lives in Freeport. He goes by the handle Kam. And he's still in the game, producing, making beats. Being real to who he is. I guess that's all hip-hop can ask of anyone. Black or white.

6

MY UZI WEIGHS A TON

I still owe Chuck D five grand. We all do. Me and my mates from college—Mark, Dale, and John. At various times over the last eight years the fact has popped into my head. A little voice piping up to announce, "Hello, you owe a debt to one of the most important MCs of all time." We always meant to pay Chuck back. Really. Just never did. But it was perhaps the timeliest five grand any of us had seen to that point. Probably saved our butts from being locked up. Well, saved mine anyway.

This was the early nineties. The four of us were underclassmen at Princeton University. But we called it The Yard. I don't recall why we dubbed it such. After all, that name hardly encompassed the grandeur of the place, the scope and the scale. It possessed fields upon fields of grass. Some laid flat. Some sloped this way and that with gently undulating curves. My favorite was Cannon Green. So named for the ancient iron cannon that kept silent, solitary watch in the middle of the lawn. The Green was centrally located, an oasis that the students constantly wandered around and through. It became a sea of shimmering jade in the warmer months, an expanse of eye blinding white during the colder ones.

We all hailed from the New York area and hip-hop flowed in our veins. John was from Co-op City in the Bronx, Mark from Harlem, Dale from Montclair, New Jersey. John, Dale, and I were all DJs. Mark made beats and played guitar. Together we exploited every opportunity Princeton gave us to propagate and profit from our love for hip-hop. Under the acronym FOPO DJs—short for four poor DJs—we would spin two to three parties a week, charging the various student groups on a sliding scale, $200 to $300 for friends and those with little dough, $400 to $600 for everyone else. At FOPO's height we had two full party sets—turntables, mixer, amp, speakers, lights, fog machine—and we'd split up when the demand grew great, doubling the income. We'd parley our wares off campus as well, occasionally spinning the good times at neighboring colleges Rutgers, Rider, and Trenton State.

Princeton also had a near-commercial-strength, thirty-thousand-watt radio station—WPRB, 103.3 FM. Every Thursday night from 10:00 P.M. to 1:00 A.M., between the years 1992 and 1995, we hosted a hip-hop mix show called Vibes and Vapors. The show became enormously popular in the South Jersey/Philly area. And it was strategic as well as fun. Since all the labels had us on their college mailing lists we got the latest hip-hop records for free. They also sent radio drops and promos from their artists who'd give props to us and the show, "You're listening to 103.3 with J, D, and Seyfu!" And we built a strong rapport with the local artists, many of whom came by at one time or another to freestyle during our open mic segments.

Most hip-hop DJs eventually try crafting their own music and Princeton provided that opportunity, free of charge, as well. There was a studio located in Woolworth, the campus music building. Mark interned there. He painstakingly showed the rest of us how to navigate the equipment—the Roland drum machine, EPS keyboard, two-inch reels, computer with Performer. Soon enough, whatever time not spent hunched over the turntables was spent hunched over the studio's mixing board, cranking out beats until the wee hours of the morn.

We had all a group of twenty year olds could demand from hip-hop: the opportunity to shape and interact with the culture in a manner we thought significant. And it delighted us to no end that the tools of our opportunity were provided by an Ivy League institution, an environment that, on the surface, would appear to have no ability or desire to sustain anything having do with hip-hop. One year, Congresswoman Maxine Waters came to Princeton to receive a student prize for her staunch work on behalf of the disempowered. The organizers asked us to participate and we obliged, providing artists to open the proceedings.

"Well," Congresswoman Waters began after the music faded away, "hip-hop at Princeton. I've got to tell someone about this." She beamed. We beamed back.

By 1992 we'd connect with a group of my friends from Freeport, Long Island. Jamel Bazemore, Sean Chaplin, Grendel Thompson, and Vick Brownlee—collectively known as the Punk Barbarians, or PBs—were high school buddies who'd gotten together to form a rap group. One day I brought them to Princeton so they could meet this other crew of mine I'd always harp about on trips back to Long Island. The guys trudged onto Princeton's campus like explorers on Mars, peering curiously at the sights around them: the buildings, majestic structures with ivy crawling about their stone facades; the students bustling around on concrete walkways and grassy meadows. Princeton peered back. At these four big guys dressed in baggy clothes, walking through the campus with slow, loping gaits as they spat rhymes to each other. All of them carting paper-bagged forty-ounce bottles of Olde English in one hand, donuts in the other.

"Yo, this place is type ill!" Vick, the youngest, exclaimed with characteristic enthusiasm.

"Word," the other guys muttered, still steering around. "Where the studio at?"

That first night we worked until dawn, once we'd avoided campus security and snuck into the Woolworth Building.

Fortune smiled on us a year and many recording sessions later—Jamel and company hooked up with the guys from Public Enemy who were interested in managing them and securing a record deal. By this juncture my college crew had pretty much exhausted all the Woolworth studio had to give us. There were simply too many constraints: pesky grad students looking to do work of their own; the fact that we weren't supposed to have nonstudents in the studio; and the constant late-night sessions required to get by both of those issues. We had to get our own spot.

A building on nearby Nassau Street offered us the real estate. We just needed to buy the equipment. First we tried it the Princeton way, drawing up an elaborate business plan that spelled out the nature of our fledgling production company, Poisoned Ivy, and asked for a thirty grand investment so we could outfit our studio. There happened to be a black alumni luncheon two weeks away, so we rushed to get the plan done, certain that we would get someone to hand over a check. We simply could not fathom any other possibility. When the time came the four of us strode confidently into the building where dozens of black Princeton alumni stood around chatting, several copies of the plan carried in bags slung about our shoulders. We struck up multiple conversations, including one with BET founder Bob Johnson, an alumnus of the graduate school, who nodded sagely as he listened to John, our designated pitchman. The listeners were liberal with advice and approval; but no one broke off the dough.

Then we took the New York hustle route. We acquired as many credit cards as we could qualify for, except yours truly who'd already wrecked his credit halfway through freshman year. Then we simply went into stores that sold the necessary equipment, like Sam Ash, and ran the cards to the hilt. We also picked up some extra stuff with the just 'cause tax. Just 'cause as in, "I'm spending a couple thousand dollars here so I should take some extra stuff without paying for it . . . just 'cause." Headphones, cables, audio tape, anything not tied down securely found its way into large jacket pockets and beckoning bags. We became light-fingered specialists. Well, I did at any rate, walking around with the guilt of not shouldering credit card debt like the other guys. I grimace now at how casually I risked grand larceny charges and probable expulsion. But at age twenty-one immortality still held its grip. The dumb gene had not yet been beaten out of me.

There was one vital piece of equipment we needed. A Tascam DA-88 recorder. With that in hand we could complete the recording of the new PB demo that Chuck D needed for a round of meetings. Problem was the Tascam cost upward of $4,000 and we only had some $1,000 left on our collective credit cards.

One afternoon Mark and I headed to a Sam Ash store to pick up some equipment. I was determined to pick up the Tascam, as well. We took Dale's car, a beaten, worn Nissan that served us faithfully for years, ferrying bodies and equipment to and from parties. Mark drove. I kept watch. He had a habit of falling asleep when driving, and he slept with his eyes open. So if you weren't attentive the first sign of a problem would be the highway guardrail. But we managed to arrive at Sam Ash in one piece. Mark jerked the car into the store's parking lot. We got out, stretched, and casually walked inside, separating slightly. The store was crowded, typical for a Saturday afternoon and key for the plan. Patrons wandered around stacks of equipment, ears attuned to the salespeople drifting through them like whale sharks through plankton, gulping down order after order with nary a pause.

Mark signaled a salesperson and struck up a conversation. They floated from aisle to aisle, Mark pointing out items he wanted, the salesperson nodding eagerly. I strolled in their wake. One of the items Mark ordered was the Tascam. According to the plan, it would be brought up from storage and placed by the security desk at the front of the store where guards checked receipts against items. Mark, however, would change his mind about purchasing it once he reached the cashier. But the Tascam would still be sitting by the front, vulnerable to sleight of hand.

As Mark and the salesperson continued their rounds, the Tascam emerged from basement storage and sat by the front door. I ambled over. The guard on duty paid me no mind. Mark did his business with the cashier and arrived at the front, he and the salesperson bearing a few items. They set the boxes a few feet away from the Tascam and shook hands. The salesperson moved back into the Saturday hubbub. The guard, bored with the routine, took the receipt and peered at the boxes on the ground. Mark, standing between him and the Tascam, helpfully pointed them out. He nodded, stamped the receipt, and handed it back, then slouched behind his desk, weary eyes already fixed elsewhere in the store.

"Hey," Mark called out to me. I'd been several feet away the whole time. "I'm gonna pull the car up. This is our stuff." He waved a languid hand at the items on the floor then walked through the front door. I made my way over with a hand truck and stacked the boxes, placing the Tascam on the bottom of the pile with another box in front to obscure the markings. I nodded at the guard as I pushed the hand truck outside. He ignored me.

Mark already had the car waiting and the trunk open. Working quickly, my heart for the first time thumping with nerves, we loaded the boxes into the trunk. Hurriedly, I pushed the handcart away and hopped into the passenger seat. The car pulled off before the door shut, swinging out of the lot and back onto the main road, heading to Princeton.

We looked cautiously at each other. Then erupted into a fit of whooping laughter, thumping each other on the back and slapping hands.

"I can't believe . . . I can't believe," Mark struggled to get the words out through a fit of giggles ". . . can't believe you just walked out with that shit!"

We cackled on and on for several minutes, scoffing at the inability of mere peons to resist our clever scheming, when Dale's car phone rang. Mark picked it up.

"Hello?" Almost instantly his eyes widened and he thrust the phone at me. Curious, I grabbed it from his hand.

"Hello?"

"Yo." It was Dale. "Sam Ash just called."

"Oh shit." I shot a glance at Mark who was rapidly shifting his gaze between the road and me.

"What'd they say?"

"That two of my associates may have taken an item from the store by mistake," Dale replied in his usual cool, measured tones.

"I mean, did they sound pissed, like, as if something was wrong?" I blurted out.

"No. But you should take it back now." Dale hung up.

I looked at Mark. Visions of handcuffs flitted before our eyes.

"We gotta go back."

"Damn! I mean . . . do you think . . . ?"

"Look, it's cool. That's why we did it this way. We say you meant to buy the Tascam but changed your mind. We didn't communicate in the store so I just assumed you had bought it, and you'd already gone outside when I started to move boxes. Simple mistake."

We returned to Sam Ash. My eyes darted around the parking lot, searching for police. Didn't see any. Got out of the car and grabbed the Tascam from the trunk. We walked inside, steps leaden. Mark met an assistant manager by the door; I stood with the offending item in my hands. They held a quick conversation, apologies gushing back and forth. Mark, all Ivy League charm, regretted our absconding with store property over a simple mistake in communication. The assistant manager, well aware of the fifteen grand or so we'd spent in his store in the last few weeks, regretted making us come all the way back, and did we want to reconsider getting the Tascam after all? Soon we were again on the road to Princeton, less one Tascam. I took what seemed like my first breath in fifteen minutes.

A week later I sat in Chuck D's Roosevelt, Long Island, office, telling him of our plight, minus the illegal attempt, of course. We simply were not going to be able to record the demo he wanted. Chuck listened carefully.

"I'll lend you the money," he finally declared in that stentorian voice made famous on countless Public Enemy recordings. "You guys can give it back when you can."

Public Enemy helped define my college life. In the late eighties and early nineties, freshman and sophomore years, my emerging political consciousness—like that of many students across America's campuses, particularly black students—took shape to a Public Enemy sound track. Then, during later college years, Chuck and company became mentors of a sort because of their relationship with my high school buddies, the PBs.

Public Enemy singlehandedly stirred up the phenomenon of politically self-aware rap music. Unlike earlier groups whose narratives occasionally veered into the territory of social commentary—1982's "The Message" by Grandmaster Flash and the Furious Five being the earliest such instance—Public Enemy locked in with laser-beam focus on the sociopolitical conditions of black folk in America, the persistent tentacles of racism, and the uneven distribution of power that underscored such an existence. With a philosophy drawn from a spectrum of black nationalist thought—Marcus Garvey, the Black Panthers, the Nation of Islam—and a booming, commanding baritone, Chuck D delivered social and political harangues atop the group's equally revolutionary sonic production—dense layers of samples, wailing sirens, and deafening percussion, courtesy of the Bomb Squad, PE's beat-making unit comprised of Chuck himself, the Shocklee brothers Hank and Keith, and Eric "Vietnam" Sadler. Public Enemy's compositions of beat and narrative didn't merely engage in reflective analysis; they issued calls to action: Fight the Power; Burn, Hollywood Burn; Don't Believe the Hype; Bring the Noise. These were radically aggressive statements for pop music in the eighties, let alone hip-hop.

The group grew out of Long Island, or Strong Island as they termed it. In the early eighties Chuck and Hank Shocklee, along with Bill Stephny, who would become the group's spin doctor, were students at Adelphi University in Garden City. Chuck was a DJ on Adelphi's student-run station, WBAU. They shared a hankering for politics as well as hip-hop, and by the mideighties Chuck had come up with the concept for a revolutionary new group, partly in response to urgings from Def Jam cofounder Rick Rubin, who'd heard Chuck rhyme on a demo tape and courted him eagerly. Chuck turned to childhood friend William Drayton, subsequently known as the inimitable Flavor Flav, the humorous, huge clock-wearing sarcastic foil to Chuck's grave mien; Norman Lee Rogers, better known as DJ Terminator X; and Richard Griff, who as Professor Griff organized the choreographed, martial routines carried out onstage by the S1Ws, Security of the First World, the group's faux-paramilitary wing. Public Enemy was born.

From the beginning they owned Long Island, certainly Nassau County where Roosevelt, the town Chuck and

Flav called home, was located. These lands east of New York City flourished in the late eighties. Seminal hip-hop acts like EPMD, Rakim and Eric B., and De La Soul all sprang from the Island. But those artists emerged from towns further east, in Suffolk County—Brentwood, Wyandanch, and Amityville respectively. Public Enemy came from a small cluster of Nassau towns with heavy black populations: Roosevelt, Freeport, Uniondale, and Hempstead.

We were in tenth grade at Freeport High, 1987, when Def Jam released Public Enemy's debut, *Yo! Bum Rush the Show.* One afternoon I trotted up St. Mark's Avenue on Freeport's south side to Jamel Bazemore's house. His older brother Derek grabbed me excitedly.

"Yo, come check this out." He pulled me into their bedroom. In those days our crew had a ritual. Whenever an anticipated album hit the stores someone would purchase it and bring it over to the Bazemore home. There we would crowd into Jamel and Derek's bedroom, spreading our limbs over beds, carpeted floor, and walls. The tape would go into the faithful, beaten-up system that sat atop a wooden dresser. Then we'd listen carefully, tomb-silent during songs, opinionated yammering in between.

That afternoon Derek had the Public Enemy album. We put it on and cranked the volume up. The sheer force of Chuck's voice, and the beats, almost harsh in their sparseness, struck me. I glanced curiously at the album artwork, the photograph of the group on the front, huddled about a record spinning on a turntable. They looked serious, intent. As if planning something vaguely dangerous. A bold phrase ran across the bottom of the album in small, repeating type: *The government's responsible.* This was completely different stuff from anything else going on in 1987, like Boogie Down Productions' street opus *Criminal Minded*, Eric B and Rakim's masterful lyrical display on *Paid In Full*, and LL Cool J's braggadocio-filled *Bigger and Deffer*. Although Chuck's politicized rhetoric on songs like "Public Enemy No. 1," and "Miuzi Weighs a Ton" was in its formative infancy relative to what lay ahead, Public Enemy stood clearly separate from the rest of the rap pack.

A year later, spring of 1988, I sat in my bedroom for the Tuesday night ritual: doing homework while listening to New York University's hip-hop show hosted by P-Fine. The low-key P-Fine never failed to disappoint the ear hungry for the new. Nor did he that night. I looked up as he said something about a new Public Enemy song and automatically reached over to depress the pause button on a tape set to record. Just in time. The unmistakable voice of Malcolm X rang out, "Too black, too strong." Then a stuttered beat coated by a shattering siren dropped in right behind. Flavor Flav emerged, riding the introduction, calling out directives to his partner, "Yo, Chuck, these honey drippers are still fronting on us. Show them that we can do this, 'cause we always knew this. Ha-ha. Yeah, boyeee!" Then came Chuck:

> *Bass! How low can you go?*
> *Death row, what a brother knows*
> *Once again, back is the incredible*
> *The rhyme animal*
> *The incredible D*
> *Public Enemy number one*
> *Five-O said, "freeze!"*
> *and I got numb*

Next day the high school's hallways hummed with the illegal hiss of Walkmans. We'd been introduced to Public Enemy's *It Takes a Nation of Millions To Hold Us Back,* a record acknowledged today as perhaps the greatest rap album ever and certainly one of the most significant records in modern pop music history. With *Nation* the Bomb Squad perfected its dense, signature sound and Chuck's writing gained an intellectual breadth and rhetorical focus that the group's sterling debut had only hinted at. On songs like "Don't Believe the Hype," an admonition to a media hostile to rap, "Night of the Living Baseheads," a harsh attack on inner-city drug dealers and users alike, and "Black Steel in the Hour of Chaos," a brilliant indictment of the prison industrial complex and the justice system that feeds it, Public Enemy displayed a narrative ability never imagined in rap. *Nation* probed at the underbelly of the African-American experience in a way not seen in black music since Marvin Gaye's *What's Going On?* Rock critics fell over themselves in praise of the record and Public Enemy suddenly found itself with a commercial and critical smash, a fan base that now included white kids, and hailed as the leaders of some burgeoning rap revolution.

But with higher visibility the group's fierce, uncompromising stance began to draw fire. Detractors sniped at Chuck's seeming endorsement of Nation of Islam leader Louis Farrakhan. And in the summer of 1989 "Fight the Power," the group's lead single from the Spike Lee joint *Do the Right Thing,* stirred up more outrage among some in the mainstream for blasting Elvis Presley and John Wayne: "

Elvis was a hero to most
But he never meant shit to me you see

Straight-up racist that sucker was
Simple and plain
Motherfuck him and John Wayne

I set out for college midway through that summer and "Fight the Power" was the anthem, never mind critical harping. Hip-hop's political consciousness found its heart in 1989. Gold chains festooned about necks began to give way to African medallions and Malcolm X T-shirts. We were new adults fresh out of high school. Tired of the domestic policies of the just-ended Reagan era. Tired of the drug wars that had devastated too many of our neighborhoods in the eighties. We sniffed change in the air, and Public Enemy stoked the fumes. No criticism could dislodge them, or so we thought.

Real controversy embroiled Public Enemy by summer's end. Professor Griff, leader of the S1Ws, stood accused of making clearly anti-Semitic statements in the *Washington Post,* labeling Jews as being responsible for "most of the wickedness around the world." Public Enemy reeled in the resulting firestorm. We heard wild stories on campus that fall: Chuck fired Griff, Chuck rehired Griff, Chuck disbanded the entire group, Griff attacked Chuck and Public Enemy in print. The group issued a public apology. Yet, for a moment their future stood in doubt. Then the Enemy struck back in early 1990 with "Welcome to the Terrordome," the first single from a forthcoming third album, *Fear of a Black Planet.* It was an intense, powerful composition, even by Public Enemy's standards. The Bomb Squad's urgent beat conjured images of fleeing antagonists while Chuck rhymed with a rapid, controlled fury.

"I got so much trouble on my mind/Refuse to lose,"

he began before unleashing a rhetorical scattergun with targets wide and varied, like Yusef Hawkins's 1989 killing in New York:

It's weak to speak and blame somebody else
When you destroy yourself
First nothing's worse than a mother's pain
Of a son slain in Bensonhurst

Or betrayal from within and without:

Every brother ain't a brother
Cause a black hand
Squeezed on Malcolm X the man
The shootin' of Huey Newton
From a hand of a nigger who pulled the trigger

Chuck's diatribe took the breath away. But it would spark further controversy. Chuck had lashed back at the tormentors still on the group's case even after Griff's dismissal and a public apology for his statements, but with four lines—*Crucifixion ain't no fiction/So called chosen frozen/Apology made to who ever pleases/Still they got me like Jesus*—those tormentors had additional fodder, seizing on Chuck's lines as anti-Semitic utterances.

But Public Enemy kept the ship upright, landing *Fear of a Black Planet* in spring of 1990. *Fear* built upon *Nation*'s success, garnering glowing reviews and charting high. Aside from "Welcome to the Terrordome" and "Fight the Power," the record also contained future hits "911 Is a Joke," a humorous, yet deadly serious critique of the 911 system in the inner city, and "Brothers Gonna Work It Out," one of the most hopeful and optimistic songs in the group's discography. Although *Fear* lacked *Nation's* consistency, Public Enemy had clearly won again.

And by 1990 they no longer had to do the work alone. Between the 1988 release of *Nation* and *Fear's* entrance in 1990, others had carved their own path into the realm of sociopolitical consciousness. After the tragic death of partner Scott La Rock, shot in the street while trying to settle an argument, KRS-One of Boogie Down Productions had evolved from the mean street-focused MC of 1987's *Criminal Minded* into a visionary in his own right, championing self-awareness and education on 1988's *By All Means Necessary*, 1989's *Ghetto Music: The Blueprint of Hip-Hop*, and 1990's *Edutainment*. The Jungle Brothers and A Tribe Called Quest expressed bohemian Afrocentrism on the former's *Straight Out the Jungle*, 1988, and 1989's *Done by the Forces of Nature*; and the latter's 1990 classic, *People's Instinctive Travels and the Paths of Rhythm*. Brand Nubian delivered Islamic philosophy on 1990's *All for One*. And X-Clan—helmed interestingly enough by Lumumba Carson, better known as Professor X, son of activist Sonny Carson—expressed militant Afrocentrism on their 1990 debut, *To the East, Blackwards*. Even N.W.A.'s 1988 debut, *Straight Outta Compton*, a record that stunned me on first listen with a profanity and graphic imagery way beyond anything produced by New York artists, had a vital role. Although N.W.A. would later fall into the self-parody that would birth gangsta rap, hip-hop needed the perspective of songs like "Fuck tha Police" and "Straight Outta Compton." For if Public Enemy represented the intelligentsia of hip-hop's sociopolitical moment, then early N.W.A. represented the proletariat.

But moments pass. The following year Public Enemy

released *Apocalypse '91*. Although the record met with
favorable press and contained expected Public Enemy
fare—"When I Get to Arizona," a pissed-off commentary
on that state's refusal to celebrate Martin Luther King Jr.
Day, and "Shut 'Em Down," directed at liquor stores in
black communities—it didn't have the steam of prior
work, a state of affairs partially due to the dissolution of the
original Bomb Squad. In 1992 they released *Greatest Misses*,
a compilation of six new songs and six remixes. The album
felt unsure, uncertain. For the first time Public Enemy's
musical chops were looked on askance. By the time my
friends and I came within Public Enemy's sphere in 1993,
hip-hop had moved on, as well. Ironically, the marketing of
the latest film from PE's nationalist soul mate Spike Lee—
the 1992 Malcolm X biopic, *X*—probably hastened the sea
change by helping to commodify black consciousness.
Prior to the movie's release, X hats, shirts, and black
nationalist tomes of any sort were all the rage. Later, as the
film floated from public conversation, these accoutrements
of black nationalism slipped away with it, now disposable
as all commodities become. By then gangsta rap's runaway
chart success had completely supplanted nation consciousness, and Public Enemy's brilliance in the late eighties
already seemed the stuff of legend. This was a new time in
America. And under the leadership of an enthusiastic
Democratic president, supposedly focused on domestic
problems, there seemed little motivation to rail against the
bogeyman government of the past decade. The good times
were here now, folk assumed. The need for cultural revolu-
tionaries had passed.

We loved to sit and listen to Chuck. And he required little
encouragement to talk. He'd stride into Public Enemy's

Roosevelt offices where we'd inevitably gather. Chuck was a husky guy of medium height. He seemed a lot bigger than in videos of old, as if he'd been lifting weights during Public Enemy's downtime. He dressed casually—jeans, sleeveless Ts in the summer, athletic cap turned backward. Chuck had tremendous presence. As soon as he came within eye or earshot, calls would ring out, "Chuck! . . . wassup, Chuck . . . yo, Chuck!" If he were not too busy he'd slide over and strike up a conversation, regaling us with everything from political opinions, his views on the state of hip-hop, and Public Enemy lore.

Chuck looked out for the PBs during the time they spent under his wing. The guys went on tour with Public Enemy, contributed a song to Terminator X's 1994 compilation, *Terminator X and the Godfathers of Threatt*, and performed backup vocals on Public Enemy's 1994 comeback, *Muse Sick-N-Hour Mess Age*. But, like young MCs everywhere, they were impatient to land their own recording deal and when things seemed stagnant they left the nest, signing a contract with a small, New York independent called Lethal Records, owned by Public Enemy's former lawyer, Ron Skoller. Chuck wasn't happy, but he understood the impulsiveness. The PBs put out an album in 1996, *Sex, Props, Cream and the Drama in Between*, along with three singles accompanied by low-budget videos. DJ Red Alert gave 'em burn for a while on his Hot 97 afternoon mix show. And then, like 99.9 percent of rappers, they melted into the landscape.

Public Enemy's *Muse Sick-N-Hour Mess Age* was met with the harshest reviews of the group's career. But they would move forward. Chuck put out a solo album, 1996's *The Autobiography of Mistachuck*, and become an online music pioneer, establishing a highly regarded website, Rapstation.com, as well as an online label, Slamjamz.com. And the group even experienced a revival of sorts with the well-received *He Got Game,* the sound track to Spike Lee's 1998 movie of the same name.

Today a huge vacuum sits atop the stage Public Enemy once strode. The idea of a politically conscious group of hip-hop radicals achieving great commercial reward seems, well, radical. Hip-hop has grown comfortable in its nineties success, comfortable in aping the money and material-obsessed boom mentality of the economic expansion that characterized the nineties. The space between a bottle of Cristal and an iced-out Rolex is too scant for protest. The desire for a Bentley doesn't inspire one to break the system, only coopt it for a spell. Indeed, contemporary hip-hop embodies counter-culture's near inevitable evolution into the new status quo, with a distinct tyranny of its own to boot.

What's left of Public Enemy's hip-hop legacy sits on the fringes, in the work of groups like Dead Pres and Black Star, critically acclaimed acts for which the commercial market has shown relatively meager appetite. Many who enthusiastically received Public Enemy's message in the eighties and early nineties bemoan that fact. But the truth of the matter is that commercialized art springs from, reflects, and exploits the demands of its market. And demands change like the tide, often sweeping artists along. In the end, our yearning for Public Enemy simply speaks to the dearth in our everyday political life. For hip-hop the next frontier of political struggle lies in the world beyond the sixty minutes of a CD. The hip-hop generation has proven that it can move in near unison behind trends. It has proven that it can, by virtue of will alone, deposit dollars in pockets around the world, enriching anyone with a product to sell to young people. The great unproven rests in the political arena. Think celebrity rappers sell products well? How about selling a political agenda? Tell you what; if Lauryn Hill told any of my young, twenty-something cousins to vote for a candidate, they'd be in a booth tugging levers in a heartbeat. And should Chuck D ever decide to run for office, I'd be first in line with a $5,000 campaign donation.

7

ILLS OF A NATION

There exist few beings more neurotic and insecure than writers. Any writer who has ever stared at a blank computer screen for hours is well familiar with the feelings of ineptitude and you-suck syndrome that inevitably arise. Similar emotions crop up when you revisit work. Many a time have I found myself staring at an old piece of writing, marveling that I'd ever composed such, convinced that I'd been a heck of a lot smarter and better in seasons past.

One day I came across an essay I'd written as a twenty-two-year-old student in college. It had been published in the *Vigil,* a literary journal I'd worked on during my years at Princeton. The essay was the first piece of hip-hop criticism that I'd ever had published. Fascinated, I settled down to read it and quickly realized that the issues and topics I was trying to sort out in 1993 still held great currency. After a few aborted attempts at updating the piece I accepted the futility of changing history. The thirty-year-old me is too different a being than my younger self. However, that younger self wrote with a raw fire that deserved a space all its own. So I decided to include the essay as originally crafted.

This piece is shot through with an idealism that has been tempered by time. And some of its convictions have since drifted away, whether due to my own maturation or hip-hop's evolution. But more than anything else, the piece is an act of love, the work of a young mind struggling to reconcile the complexities of this hip-hop culture that so clearly captured his soul. I've missed that guy in recent years. Nice to welcome him back.

These days I often fear for my nation. Brown and black bodies vibing on asphalt. Hoodie-wearing, dread-growing beat monsters moving to sharp thunder. Liquid flow gliding on and through ears. And the beat, the beat rushing up through the foundation into the feet, trembling the thighs, shaking the ass, clutching the heart and bursting into the air as it screams out, "O Lord, I been freed!"

Seems like I can't go anywhere, like I can't turn around, can't breathe without feeling that fear. As if something were creeping up behind me, masking its approach inside the pulse of the beat in and outside my head. It's become very easy to lose myself in the nation, to become drunk on the growth and success of what was once called a fad and a passing thing, to embrace a culture that touches and gives voice to mad amounts of people. It would be simple to look back at '92 and scream out, "Yeah, I told you. We went and took over. Hip-hop is everywhere, in your backyard, on your front porch, in your face!"

I could do that. But I won't. I don't measure success that way. Oh, don't mark me wrong. We are large, no doubt. It's difficult to deny that in the face of the representations of hip-hop that bombard me daily. The Kris-Krossing, Arrested Developmenting, Naughty by Nature economic windfall and mainstream penetration. The endless stream of ridiculous "rap" commercials touting every product under the sun. You can't pick up a magazine without seeing some high-class (please) model sporting someone's idea of "street clothing." Sarcasm aside, it's probably all very well and good that kids in Iowa get to see *Yo! MTV Raps.* But despite all of that, I live in fear of the external and internal ills that beset the nation, and of what could happen if we don't issue out a massive head check.

So just what the hell is this Hip-hop Nation? Aren't you just talking about rap music?

Well, yes, I am talking about music but rapping, the vocal art of rhyming over percussive tracks, is simply one element of hip-hop culture. The other elements are Djing, Graffiti, and B-boying. Hip-hop is a diverse array of griots speaking to and on a number of issues and subjects. It's a mass of people, an entire generation, listening with fist-clenched approval of the dope stuff and snickering dismissal of wack shit. It's turntable technicians working wonders, aerosol artists creating brilliant canvases, athletic dancers cutting a swath on cardboard and linoleum. It's baggy jeans and baseball caps in Harlem, skullies in Brooklyn, hoodies and flannels in Cali. It's the kid, once ignored by mainstream society, who grew large and shook the tree.

And oh, how the fruit have fallen. Some of it sweet like economic success. Some bitter like negative stereotyping and misrepresentation. Just the other day I read a brief piece on Arrested Development in *Time* magazine. It began like this, "Tired of the rage and misogyny of rap . . ." and then went on to offer Arrested Development as a refreshing alternative. Now no one is going to dispute the presence of rage and misogyny in hip-hop music, not to mention larger society, of course. But this pat construction results not only in placing all present and prior music in neatly manufactured corners, it also significantly disempowers Arrested Development in an effort to confer some sort of legitimacy.

Time went on: "These rappers get angry, too . . . but theirs is righteous anger." Righteous anger? This is what separates them from the likes of Public Enemy, Ice Cube and X-Clan? By no means am I denying Arrested Development their own particular and deserved niche, but the simple fact is that some of the same things they get angry about are things that people have been getting angry about for years. The complexity and novelty of Arrested Development's rage is such that it does not come at you with a cacophony of beats, sirens, and vocals. Nor does it make itself an easy target for containment by screaming out "Fuck the white man and his system." So folks just carry on dancing to the "righteous anger" of songs like "Tennessee" and "Revolution," usually in heady oblivion to the words and message.

You don't want us to go get a gun now, do you? Arrested Development's Speech from "Revolution."

In any case, no matter the constructions and perceptions Arrested Development has dealt with, they have still enjoyed critical and commercial success. Misrepresentation does not always work that well. Sometimes it simply supports the perception that most hip-hop is simply a bunch of angry niggas speaking to a bunch of equally angry niggas with their fingers on the triggers. How else to explain the furor over Ice-T's "Cop Killer"? Never mind the fact that this is an artist creating a work. Never mind the not too subtle implication that Ice-T's listeners wouldn't have the complexity of mind to understand that this was a work of fiction, and not a command for people to go and dust some cops off. Of course we ignore the nonfiction reality that would make such an occurrence likely.

It is completely within rights to disagree over the content of an artist's speech. But applying an Orwellian maneuver—especially when cops and all other sorts of folk get blown up and dusted off all over the big screen all of the time—sends the ugly message to the hip-hop community that what we say and the platform upon which it is said can be yanked away at any time. Start controlling the things people say and control over what they hear, see, feel, and think may be closer to reality than the black and white of *1984.*

America is the land of opportunity, and that usually translates as economics. Hip-hop has finally climbed to a point where it can look the upside of capitalism in the eye. No more small, local markets, hip-hop has gone bicoastal, transglobal even. But who is really making the money and at what price? Exploitation and black culture have had a long, sordid history in this country. The maximization of the economic potential of a black art form, indeed any cultural product from the margins, usually occurs when the mainstream picks up and capitalizes upon it. Jazz, rock and roll, and hip-hop all lay within this tradition. The full ramifications have yet to play themselves out with regard to hip-hop, but as for the other two. . . . These days black jazz musicians find themselves playing to mostly white crowds and have little communication with black youth, although there has been some resurgence of interest in jazz because of hip-hop's growing appreciation and even affiliation with it— GangStarr and Branford Marsalis, A Tribe Called Quest's work with the likes of Ron Carter on their classic *Low End Theory*. In fact, jazz has become the classical music of American society. I find it fascinating that so many of the white people that I encounter can speak fondly of Miles and Coltrane, and yet seem to disconnect jazz from its cultural specific, i.e., black folk. Now it's just our American thing.

Rock and roll is so disheartening to discuss beyond a few points of historical note: the songs by black artists in the fifties that went on to greater commercial success when appropriated by their white brethren; the fact that the King was only the King because he could sing and dance like a black man; the eventual turning away by black youth from the music birthed by the likes of Little Richard and Chuck Berry; the fact that bands like Living Color and Eye and Eye had to fight so hard to get and maintain recording deals in an industry that could not figure out how to deal with the novelty of black rockers; and the crowning irony that there exists a Black Rock Coalition to help preserve black involvement in an art form they helped originate in the first place.

There is little wrong with the notion of cross-cultural exchange. That is how the family of humanity lives, breathes, and advances. But there is a line between exchange and exploitation, between sharing and unabashed thievery. In light of America's history in this regard, it is no wonder that the hip-hop nation casts doubtful looks upon the growing popularity of the form. On the one hand there is the cultural exchange, the passage of information, white kids listening to Public Enemy. On the other there is a Vanilla Ice who can come along in brazen-faced mockery and sell more records than anyone, a fact that falls in line with the tradition of black art being more commercially palatable when it is identified with a white face.

Given that history and tradition, the question rises as to how the hip-hop nation deals with the extension of its boundaries to include the white kids on the corner, suburbs, or elsewhere, with their baseball caps, baggy jeans, pumping Das EFX on car systems as they roll by. Do we extend an open hand or a closed fist? How does one react when something that is so far beyond music, that is a culture close and near to the heart, is experiencing the influx of an element it so often rails against? Of course the railing is often done against specific parts of an establishment and not all white folk. But the question remains: Can this element really empathize with the message, the music, the feeling? I must admit that I know several that seem to, and then there are artists like MC Serch, formerly of 3rd Bass. But in all honesty I'm not sure whether this is all fine or if it means that I have to look forward to the Black Rap Coalition in a couple decades or so.

But we sure don't make it any easier on ourselves, the hip-hop nation in particular and black people in general. Oftentimes it seems as if mainstream society is more willing to support hip-hop music, exploitative purpose notwithstanding, than the older generation of black folk. It is truly ironic and telling that you can tune into a "power" radio station and probably find more daily hip-hop programming than a large number of so-called black radio stations. Hip-hop has long had a troubled affair with black radio. It is cut out of daily programming and shuttled to after-school hours, or to late-night specialty shows, or sometimes out of programming altogether. The stated reasoning generally has to do with advertising. We've all heard the song that goes "the hip-hop audience does not represent our advertisers' target audience, advertisers threaten to pull their ads if we play them during hip-hop programming, etc., etc." Somehow none of this prevents "Power Whatever" from unleashing a daily barrage of House of Pain, Kris Kross, and the like. Plainly speaking, the issue is simply a lack of support for hip-hop by older blacks. This is not to imply that African-Americans above the age of thirty do not support hip-hop. But I believe that there is a severe conflict between generations involved here. One mired in genuine fear and concern, escapism and misunderstanding.

Hip-hop's explosion across the mediums of communication has afforded a once absent insight into an entire generation, but it has also been a flaunting, naked display of the innards of black America, a display that leaves many uncomfortable. Black folk are an insular people. We don't like to air our laundry, to let others catch an unpleasant smell. Hip-hop has done exactly that. It assaults black parents with images that they are not comfortable with for themselves, and certainly not for their children. *Gun-toting gangsters? Gold-wearing hooligans? Misogynist, bitch-swearing, corner-hanging thugs? The ghetto? That's not me. And that's not what I want for my children.*

Those images do not represent the full spectrum of hip-hop. But negative images and stereotypes are easier to retain than to let go. And the insistence of the majority of mass media in portraying the negative as the norm and groups like Arrested Development as a sort of pop culture exception does not aid matters.

It makes it easy to dismiss the music and the culture as a whole. And the resulting defensiveness and entrenchment by the hip-hop nation only deepens the lines. For a number of us it is a deep hurt indeed to receive hostility to our music and culture from our parents more biting than that of those whom we would term adversaries. For me it is particularly difficult to accept that a generation bred in the contrarian sixties could be so hostile to a creation of their children.

But our parents coming to terms with this fear of the ugly child is not all there is to it. Much more rests in the hand of my generation. It lies in recognizing what is valid in our parents' discomfort and communicating this realization. Hip-hop music is a multifaceted, open soul: weak, strong, beautiful, ugly. That is its power. It doesn't hide behind crooners wafting endlessly about boy meets girl, boy gets girl, boy loses girl. It gets in your face, in your head, and challenges you to do something about it. It is loud, confrontational. And it is often wrong. This is what members of the nation need to accept on a wider basis and thus understand some people's reluctance to embrace the music. We need to acknowledge that homophobia is rampant and virulent within hip-hop. We need to acknowledge that sexism is rampant and virulent within hip-hop.

Hip-hop is an incredibly powerful vehicle and it is up to us to maximize it. The music and nation are products of an enormously sexist, homophobic, violent, and racist society. It is only logical that some degree of baggage comes along with this soul-baring music. The challenge lies in stepping beyond the baggage. I realize the shortcomings and the steps involved, as do many others. But this is something that detractors of hip-hop often seem to ignore. Some of us are quite capable of being highly self-critical. The difference is we see that as part of a whole, a necessary part of a growth process, while others only seek to condemn and dismiss. It would be interesting indeed if the rest of society were as open and honest as hip-hop. Perhaps then we would more clearly see the sexism hiding between judicial robes and the racism and intolerance in Executive actions.

But in the final analysis it is not merely the detractors to whom this is directed; it is to the hip-hop nation itself. It is to ask that we not squander this voice that we have developed. It is to plead that we come out on top of the popularization equation this time around. It is to point out that here is something with power, economic and otherwise, that needs to be cultivated and developed with care. It is to say kill the ill shit or by God, one day it may kill us.

8

THE SOURCE OF IT ALL

The Wu-Tang Clan kidnapped me on my first assignment for *The Source*. Okay, I was a willing participant. But it seemed like abduction nonetheless. I'd been assigned a Wu story for the August '95 issue. Raekwon's *Only Built for Cuban Linx* would soon be released. And the nation's foremost hip-hop magazine wanted to showcase perhaps the strongest Wu-Tang album since their explosive '93 debut, *Enter the 36 Chambers*, with the most coveted real estate a magazine possesses—a cover.

Adario Strange, the senior editor at *The Source*, had given me the assignment. At that moment, early summer of 1995, I'd been writing heavily for the *Village Voice*, the leading New York City weekly, for eighteen months. I'd originally come to the *Voice* under the auspices of a writing fellowship the paper offered to minority students. In August of 1993 I'd made up my mind to take a year off from school in order to write and the *Voice* seemed the perfect home. So I filled out the necessary paperwork and sent it in, along with a few writing samples. One cold, fall morning in 1993, Lisa Kennedy, the paper's arts editor who also administered the fellowship program, welcomed me into the *Voice* offices at 36

Cooper Square. We sat down at a long conference table. She looked at me musingly.

"You've got a well-developed voice for such a young writer."

With that my *Village Voice* experience began. But by 1995 I'd woken up to the stark fact that survival as a writer in New York would not come by *Voice* checks alone. Lisa and Ann Powers, another mentor at the paper, helped me sketch an angle of attack. Subsequently, I sent out clips and cover letters to several magazines, including *The Source.* Strange called back for a meeting that promptly yielded the Wu-Tang assignment. I was excited. The magazine was rebuilding after a walkout by the founding editorial staff, but a cover profile at the still-leading hip-hop publication remained quite a get for a young, hip-hop-obsessed writer. At the *Voice* I'd mostly done critical essays and thought pieces, along with a decent bit of nonmusic reportage. So the Wu-Tang story wasn't merely my first magazine cover, it was my first genuine profile.

Those thoughts were far from my mind as I stood on a darkened Staten Island street near the Stapleton Projects, where Raekwon had left me. I wasn't alone though. To either side and all around me lurked members of the Wu-Tang faithful. They cut lean outlines in the dusk. Many had outlandish hairstyles. Wild Afros or half-braided heads of hair. All gazed at the interloper with interest. Not threatening. Just curious. Their eyes slid from me as Raekwon and Ghostface returned, the stocky Rae in front, followed by his taller, leaner partner.

"Ay, yo, son, we 'bout to ride down to do this show in Philly," Raekwon began. "You rollin'?"

I considered for a spell. Raekwon and I had hooked up

earlier in the day at the photo shoot for the cover. All of the Clan members had been there, so I had most of my secondary interviews. But I had yet to spend significant face time with Raekwon. So when he and Ghostface, standing on busy Broadway after the shoot, nodding at gawking passerbys, said that they "needed to make a run to Shaolin" and I could tag along if I wanted to, I'd jumped at the chance. Now he was proposing another run.

"No doubt," came my affirmative reply. It took all of two seconds.

We piled into a van. Raekwon took the driver's seat. Ghostface sat next to him. In the back I burrowed in between five or six of their crew, who were making the trip down, as well. The van pulled onto the New Jersey Turnpike, heading south.

Then came the topic of conversation—the Notorious B.I.G. It was an awkward time between Biggie and the Wu-Tang Boys. The streets buzzed with murmurs about a skit on Raekwon's album where Ghostface clearly leveled a diss at Biggie, and Biggie's resulting displeasure. Earlier, Rae and Ghost received word that a street team employee from their label, Loud Records, had been putting up posters in Brooklyn for the *Cuban Linx* album when he'd been roughly accosted by cats down with Biggie. The folk in that van weren't too happy with Big Poppa, especially the crew in the rear.

"We need to get that nigga, son. Word," someone spat.

"Yeah, for real."

"We should stab that fat nigga, son. You know fat niggas is scared of gettin' stabbed."

Laughter. I sat quiet. Unsure whether they were joking or deadly serious. But resolved to remain as innocuous as possible.

"We should catch him next week at *The Source* awards, son. Roll up, PLO style and shit, catch that nigga out there."

More laughter.

"Yo," one of the crew said and turned to stare at me. "You from *The Source*, right?"

I nodded.

"Yeah? So if this get out we gon' know where it came from."

He continued to stare dead in my eyes. The van went silent. I recognized the moment: a test. Whether they were joking about Biggie or not, the implicit threat rang clear. I looked at my interrogator.

"Yo, I just write for them, man," I said as reasonably as I could. "All this ain't necessary."

Raekwon laughed from up front.

"Ay, yo, son is cool."

The crew turned their attention away.

Three hours later the van pulled into Philadelphia. First stop, radio station 98.9, where Ghost and Rae plugged the album with Philly hip-hop jock Cosmic Kev. Then we headed to the Red Zone, the venue for the promotional show.

The club was a small, nondescript space; but it was filled with hungry hip-hop heads, eager to witness the latest from the Wu-Tang camp. Ghost and Rae did not disappoint, hitting the crowd with joint after joint from the now classic *Cuban Linx*. All of the Wu-Tang, with the exception of Ol' Dirty, made it to the show, leaping onstage to lend their support. RZA even took over from the house DJ, turning the evening's sounds into pure Wu-Tang medley. The crowd, expecting only a small promotional show, maybe just a couple of songs, rocked with ecstasy.

Afterward we filed over to a local hotel, our van crew now joined by the other Wu-Tang members—RZA, GZA, Method Man, U-God, Inspectah Deck, and Masta Killa— along with a few Loud Records personnel. Laughing and chuckling with exhilaration, the Clan members made their way to their rooms.

"Yo, tomorrow, son." Raekwon called out as the doors to the elevator hummed close.

It dawned on me that I had no place to sleep. And with little money in my pocket, no credit card, and no per diem from *The Source,* procuring a room was out of the question.

"Yo, *Source* guy, you need somewhere to sleep?" One of the Loud staffers asked sympathetically.

I nodded.

"You can chill with us," he said. "Might have to get the floor though."

The floor sounded wonderful.

The next morning, Saturday, I rose early and headed to the lobby. I sat in one of the chairs and began transcribing some of the material from the day before. An hour passed before Raekwon ambled by. He caught sight of me.

"Yo, we gon' head down to D.C. for some promo shit. You comin'?"

I didn't even reply that time. Simply gathered my stuff and trailed behind him. That leg of the trip was accomplished via car. Again, Raekwon drove. A Loud Records staffer occupied the passenger seat. Ghostface and I sat in the back.

Raekwon took off, pealing down the road, heading for I-95. He hit the highway and opened the engine even more, hurtling past slower-moving vehicles.

"Hey," I had to raise my voice above the howl of the wind slicing through the open windows. "Y'all wanna talk now?"

Ghostface nodded. Raekwon grunted assent. I broke out the microcassette recorder. For the next two hours Ghost fielded questions, Raekwon chiming in from behind the wheel. The two spoke like they rhymed. Piling one atop the other, each excitedly finishing his partner's thoughts, getting almost metaphysical in their musings.

"[To write this album] me and son jetted to Barbados on some Marvin Gaye shit, " Raekwon shouted over the highway din. "On some 'we gon' sit across the way on the other side of the world and just observe the water and the world' type shit. It just took my mind to another level, like, 'Damn nigga, you hear for something.'"

Ghostface murmured agreement.

The sights of Washington, D.C.'s buildings soon greeted us. The Wu-Tang caravan pulled into a hotel close to the city's Union Square train station. I stepped wearily from the car, glancing down to tuck away the valuable interview tape.

"You got what you need, son?" Raekwon asked.

"I'm cool."

"So wattup? We gon' do some shit here in D.C., then we heading down to VA."

"Think I'm gonna pass. Have to get back to New York to write the story."

"Aiight. Make it good." Raekwon gripped my hand in a quick farewell and drifted off.

The Loud Records staffers moved over.

"So you cool?" one asked.

"Actually, I may need some help getting home." I smiled ruefully.

They bought me an Amtrak ticket. Soon thereafter I rumbled back to New York, fingers already flying over the keys of my laptop.

Four weeks later. I'm leaving a Soho restaurant called Noho Star with Ola Kudu, then the art director of *The Source,* when a red Lexus screeched to a stop in the middle of the road before us.

"Yo, man, that article was wack!" A loud voice rang out. Kudu and I stared at the car in momentary confusion.

"Isn't that Raekwon?" Kudu wondered. I squinted through the summer haze.

"Think so."

Jogged out to the middle of the road. It was Raekwon. Extended my hand in greeting. He gripped it quickly. Then scowled.

"Ay, yo, son, that article was wack, man. Shit had too many big words. Couldn't understand that shit."

I was taken aback. But a reply was already tumbling from my mouth.

"You know, that's just my art, man. The same way cats may not necessarily catch your lyrics the first time around. That's just what I do. It's a good piece, man."

Raekwon scowled again. Less forcefully this time.

"Aiight, son," he replied. "Peace."

The car screamed off. Me and Raekwon been cool ever since. But I never told him he was absolutely right. That article did have too many big words.

The story of *The Source* magazine reads like some Horatio Alger publishing tale. Founded in 1988 by

David Mays, a student at Harvard University, as a two-page newsletter sent to the listeners of his hip-hop radio show, *The Source* would eventually evolve into the top-selling music magazine on America's newsstands, a magazine with a circulation near 500,000 and a total readership of three million, a magazine nominated for a National Magazine Award for General Excellence, alongside the likes of *GQ* and *The New Yorker*, a magazine chock-full of ad pages, capable of stirring incredible passion and exerting incredible influence within the hip-hop community, and a magazine that would provide a home for a generation of writers. But when I arrived in September of 1995 *The Source* was only baby steps along that path, and still recovering from events that had threatened to derail the journey altogether.

Dave Mays didn't grow his newsletter all by himself. At school he was joined by fellow Harvard man Jon Shecter, also a young, white hip-hop fan who would become founding editor in chief. They soon added H. Edward Young Jr., an African-American student who'd had some experience in publishing at *The New Republic*. Young and Mays would run the business side of the magazine. Editorially, Shecter would be joined by two other African-Americans: James Bernard, a student at the law school who would become senior editor and the fourth founding partner; and Reginald Dennis, the founding music editor. By the time Mays and Shecter graduated in 1990 *The Source* had become a nascent publishing enterprise. They had healthy advertising revenue, the bulk supplied by young rap labels like Jive, Tommy Boy, and Def Jam who were all eager to have access to a media outlet, albeit a small one, dedicated to hip-hop. Mays and company had discovered a clear niche. To that point in time the only regular ink on hip-hop cropped up in trade magazines like *Billboard,* alternative weeklies like the *Village Voice,* and teen fanzines like *Right On* and *Black Beat.* But no one had sought to make hip-hop its exclusive purview, no one treated it with real gravity. *The Source* crew used early *Rolling Stone* as a model and devised a magazine that regarded hip-hop as a cultural movement. They took their mission quite seriously; creating an editorial mix that went beyond music and deep into the cultural and sociopolitical issues that swirled about the hip-hop generation. It was a winning formula. By 1990, when they moved to their New York City offices at 594 Broadway, *The Source* had firmly planted the flag on a once unclaimed planet.

Between 1990 and 1994 *The Source* grew organically. The wildfire circulation surge that the magazine would experience in the latter nineties was still some ways off, but during this period *The Source* built its reputation as the bible of hip-hop. On the business side Mays and Young made slow but steady progress. Despite the emergence of Larry Flynt's *Rap Pages* and another publication called *Rap Sheet* in 1991 and 1992 respectively, both out of California, the music labels continued to reward *The Source*'s first-mover status by buttressing advertising revenue even as Mays sought, sometimes in vain, to bring other categories into the magazine. He had his work cut out convincing skeptics that the hip-hop audience was a viable market. But, with the dogged persistence that became his hallmark, convince he would.

Shecter's team didn't sit still during this period. They continued to hone the magazine's editorial. James Bernard helmed the political coverage, giving the magazine an almost nationalist bent and an edgy tone. Reggie Dennis was in charge of music, imparting an earnest, highbrow sensibility to the magazine's critiques. Dennis could be incredibly scathing, and he often was. But that didn't detract from his obvious creativity. The music coverage had many clever elements, such as a column for the best rhyme of the month, and handing out microphones to grade record reviews instead of stars. These items became things tracked as hungrily by artists as by readers, generating debate and argument. The Mind Squad, as the editorial staff called itself, had succeeded in making their magazine a thing of passion and prominence in the lives of their readers.

That accomplishment would nearly tumble off the cliff in 1994. By the fall of that year I'd returned to complete school after my year at the *Voice*. One afternoon someone at the paper's New York office sent me a fax. I looked at it curiously. It was a petition of some sort. And it had come from James Bernard. In it he accused Dave Mays of every publishing evil under the sun and demanded that Mays step down as publisher of the magazine. The petition asked for writers' signatures as a promise to boycott *The Source* as long as Mays remained.

I called a friend in New York for information. The story came pouring back; it was big news in hip-hop circles. The dispute stemmed from an article in the November '94 issue of *The Source*; a two-page profile of a hip-hop group out of Boston called the Almighty RSO. I remembered reading the article and thinking that the tone rang odd for a *Source* profile. It seemed little more than a platform for the artists. Turned out that the group in question had been associates of Mays since his Harvard days. He'd long been trying to get them into the magazine and the editorial staff had steadfastly refused. So after the October issue closed, Mays inserted a story of his own devising. The staff only discovered it after the issue was already at the printer.

The drama ran hot and ugly in the press. Dennis and Bernard accused RSO of a history of threatening, intimidating behavior toward the editorial staff, citing that, along with their negative opinion of the group's talent, as the reason they'd refused to cover them. Mays didn't say much beyond a few blanket statements from PR drones, though in later conversations with me he'd caustically accuse Dennis and Bernard of their own power shenanigans and deride them as editors gone drunk with power, prone to squabbling with artists in the magazine's pages, and intent on using the RSO incident as a lever in a struggle to control the magazine. Mays scoffed at the demands that he step down. Eventually, Shecter, Dennis, Bernard, and the majority of their staff left, taking most of the magazine's major writers with them, scribes like dream hampton and Cheo Coker. Mays and Young stood alone. Things looked bleak. But the dogged Mays found help from other *Source* writers like Ronin Ro and Adario Strange. They managed to keep publishing, though the editorial void was evident for some time.

Adario Strange called me a few days after I'd finished the Wu-Tang piece.

"Listen, I got another one for you. But you're gonna have to turn this around just as quickly."

"Who is it?"

"The Pharcyde."

The Los Angeles foursome with the creative flows and

B-boy moves was one of my favorite groups at the time. I immediately said yes. Between interviews and writing, the story took about four days to complete. When that, too, had been handed in successfully, Strange called yet again.

"Listen," he said, "would you be interested in a job?"

I was flabbergasted.

"Umm, what exactly?"

"Music editor. Why don't we meet and discuss it?"

"Yeah. Sure."

I hung the phone up. A giddy feeling seized my limbs. The next day I trekked into Manhattan to meet Strange. The magazine's offices were on the fifth floor of a building on Broadway, just below Houston, in the Soho area. There I met the building's turtle-slow elevators. They often left one in danger of overheating in the summer months, or chattering to death during the colder season. Upon exiting the elevator a swift right-hand turn and trip down a winding, wooden hallway revealed the simple black door that allowed entry into the *Source*'s waiting room. Strange met me there and we walked back downstairs to the street.

We strolled up Broadway, chatting about the future. Strange, a tall, physically commanding man, loped with ground-eating strides as he talked about *The Source*'s quest to rebuild, his vision for accomplishing that goal, and his belief that I could play a part. He spoke with fervor and passion. Adario Strange was an ambitious man. I listened carefully, quickening my own strides to keep pace.

"What about Dave?" I asked after several minutes. Strange knew what the question meant.

"Well, he doesn't say it much. But he's admitted to me that he knows what he did was wrong."

Three days later I reclined in a chair in Dave Mays's sixth-floor office. Mays sat across from me, behind a large desk. Bakari Kitwana, the executive editor, sat to my left. I'd only met Mays briefly before. Strange had introduced us after the Wu-Tang piece. Now I carefully studied this man who'd given hip-hop journalism a home. He seemed fairly nonassuming—just over six feet in height, medium build, hair and goatee trimmed in the close-cropped style preferred by many white hip-hop aficiona-dos. His eyes were his most distinct feature. They'd shift around the room, seldom resting in any one place. But when they did settle they churned with intensity. Kitwana was a shorter, compactly built black man. He wore small spectacles which, combined with the few years he spotted most of the staff in the age race, gave him a benign, professorial aura.

The two interviewed me formally, Kitwana peering at my scant résumé every now and then before asking a question. I couldn't shut up, running on about what I'd learned about journalism at the *Voice,* and my experi-ences in hip-hop dating back to Guyana. They were intrigued, and offered me the job.

I thought about it hard before I accepted. Despite Strange's assurances I was still deeply bothered by what had transpired just a year ago. And although I didn't know any of the *Source* writers or editors who'd walked out, I still felt some kinship with them. One afternoon at the *Village Voice* I ran my concerns by Greg Tate, a writer whose work I greatly respected.

"You should take it," Greg said, almost at once. "At your age, you don't get too many chances to play an important part in building a magazine back up." My decision was made. But in retrospect I've sometimes wondered if the decision would have been the same if I'd known all the nuances at the time. If I'd realized that this wasn't merely a case of another power-tripping magazine publisher riding roughshod over editorial precedent and prerogative, as such publishers are wont to do. If I'd known more about the physical confrontations, and the alleged death threats and guns brandished in the editorial offices. And if I'd caught sight of the thin, choking rope with which Raymond Scott, leader of the RSO, had securely trussed up Dave Mays.

Once past the main entrance, the office at 594 Broadway split into distinct hemispheres. The editorial team lived on the left, the business guys on the right. There were some six offices on the editorial side, scattered in a rough semicircle around an open area, separated by no more than a few broad steps. Omnipresent sounds from each office's sound system would leak out to collect and mix in the common space, providing a curious blend of continued chaos and calming routine. The entire place screamed with youthful energy. Colorful stickers, posters, and graffiti scribbles adorned every inviting space: desks, walls, filing cabinets. And the evidence of a young music staff at work lay everywhere—discarded tapes from rapping hopefuls, CD discs and jackets, black-and-white promotional photographs from labels now consigned to life as step-upons.

We had a small editorial team. The magazine boasted only two other staffers besides Strange, Kitwana, and myself—Angela Bronner, the editorial assistant, and staff writer Alan Gordon, an Oakland transplant who began the same day I did. Our art department counterparts also numbered few: art director Ola Kudu, art assistant Diana McClure, and Eric Russ, the photo editor.

A fellow named Jeremy Miller—or J-Mill as we called him—held the music editor's job before I came along. Actually, he worked in circulation. But he'd been moonlighting in an editor's role since the departure of the founding editors a year prior. A big, affable kid from Okalahoma, J-Mill looked at me with clear relief when I walked into his office that first day.

"Great, a real editor," he said, a slight midwestern tinge lacing his words.

He grinned at me. I grinned back, but more than a bit of anxiety danced beneath my composed expression. The look in J-Mill's eyes seemed akin to the relief of a weary, long-activated National Guardsman, thankful to return to familiar pastures now that the regular army had swooped in to take over. Delta Force trooper, however, I was not. Sure, I'd been edited by some of the best in the business at the *Village Voice*, legendary music editors like Bob Christgau and Joe Levy, but I'd only been walking in my own editor's skin for mere hours. J-Mill's experience at that moment dwarfed my own, and he'd done a damn good job of holding the section together while performing his regular duties in the circulation department. All this ran though my mind in the fraction of a second it took me to respond with aw-shucks assurance.

"Hey, great to meet you, man." I extended my hand confidently. "So how does all this work?"

For music magazines there is no post more critical than that of music editor. The editor in chief paints the broad strokes of the overall vision. Senior editors fill out those strokes. The managing editor keeps the trains running on time and on track. But the music editor feeds the entire machine: album release schedules, who may be in the studio or on tour, new artist signings, new records, new trends, all and more fall within the purview of the music editor, and this information shapes much of the edit calendar. Aside from providing this fuel, the music editor has his or her direct page responsibilities. These can vary from publication to publication but they almost always include the review section of the magazine. At *The Source* no piece of edit held more import. The review section, or Record Report as we termed it, meant the mics, the system by which we ranked albums. And nothing *The Source* did, even the cover, caused as much controversy and consternation as the mic awards. As music editor I would assume control of the entire process, which, aside from assigning and editing review copy, also included dubbing and distributing the albums under consideration and running the meetings at which key staffers decided on ratings. In those days that meant Dave, Adario, Alan, and me. I would also now be the main point of contact for the inevitably irate artists and label personnel for whom a rating could never be high enough. Don't think J-Mill minded handing over that responsibility.

J-Mill also gave me Riggs Morales.

"I've got this one writer," J-Mill explained. "He's a seventeen-year-old kid from uptown. He's still raw, but he loves the music and *The Source* and he really wants to get more involved. He could be a great help to you."

I shrugged.

"Well, okay, tell him to give me a call then."

I took my leave. Riggs called soon thereafter. He wanted to come by the office; meet the new music editor.

"Sure, come on by."

He materialized the next day. Riggs was a lanky kid, lean with a ball of energy curled inside. It gave him that springy, confident walk so common on the streets of Washington Heights from whence he hailed. Riggs had a ready grin, and an impossibly sunny disposition. I liked him right off the bat. He reminded me of my younger brothers. We chatted for a while that first day and he left with an album review as an assignment.

Riggs began to hang around a lot; collecting what assignments he could and being as helpful as possible. One afternoon, some two weeks later, he popped into my office with his customary bustle of energy and dropped onto the couch that faced my desk. I glanced up at him.

"Um, Sel," he blurted out, a high-wattage gleam in his eyes, "I was thinking I'd really like to be your intern. I could help you out. What do you think?"

He looked at me expectantly. An intern? I was still learning this editing thing, did I really need to figure out someone else's role? Riggs waited, hope, ambition, and eagerness practically radiating from him. The answer came easily.

"Well, sure," I replied, unable to contain a chuckle at his exuberant response.

"Dope! So what do I do now?" He asked.

I cast my eyes around my new office. The black couch against the right wall, the bookcase opposite, liberally sprinkled with a glut of CDs, tapes, and unopened packages. And just outside my door—the Wack Box. A grin stole over my features.

"See that," I gestured at the large cardboard box, another thing bequeathed to me by J-Mill. Riggs turned to look. The Wack Box sat there, large and foreboding. Originally meant as the repository for the most hilarious of the up to seventy submissions that came in weekly for the magazine's Unsigned Hype column, over the last year the box had ended up storing the majority of those submissions, good along with bad. J-Mill simply hadn't had enough time to go through all of the tapes.

"There's probably some good stuff in there," he'd told me almost sadly when we discussed the Wack Box. I thought he was right in all likelihood, since the magazine possessed quite a track record of discovering new talent—the Notorious B.I.G., Common, Mobb Deep, and many others. J-Mill himself had recently put the then unknown Queens duo CNN in the column. But no one could sum up the energy to plow through what looked to be several hundred, if not a thousand, tapes and bios from hopeful artists. Except for Riggs, that is.

"Right there," I told him, motioning to the box. "That's all you."

No more needed to be said. Everyone in edit knew the dilemma of the Wack Box.

A couple weeks later he tapped on my door. I looked up.

"Hey, I finished the box," he said.

I eyed him suspiciously, then glanced out the door. I could still see the Wack Box. Got up and made my way over to it. It was cleaned out, save for a few tapes and photos.

"I kept some of the really funny ones," Riggs said hurriedly, "like this one from these kids in Sweden." He showed me a picture. They looked like a rapping ski patrol.

"And here's all that's worth keeping." Riggs gestured to a smaller box in his arm; it contained about a dozen tapes.

"That's it?" I inquired, rummaging through them.

"Uh-huh, but these are all pretty tight."

"Good job, kid."

He grinned.

The success of *The Source* in the mid-to-late nineties begins with people like Riggs. Young. Passionately devoted to exploring hip-hop. Painted through and through with boundless energy and the sense that things would, more often than not, land right side up. Those qualities kept us buoyed when the surf got choppy. After all, there was little reason, less logic, and no paradigm for a group of young, minority journalists with scant experience to expect that they could grow a niche publication into a commercially successful magazine. Because of the walkout, we had little connection with the first set of editors to take a stab at that notion. We were truly mavericks, skiing downhill on fragments of institutional memory mixed with dashes of in-the-moment creativity. Most times the descent felt liberating. Frankly, we probably didn't know enough at the time to be anxious. But it did grow daunting for me on occasion. I'd left an environment where I was a clear junior, surrounded by proven mentors, to take a position where others would now lean on me in the same manner in which I had once leaned on the likes of Joe Levy and Ann Powers. Intellectually, I knew I wasn't there yet. Still, for this young staff I had to be.

The readers made the job easier. They were a passionate bunch, fierce in their criticisms, unwavering with their support. Since its inception *The Source* had done a remarkable job of making the reader central through a combination of strong editorial product and clever grassroots efforts, like the Source Van. The Source Van was exactly that—a souped-up piece of automotive machinery, laden down with video monitors and a punishing sound system with which to disseminate the latest in hip-hop. The Source Van and its driver, wild-haired, wild-eyed Ousman Sam, traversed the countryside to stop at diverse locations—schools, malls, record stores, hip-hop events—and hand out cool stuff: promotional CDs, videos, stickers, posters. For the fans it was more tangible evidence of *The Source*'s passion for them and the music they loved.

I hitched a ride with Ousman just once, in October of 1995. Several *Source* staffers had traveled to Miami's South Beach for a hip-hop industry convention called How Can I Be Down? On this afternoon Ousman and the van were heading to a record store in North Miami, just to let the kids know that *The Source* wasn't content to hang out in tony South Beach while we were in town. Seemed simple enough. I volunteered to come along since I'd never been on the van before. Ousman grinned broadly and invited me aboard.

"Come on, come on," he urged, voice painted a deep, smoky husk.

I clambered on. My backside had barely touched leather when Ousman took off, foot jammed down on the accelerator. The van hurtled onto and up Collins Avenue, a monstrous, aerodynamic shape cutting a silver swath through the Miami sun. Ousman drove the van like it was a Formula One car. Accelerating and decelerating with rapid abandon, hurtling past slow-moving drivers. He'd yank the steering wheel from side to side, his whole frame moving in the direction of the turn, like some peculiar body English. All of this done to the tune of high-decibel music. I sat shocked. Stomach lurching with every move of the van, breakfast threatening to reappear. Eventually, thankfully, Ousman pulled into the lot of a local mall. It was a toss-up as to who was the more grateful—me or the excited kids who soon gathered around.

The increased velocity of the surrounding murmurs caught my ear first. I looked up, wondering what had caused the upsurge in the conversation levels. The answer came swiftly. It was impossible to miss him, impossible to miss them. From beneath the canopied tent on the east side of New York City's Bryant Park I could clearly see Suge Knight making his way through the VIP entrance for this after party to MTV's 1996 Video Music Awards, completed moments ago in nearby Radio City Music Hall. Knight wore red. Whether suit, shirt, or sweater I don't recall. Just the crimson splash so clear to the eye, draped as it was upon a six foot plus, three hundred-pound frame. Knight had not come alone. Some two dozen associates floated in his wake. And Tupac Shakur strode alongside. There were vague mutters of surprise from some of the observers marking the posse's entrance. After all, Knight, Tupac, and their Los Angeles-based Death Row label were still in the midst of a bitter verbal and emotional conflict with Sean "Puff Daddy" Combs's Bad Boy label, home of the Notorious B.I.G., a conflict that media outlets would elevate into the so-called East-West war.

I remember Tupac's eyes more than anything else. They burned with a deep fire clearly visible even from yards away, marking all in his path. One well-wisher came up to greet him. Tupac stopped to listen, nodding slowly at the proffered words, those cavernous eyes drifting to and fro, swallowing everything within their field of vision. Briefly, his gaze met my own; then moved on.

I had never met or seen Tupac in person before. That sighting would be the first and last time. On September 7th Tupac, riding in the front seat of a car driven by Knight, would be shot after leaving a Mike Tyson fight at Las Vegas' MGM Grand. Four shots hit Tupac in the chest; shrapnel grazed Knight. Back in New York the news struck *The Source* with sledgehammer impact, yet it did not come entirely as a surprise. Specific circumstances aside, Tupac himself had long been predicting such an end in deeply fatalistic songs. And his life of late—the angry assaults on the Notorious B.I.G. and Bad Boy in the media and on records; his 1995 incarceration on sexual assault charges; the 1994 robbery in Times Square that left him shot several times; the numerous run-ins with police, including a 1993 shootout with off-duty cops in Atlanta— seemed permanently touched by controversy and near tragedy. Tupac was an ember in constant search of a bonfire. Las Vegas proved the final conflagration.

Still, he'd long seemed invulnerable. So we scrambled to prepare two sets of editorial in the event that he lived or died. Los Angeles-based senior contributor Frank Williams immediately went to Las Vegas to report, joining the throng of media, teary-eyed fans, and the curious who had flocked to Tupac's hospital, the Nevada Medical Center. Back in New York we made our assignments, mocked up a cover, and then waited to see if Tupac would pull through yet again. He would not. On the evening of September 13th I sat tiredly on a couch in my girlfriend's living room, wrung ragged from the intense hustle to rearrange the issue, when my cell phone rang. It was Dave Mays.

"Yeah," his voice, too, seemed weary, "Tupac just passed, man."

"Shit." After six drawn-out days the finality seemed surreal. "I'm gonna head back to the office."

I trudged back downtown to *The Source*'s new office space at 215 Park Avenue South, then penned an emotional essay that would open the editorial package on Tupac. But some of that essay's sentiment would raise the ire of Adario Strange, who was now our executive editor. In the essay I cast a wide net of responsibility. I was convinced that all of us—fans, the media, and music industry—had played a role, if not in Tupac's death, then in nurturing the soil from which the possibility sprang. In my estimation we stood guilty—whether through production, dissemination, or consumption—of allowing young black men to believe the myths of invulnerability they spun about themselves for far too long. Strange took deep exception to that point of view, although, to his credit, he didn't edit it out.

"I don't know about you, but I didn't have anything to do with Tupac's death," he snapped at me once he'd read the essay. I don't know if he felt I was pointing a specific finger at him, since he'd conducted an interview with Tupac for a *Source* cover story earlier in the year, which Tupac used, in part, to further his verbal assault on Biggie and Bad Boy. And I'd made no secret of my disgust for an earlier *Vibe* magazine cover that featured Biggie and Puffy with the alarmist banner headline "East vs. West," crystallizing a dispute between two artists, two executives, and their respective labels into a regional conflict, a designation that the mainstream media would pick up and toss about for years. Perhaps Strange thought the implication in my essay lumped him into the same irresponsible pot. But that was not my intent. And I never equated his story, or anything *The Source* did at the time, with *Vibe*'s actions.

Things were a tad uneasy with Strange and I in the fall of 1996. Earlier in the year he'd maneuvered his way to a co-executive editor role with Bakari Kitwana who, tired of the wear and tear of the job, eager to spend more time with his family and preferring to concentrate on the political beat he loved, eventually ceded the role completely to become the magazine's national affairs editor, a part-time position he'd be able to fulfill from home. By spring of 1996 Strange possessed the gig he'd clearly itched for from the moment we first met: running editorial at *The Source.* He was excited and charged. In contrast, my own tank was running low. *The Source* had ballooned over the course of the year—ad pages, edit pages, circulation; all were on an upward swing. I thought it important that we add talented staffers in order to meet the demands of that growth. But Strange felt differently, or so it appeared to me since he wouldn't hire anyone. I would funnel résumés and talented folk his way, only to have them shot down. All the while my edit load grew exponentially. We had a staff that could only react to the moment, lacking the resources to work two, three, four issues ahead. And my editor now seemed hostile to the very notion on which he'd originally sold me: rebuilding the staff. I didn't know whether Strange felt threatened by the idea of surrounding himself with too many talented people, whether he felt there simply weren't any such folk available, or if Dave Mays hadn't given him the budget. The result was still the same: we were stagnant and stood in real danger of falling behind our own growth curve. By the fall Strange also became withdrawn and disenchanted with hip-hop in general, as well as with some of the young folk who'd begun to gather about me: staff writer Alan

Gordon, whose writing abilities Strange openly derided, passing him off to me as a hopeless case in need of a permanent editor, my intern Riggs Morales, and Carlito Rodriguez, a Bronx cat whom I really wanted to hire. Back at 594 Broadway, Rodriguez, who'd recently done a five-year bid in the fed, handed me a piece he'd written in prison. I realized he was a hell of a writer and decided to groom him for a place at the magazine. Strange disagreed. Patience was fast fleeing.

I'd had a brief flirtation with *Vibe* the past summer. Then music editor Danyel Smith, whom I'd written for before I accepted the *Source* gig, took me to lunch at Noho Star in Soho, the same restaurant where I'd run into a disgruntled Raekown the year prior. Smith didn't mince words. After the requisite small talk she asked me to come work with her at *Vibe*, as the associate music editor. I digested the offer. Told her it sounded intriguing.

A week later I journeyed to the magazine's offices on Lexington Avenue. I was stunned. From the size of the space, to its interior design, to the sheer number of staff hustling about, everything seemed several orders of magnitude grander than *The Source*. These folk had money and didn't seem shy about using it. Smith took me into the office of editor in chief Alan Light. A bit later Keith Clinkscales, then CEO of *Vibe*, strode in. Clinkscales, a brash, dynamic man, pumped my hand in greeting. The four of us had a quick conversation before Clinkscales bid farewell and strode out with the same purposeful energy with which he'd entered.

Smith called me a few days later with their offer. It was a decent offer, more than I was making at *The Source* for a lower masthead position. But I thought *Vibe* could do better, particularly since they were stealing a key element from a competitor. So I gave Smith a counter offer, explaining my logic and adding that it would make particular sense for *Vibe* to pay me more, especially since the magazine had recently taken a pounding in the press for underpromoting and underpaying African-American editors. I hung up, satisfied that I'd made a compelling and clever case. Too clever by half, as it turned out. *Vibe* gave me a polite no thanks and that was that. End of flirtation. I'd run into Clinkscales a month later at the *Vibe* Music Seminar, a weeklong event at the Waldorf-Astoria. He spotted me one night through the smoky haze of a cigar party in a Waldorf suite. Motioned me over.

"So what happened?" I figured he must have known, so I shrugged noncommittally.

"Money just didn't work out, I guess."

Clinkscales shook his head and wagged a finger at me.

"Next time don't worry about the money, just grab the opportunity," he said before moving deeper into the party.

I had not told Dave Mays about *Vibe*'s approach. Chalk it up to inexperience. Still, I reasoned, there was no reason why the *Vibe* offer couldn't work for me now. If I needed a hammer to get what I wanted at *The Source,* then *Vibe* and Clinkscales, with whom the similarly competitive Mays had an acrimonious relationship, would be that hammer. I walked into Mays's office in October of 1996, two months after things had cooled with *Vibe.*

"*Vibe* made me an offer, and it's a good one. I'm really thinking about it."

Mays leaned back in his chair and assumed his thinking pose—eyes narrowed, chin cupped between thumb and forefinger.

"Well, we don't want you to go anywhere." He paused. "What do you need?"

No mystery there, just more money and the power to actively recruit people. And I wanted to bring those people straight to Mays and co-owner Ed Young for hiring consideration. Mays agreed.

I moved rapidly, recruiting Tracii McGregor, a talented journalist from California who'd been marking time as a publicist, for the lifestyle editor post, and Elliot Wilson, cofounder of the well-regarded underground tome *Ego Trip* and then serving as an editor at *CMJ*—the trade paper *College Music Journal*—for the associate music editor position. After sitting through a grilling in Mays's office, administered by Mays, Young, and a skeptical Strange, both editors were hired. They formed the core of the creative team that would evolve over the next year. In a few months we officially added Carlito Rodriguez as staff writer. Strange grew more and more distant from this emerging staff. And by February of 1997, after the March issue hit the stands, he'd left us. It was an awkward moment. On the one hand I felt no small measure of guilt for the way my forceful, independent action had undercut the very man who'd recruited me. On the other, by the end of his tenure Strange exhibited such a strong desire to cast off the load that his departure seemed a relief to him, as well as to those who'd had to bear his frosty distance. Three months later I'd become executive editor. Three years later I'd understand Adario Strange a lot better.

• • •

I'm not sure how or where I first heard that they'd returned. But it was big news in the office—Reggie Dennis and James Bernard were back in the publishing game, at the helm of a new hip-hop magazine called *XXL*. And they intended to come for our throat.

XXL would be published by Harris Publishing, a multititle company with one other entrant in the urban-oriented field, the basketball magazine, *Slam*. *XXL* provided Harris an opportunity to delve deeper into the lucrative market cultivated by Mays and company, and it gave Dennis and Bernard a tool for vengeance of a sort, a means to demonstrate that it was their vision, not Mays's, that had pumped lifeblood through *The Source.*

The duo launched a take-no-prisoners press campaign, adapting the tried-and-true tactic of going after a category leader, *The Source* in this case, in order to set the new entrant apart. With Dennis and Bernard that strategy seemed to take a personal spin. They lost no opportunity to promote *XXL*'s pending launch by deriding all that *The Source* had become since their departure. At times the vitriol took me aback. After all, I didn't know these guys from Adam and here they were, pounding my editorial product into the mud with all the venom of an angry guy hurling insults at his ex-wife's new husband.

Between 1997 and 1998 *The Source* endured its toughest year of competition in the struggle for dominance between the urban music titles. We were under constant siege. Aside from the erstwhile *Source* crowd at *XXL*, we had to contend with *Vibe*'s combative duo of Danyel Smith, who took over the editor's job from Alan Light in late spring of 1997, and Keith Clinkscales. Dissatisfied with his ability to compete directly with Dave Mays with the broader *Vibe,* whose musical horizons stretched beyond hip-hop, Clinkscales would later launch the hip-hop upstart *Blaze,* a direct broadside aimed at *The Source*'s domination of the marketplace. And out in California Flynt Publishing's longstanding *Rap Pages*— under the editorship of former *Source* scribe dream hampton and, later, the departed Alan Gordon—still had a scrappy presence at the margins. Wherever we turned up popped snippy press items about folk ending *The Source*'s dominant run, and word of furious backroom negotiations and arm-twisting to get major artists to commit to competitor's covers and eschew *The Source* steadily leaked back. In one instance, summer of 1998, we'd secured a Lauryn Hill exclusive for our September cover, timed to hit the market with the release of her debut album, *The Miseducation of Lauryn Hill. Vibe,* unable to cajole or bully Hill's record label Columbia into a change of plans, launched a sneak attack to spoil our thunder by putting out an issue the month before featuring an unflattering, two-year-old shot of Hill on the cover. As much as it ticked me off, I had to admire their gamesmanship. Unsurprisingly, Columbia went ballistic and I urged them on, grumbling to Miguel Baguer, a good friend and Columbia's urban publicity maven, about the poor taste of it all and the possible effect on our forthcoming issue. An incensed Baguer yanked back promises already extended to the higher-ups at *Vibe,* who promptly launched an unsuccessful attempt to get him fired. Meanwhile, *The Source* quietly picked up a few more exclusives from Columbia, and when the Lauryn issue hit the stands it became an all-around home run.

We topped the competition with more than political maneuverings. A key component was the attitude of the staffers. It would have been far too easy for our young team to become caught up in the personal dynamic. Nothing wrong with taking offense at slights, I certainly did often enough, but I urged them to channel that anger into our mission, and to never lose sight of what we were here for—staying on message and on target with the reader, whom we knew better than anyone. As long as we were number one folk were going to chase us. No need for us to turn about and stoop to their level. That meant no return fire in the press, and no projection that the Johnny-come-latelies represented anything else.

An even more important component was the stark reality of the contest. I knew that for any of these magazines to win, simply being consumed with becoming the Anti-*Source* wasn't going to be enough. That fuel delivered limited miles for the gallon. After the hate, you needed a vision, staffers to execute, and an infrastructure to support. None of our competitors could consistently hit all three balls out of the park. By all rights *Vibe* should have buried us given that magazine's naturally broader reach. Indeed, they always outstripped *The Source* on overall paid circulation, but we murdered them on the newsstand, the true barometer of a magazine's heat with consumers. *Vibe* was simply too conservative, seldom venturing into the kind of serious, nonmusic reportage that helped distinguish *The Source,* and unwilling to take chances with covers. At *The Source* we bet the farm, every month, that our cover choice would be the hottest thing in the market. Most of the time we were right. Most of the time *Vibe* played it safer and slower. Only going for the sure bets, a multi-platinum-selling artist, and yet they usually didn't pull the trigger until the bet had proved its worth again through some initial success. With that modus operandi and a monthly magazine's three-month lead time you're bound to look late, and covers will almost inevitably hit the market after the wave has crested. In contrast, by the summer of 1997 *The Source* was the top-selling music magazine on America's newsstands, churning out some 318,000 copies, almost doubling its closest competitor *Rolling Stone.*

XXL and *Blaze* simply self-destructed. In late 1997, after a decent first issue, Dennis, Bernard, and company again got into a dispute with a publisher, this time over equity, and walked, promising that the next time they entered the magazine fray it would be under their own power. *XXL* would keep going with later editors Sheena Lester and Scoop Jackson. And although both editors, particularly Lester, the revered former editor of *Rap Pages* in the early nineties, would make the book respectable, it never again posed any threat to *The Source.*

At *Blaze*, helmed by former *Vibe* staffer and AP reporter Jesse Washington, idealism ran smack dab into reality. *Blaze* launched on a platform of reformation and confrontation, promising to burn away the cronyism they claimed magazines like *The Source* had with the industry, and to ratchet up the critical dialogue by bringing real heat to artists, whom they insisted, erroneously, had been getting too much of a free pass in *The Source.* But the editors at *Blaze* did not have the diplomatic skills, experience, or long-standing respect in the hip-hop community to deal with the ramifications of that point of view. Washington quickly acquired the dubious distinction of becoming the editor in chief most set upon by rappers. Just before *Blaze*'s launch he had a run-in with Wyclef Jean. In Washington's allegation, an angry Wyclef, upset at the review foisted upon his young protégé, Canibus, pulled a gun on him. Most folk who knew Wyclef scoffed at the notion, but the story quickly found its way out to major media organs and became the gossip upon which *Blaze* launched in the summer of 1998.

I saw both Washington and Wyclef moments before the alleged incident. Carlito Rodriguez and I were up at Hit Factory, the recording studio where Wyclef often worked, to meet with him and listen to Canibus's album. Wyclef liked to ask members of our staff to check out music he was working on. That night we all sat in a good-size office. Rodriguez and I, along with fellow hip-hop scribe Kris Ex, rested in comfortable, leather armchairs facing Wyclef, who lounged behind the office's large, wooden desk.

"I don't know," I shook my head after the music had faded away. "It's not that great, man; not what people are going to be expecting." The other writers concurred. We'd all admired Canibus and had hoped his debut record would be stronger. Wyclef shrugged.

"I hear you, but this is what he wants to do. You know you can't tell young MCs nothing."

Rodriguez and I chopped it up with him for a while longer, and then made ready to take our leave. Wyclef spoke again.

"Yo, I gotta go next door and meet with these cats from *Blaze.*" He waved a disparaging hand. "You know these guys?"

"Oh really? They're here?"

Wyclef nodded. Rodriguez and I looked at each other with interest.

"Let's go meet them real quick."

We got up and strode from the office into an adjoining

conference room. Jesse Washington, whom I'd never met before, and one of his editors sat at the oblong table, along with one or two of Wyclef's folk. I reached out my hand to him and introduced myself. He shook it firmly and gave me a challenging smile. I grinned in return.

"Good luck with everything," I offered. We left. The news about the alleged gun broke the next day.

Short months later controversy struck Washington again. In the midst of a heated conversation with producer/rapper Deric Angelettie over an image displayed in *Blaze*, he was physically attacked by Angelettie and an associate, and suffered some damage to his person.

After the run-ins with the rap artists Washington would have a fatal run-in with his own corporate structure. In March of 1999, he made the decision to hire Montoun Hart, the alleged killer of Jonathan Levin, son of Time Warner Chairman Gerald Levin. Then he wrote about it in an editorial, a sort of humanistic muse on restraining judgment. That was it for Washington, for although *Vibe* and *Blaze* were no longer under Time Warner's corporate umbrella, the higher-ups of owner Miller Publishing still maintained strong ties to their old company, and were infuriated by the affair. Pressure descended on CEO Clinkscales and Washington found himself dropped like a hot potato, ending a tumultuous run. Although *Blaze*, like *XXL*, would continue after its founding editor's departure—ironically, under my former style editor at *The Source*, Mimi Valdés—it could never clearly separate itself from its big brother *Vibe*, could never find and maintain an identity. Clinkscales's own departure from *Vibe* later that year would hammer yet another nail in the coffin. *Blaze* would inevitably wither and die.

• • •

When 1999 rolled around *The Source* was near the top of its game. Total paid circulation had climbed well above 400,000, most of it still generated via newsstand. We'd never made any real push to go down the more expensive subscription route. Ad pages and revenue had also climbed. Indeed, the last two years had been good for the hip-hop business as a whole. Our success was due in no small measure to hip-hop's growing dominance of America's cultural radar. Growth could be tough work, and few in hip-hop were immune from blowing off steam with spectacular hedonism or extremely conspicuous consumption. Folk at *The Source* were no exception, though our exploits were admittedly tame when juxtaposed with those of the more economically high-powered industry executives and recording artists.

One Tuesday evening a small group of us went to dinner at Puff Daddy's Justin's restaurant. Tuesday was industry night at that one-time Chelsea hot spot, and *The Source* had a regular table. We whooped it up, dinner, drinks, bottles of expensive champagne sent to tables of women we admired. By dinner's end the night was still young and appetites had barely been sated. So we kicked things up a notch, jumping in a caravan of expensive cars to head over to the swanky Royalton Hotel. The inebriated pack lumbered into the low-lit lobby of the hotel and I headed straight for the familiar face of the desk clerk. I'd recently stayed at the hotel for a spell while I'd been between apartments.

"Good evening, Mr. Hinds."

"Hey. Is the penthouse available?"

"Of course. Will this be on your *Source* account?"

I paused for a microsecond. Well, why the hell not? *Source* rule number two: Highest-ranking exec on site picks up all tabs.

"Definitely."

We took the elevator up to the penthouse suite, a cavernous space of arcing floors, metallic-festooned walls, and a balcony overlooking the winking lights and nighttime shenanigans of midtown New York City.

"Shit, this is dope, we need to set something off," someone exclaimed.

We sent for more alcohol almost immediately, and after a quick, enthusiastic discussion, the consensus emerged that the best party at the moment would involve the services of professional ladies. Swiftly, a member of the crew set off to make the requisite phone calls while the rest of us passed the time with anticipatory conversation washed down by liquor.

"So what do you do, what do you do?" one fella, RB, asked nervously. "I mean, I've never been with a prostitute before."

We were too choked up with laughter to respond. Unlike RB, I wasn't about to volunteer my own first-time anxiety. After an interminable delay, the women began to arrive in groups of twos and threes. At first we stared awkwardly. Then C-Boogie, the pro among us, moved assuredly over to them as they entered, whispering the scenario along with brief introductions. Since I was springing for the whole thing the guys insisted I have first choice. So I clasped the hand of one curvy, cream-skinned Latino beauty and moved to the confines of the master bedroom.

"You want me to take my clothes off?"

"Yeah, I guess."

She disrobed and sat on the edge of the bed. The smoky yellow light melted into her skin. Eyes locked on some indefinite spot somewhere beyond me. I walked over slowly and rested a hand on her shoulder. She lay back, her eyes now fixed somewhere on the ceiling, pointedly avoiding my own. I frowned. This wasn't at all what I'd imagined it might be. Bent over and kissed her shoulder. It was cold and rigid, like pressing lips to a sheet of metal. Embarrassment and discomfort rose about the room.

"Look, um, it's okay. We don't gotta do nothing. You could just chill here if you want."

She didn't answer. I grabbed my glass and beat a hasty retreat from the bedroom. My man Sean spotted me leaving.

"Yo, wattup, Sel, you through? What's the deal?" he inquired.

I waved a noncommittal hand.

"Not feeling it, yo."

I sat out on the balcony with the rush of night air cool against my face until they called me.

"Hey Sel, they need you to sign these credit card receipts."

But the real marker of *The Source*'s success by 1999 didn't rest in reenacted video scenes and the ability to blow money stupidly. It resided in the strength and vision of the editorial product. We'd completely locked up the bible of hip-hop identity, and held the subsequent respect. For me, the goal at this juncture was that *The Source* be recognized as a top-flight magazine, a place where important journalism took place. We were well on our way down that path. Over the past year the magazine had been redesigned, a complete overhaul of the art direction and a substantial tweaking and reorganization of the editorial. *Rolling Stone* had been the original model for Mays and Shecter back in the early nineties; but I used other reference points for my new *Source,* specifically *GQ, Vanity Fair,* and the resurgent *Esquire.* All three magazines impressed me by treating writing with great import. I admired *Vanity Fair's* outstanding photography, and sought to emulate the difficult balance that magazine struck between the relatively lighter fare of celebrity and trend reportage, and sweeping investigative pieces. *GQ* and *Esquire* both unfolded with a linear structure that I would adapt for *The Source,* creating a fast-moving front of book that encompassed our three editorial tent pegs—music, culture, and politics; a wide-ranging column well where writers touched down upon a diverse array of topics; and an ambitious feature well for the longer stories, all capped off by our infamous Record Report section. It made for a solid package that intrigued folk of every stripe. From screen legend Warren Beatty who sat me down over dinner one evening in Los Angeles while he was working on *Bulworth* in order to learn more about hip-hop and inquire, just maybe, as to whether he could end up on the cover; to Graydon Carter, editor of *Vanity Fair,* who was fascinated enough by what we were doing to take me to lunch at his downtown New York watering hole, Da Silvano. Took all my cool not to blurt out to Carter how much his magazine had influenced my maturation as an editor.

Our editors and writers enjoyed this approach. With new music editor Smokey Fontaine shoring up the bread and butter music coverage, editors like deputy editor Dimitry Leger, Tracii McGregor, Bakari Kitwana, and his eventual successor at the national affairs desk, Akiba

Solomon, could roam free. We ran short fiction; tapped star *Village Voice* reporter Peter Noel for investigative work; asked revered poet Sonia Sanchez to interview Afeni Shakur; and dispatched writers to all ends of the globe to pursue stories we thought mattered to the hip-hop generation. Amy Linden went to Paris to chase a story on that city's intersection of race and hip-hop. Jimmie Briggs flew to Rawanda to interview the young killers of that traumatized land. Marcus Mabry ruminated on slavery in the Sudan. I was particularly keen on the international stories. For me they represented a hammer with which to smash the four-block syndrome choking far too many youth of color, a means to show them their own relevance in the world beyond their immediate neighborhood. Our work in 1999 would land us a nomination for General Excellence for that year's National Magazine Awards, as well as a Gold Award from the Folio Editorial Excellence Awards. Both were firsts for the magazine. But not everyone was thrilled with this increasingly broader, smarter *Source.*

By 1999 the RSO crew had rechristened themselves the Made Men. It was an effort to shed the stigma attached to the old label and start afresh. In truth, I'd had no problem with Raymond Scott and his crew since I'd been at *The Source.* I was well aware of their dark Boston reputation—associates lost to murder, alleged gang and drug activity, persistent run-ins with police. In fact, a few years later three of Scott's crew would be convicted for the brutal nightclub stabbing of Boston Celtic Paul Pierce. But for the better part of my time at the magazine, the snarling, threatening nemeses of the old *Source* editors were just guys who'd pop in to town every other week or so and hang in Dave Mays's office till the wee hours as weed smoke, loud music, and laughter poured out. They were usually personable and friendly. And sometimes they were useful to have around. Like when Damon Dash and a bunch of cohorts from Roc-A-Fella Records stormed into our offices in the fall of 1997, screaming that Dave Mays had broken a promise to put Jay-Z on the cover.

I'd been working on an edit when a muted uproar from the lobby caught my ear. A staffer dashed in my office.

"You'd better come outside," she said excitedly. "There's trouble and Dave's not here."

I followed her out through the main passageway to the lobby of the office, only to be greeted by a scene of bedlam. To one side stood Damon Dash, CEO of Roc-A-Fella Records, along with some tough-looking individuals I didn't recognize. To the other stood several members of *The Source* business side, foremost among them Ron Horton, a forceful, weightlifting buff who sold classified ads. Arms pointed threateningly, voices raised, and bodies tensed in that physical watchfulness that precipitates an explosion of action.

"I don't give a fuck who you are, money," Ron snapped angrily at Dash. "You don't come up in here like this."

An angry retort was Dash's only answer and Ron seemed to move closer to him. The temperature jumped several degrees.

"Yo, yo, yo!" I yelled above the din, catching everyone's attention. "Ron, chill. Damon, what's going on, man?"

Dash turned to me angrily.

"Yo, your man Dave bullshitted us and we not leaving till Jay-Z gets on this cover!"

"Damon, the issue's already done."

"We don't give a fuck, we ain't leaving!"

The temperature rose once more. Ron, who seemed moments away from full-blown rage, began to gesture again. I decided to take this somewhere else.

"Everybody relax. Look, Damon, come back downstairs with me; let's discuss this." With that I moved out of the lobby toward the elevator banks. As I'd hoped, Dash and company followed.

"Ain't shit to discuss," he muttered darkly. Four staffers from *The Source* swiftly joined us. The entire throng stepped in as an elevator opened with a soft ding. Then the doors drew shut.

We stared at each other. Dash and I occupied the middle, me still murmuring reasonable statements. Four or five cats slouched behind Dash, scowls painted on their grills. To my rear stood J-Mill, ad salesman Che Johnson, big E.B., and dapper Dale Johnson. The latter two were compatriots of Dave Mays from Boston, and part of Raymond Scott's extended crew. Both held jobs on the business side. E.B. as office assistant, Johnson as Dave Mays's executive assistant.

The eleven-floor descent was largely silent, punctuated only by the muttering between Dash and I, and the laser-hot stares between the groups of men at our respective backs. The elevator hit the building lobby and as the doors hissed open we spilled out onto the bright-lit pavement of Park Avenue South. Voices began to climb again. Passersby stopped to gawk at the ten young black men yelling at each other.

"This is real bullshit; who the fuck do y'all think we

are?!" Dash exploded again, coming sheer inches from my face. "And where's fuckin' Dave Mays? He said everything was good."

I took a deep breath and stood calmly, hands folded together just below my waist.

"Damon, Jay is on the cover of *XXL*. I'm sure Dave told you that we're not going to put out the same cover as a competitor. You guys chose to go that route."

"What?! That's some bullshit. What they got to do with us on *The Source?*"

"That's just the way it works. This issue is a done deal. Let's talk about later in the year."

"Fuck that! Y'all puttin' Jay on this cover!"

"It can't be done. The issue is already printed."

Anger and frustration simmered in Dash's eyes. Che Johnson, who had his own relationship with Dash, reaffirmed the points I'd just made. Hostile side chatter flared up between the other participants in our tense circle. For one frightening moment I thought E.B. was going to smash one of the smaller Roc-A-Fella guys in the face after he'd said something particularly insulting.

"What!?" E exclaimed in that sharp tone that always heralds action in the streets. He took a step forward.

"Chill, E, chill," I implored, pushing a hand out. He ceased his forward movement, leering at the dude before him. Behind my mask of calm I desperately wanted to break the situation up. I didn't know who among this collective might be packing a gun but there was a damn good chance that someone was. I became less certain of my strategy to move the dispute into a public place to temper any explosion.

There was now a good-size crowd watching us, including my girlfriend who'd come to meet me. She, too, stared wide-eyed at this OK Corral-ish scene.

"Damon, there's nothing we can do here. We need to break this up now before the cops come."

Seconds after I uttered those words came the whoop of a police siren. All heads turned to glance in the direction of the sound, and we began to drift apart.

"This shit is fucked-up, yo," Dash uttered one last time as he walked off, just barely taking the hand I stretched out to him. His boys moved behind him, throwing dark looks and curses as they went. Silent, I watched them go.

Jay-Z got his cover later in the year. Dash and I would develop a strong professional relationship and mutual respect. But the institutional relationship between *The Source* and Roc-A-Fella remained marked by an undercurrent of distrust. And four years after the sidewalk confrontation I drifted into an epilogue rife with dark humor. One afternoon, as I drove along New York City's Houston Street, a strange car pulled abreast. The driver pointed at me in animated fashion and shouted something inaudible. Curious, I rolled down the window.

"I know you!" he barked, a scowl seizing his features. "You that nigga from *The Source* who fronted on us!"

"Excuse me?" I said, thoroughly perplexed and a bit taken aback.

"Yeah, when me and my man Dame came through. Y'all niggas fronted, yo! Your name Hinds or some shit. You like the editor, right?" His scowl deepened.

Sometimes notoriety is such an unwelcome guest. I shook my head wearily.

"Not anymore. And that was a long time ago, son." I pressed the window up and drove off.

• • •

Before 1999 Mays didn't push his crew down our throat. On occasion he'd lope down the long hallway that spanned between his office and the editorial wing to play us new music they'd been working on. Inevitably, some of that stuff would find its way onto the various song lists we published every month to highlight music below radar. It was a small give to Mays, one that we could live with. However, by the summer of 1999—with the RSO's new Made Men identity and a pending record—the stakes had grown. Mays had spent a considerable amount of *The Source's* political capital—and no small amount of money—to produce *Classic Limited Edition*, the album from the Made Men. Several hip-hop and urban music personalities were enticed to appear on the record, and more *Source* money poured into the construction of a top-flight recording studio for Scott and crew in Boston. Over the past decade Mays had helped his friends secure several recording contracts, several opportunities to pump lifeblood into their career. All came to naught. Those involved viewed *Classic Limited Edition* as perhaps their last, best attempt. By that reckoning it should have been no surprise that Mays and Scott expected the magazine to deliver a greater return on what they'd invested, despite Scott's urging me, earlier in the year, to treat the Made Men like any other new group.

Mays gave the completed Made Men album to the editorial staff in July. We assigned it for review, along with a small feature, one befitting their stature as a "new" group, to run in the September issue. Things came to a head swiftly.

One August afternoon, just after we'd gotten the first copies of the issue, Dale Johnson, Mays's executive assistant and Scott associate, stuck his head in my office.

"Meeting in the conference room tomorrow at two

P.M.," he barked brusquely. "Everybody got to be there."

I looked up in surprise. Johnson and I were pretty cool and he'd never directed such an aggressive tone at me. But before I could utter a word he pulled his head back and went striding up the editorial hallway, knocking on doors and repeating his command.

Carlito Rodriguez and Smokey Fontaine soon walked into my office.

"So what's going on?" Fontaine asked.

"I have no idea," I replied.

"It's some kind of meeting with Ray and them," Rodriguez offered.

"You know what, let me call Dave down here."

I grabbed my desk phone and dialed the three-digit extension. "Dave? Can you come down this way for a second? Need to ask you something. Cool."

I hung the phone up and looked at the editors.

"He's on his way."

Mays came down within a few minutes. His eyes widened slightly when he saw all three of us arrayed there and the ghost of a sheepish smile tickled his features. He sat.

"So what's up, fellas?"

"What's the deal with this meeting tomorrow that Dale just told all my editors they had to attend," I asked him directly.

"Oh. Well, Ray and some of the guys just want to come by and talk about their story in the new issue. They want to talk about their relationship with *The Source* and how the magazine covers them. Just air some things out, you know?"

I caught the eyes of the other two. Fontaine smiled disbelievingly. Rodriguez shook his head.

"Bad idea, Dave," I said. "Nothing good can come out of some big meeting between Ray and his crew and the editors."

"Well, I don't know. Ray has a couple of good points that are worth hearing."

I shook my head emphatically.

"Dave, you know just how it'll go down. Ray will lose his temper and flip out and that will just fuck everything up. If he's got points to make, why don't the three of us go and have lunch, outside of the office. There's absolutely no need to create some spectacle for the whole staff."

Mays considered for a moment.

"Okay, maybe you're right," he allowed. "I'll call Ray."

With that he eased up from the couch on which he'd been sitting and strode from the office.

I next saw Mays the following morning. Gone was the wishy-washy uncertainty from the day before. Now he clearly knew which course of action would be best. He walked into my office, fairly bouncing with determination.

"Listen, we're going to have this meeting at two P.M.," He smacked his fist in his palm for emphasis. "Make sure all the senior editors are there."

He'd obviously spoken to Scott who'd clearly straightened out any hesitancy. It didn't surprise me. Mays would have leaped from a bridge if the garrulous Scott demanded it.

"Dave, you're the boss," I answered. "If you say be there, we'll be there; but I'm telling you again, this is a bad idea. And if things go the way I think they will, I'm not going to react well."

Don't think he even heard me.

"This is going to be good, man, it's going to be good," he uttered as he left my office. I'm not sure whom he was trying to convince, me or some last vestige of reason buried within him.

Word spread quickly among the edit staff and the morning slumped by in a state of tense anticipation. The designated hour arrived with all the subtlety of a trumpeting elephant. From my office I could hear folk stirring in the editorial hallway and moving into the conference room. I sat still for a while. Then, after a deep, settling breath, I too headed for the meeting.

They came in slowly. Raymond Scott led the way. Scott is a light-skinned black man of relatively short stature. At first glance there seems little threat or intimidation to him. Except, perhaps, for his eyes. And his temper. A host of folk trailed him into the room: five members of the Boston crew; Marvette Britto, the publicist representing the Made Men; and two lower-level *Source* employees, Ace and Black. I looked at the latter two with particular curiosity. There was no reason for them to be in this meeting, save as members of Scott's extended crew; they didn't work for editorial. Clearly, this was shaping up to be the circus I'd forecasted.

I took a seat at the large, oval table that dominated the conference room. Several editors were already seated, including Smokey Fontaine, Carlito Rodriguez, Tracii McGregor, and Riggs Morales. Dave Mays was also there, sitting opposite from me. An awkward silence stretched for a minute as the participants considered each other. Scott spoke first. He began on a fairly even keel, recapping the long, personal relationship between he and Mays, the blowup with the original editorial staff, the black mark that he felt hip-hop journalists had imposed on his group as a result, and the fact that since *The Source* was practically home for them, too, we should carry more water, as it were.

I sat silent. My preference was to say as little as possible. I wanted to let Scott utter his two cents and have it done with. But that was not to be. Inevitably, his passions became more enflamed and editorial decisions found themselves in the bull's-eye.

"And what the fuck is up with this?" he asked, pointing to the cover of the September issue. The Made Men had a small cover line on the bottom right, one dwarfed by the larger cover lines on the left that highlighted the issue's main stories.

"Why is our shit so fucking small? I mean, you even made fucking Kool Keith bigger than us. Who gives a fuck about Kool Keith?! Tell me who gives a fuck about Kool Keith, or the fuckin' Beanuts?" His finger stabbed down on the cover as if to emphasize the point.

Almost simultaneously the editors looked over at Dave Mays for support, wondering if he'd say anything. After all, not only had I learned *The Source*'s cover line placement rationale from him—descending hierarchy, beginning in the upper-left quadrant—he saw every single cover before it printed. To our bemusement, Mays sat silent. So I spoke.

"Ray, the cover sells the magazine. We live and die on the newsstand. If I don't put together a cover that sells I wouldn't be doing my job . . ."

"Fuck your job, you gotta represent for us—even fucking *Rap Pages* represent more than you." He waved a copy of *Rap Pages* in the air, a recent issue that featured the Made Men on the cover along with a timid Q&A on the inside that gave Scott and company a platform to say whatever the hell they wanted. Scott was really steamed up now.

"Y'all send this fucking writer to hang with us for a week and this is the fucking story? I know y'all changed his shit up!"

"This is nothing like the *Rap Pages* piece, Ray," Fontaine objected. "That was a Q and A, it's totally different."

"I don't give a fuck, y'all don't know the streets," Scott screamed, pointing at me. "Y'all don't know what the fuck y'all doing!"

I'd had enough. I rose to my feet.

"Oh, so you leaving, you leaving?" Scott barked.

I walked over to him to attempt one last gesture.

"Thought we was cool, man," I said simply, reaching a hand out to shake his.

He ignored my hand.

"Fuck you, Sel!" he screamed again, jumping to his feet. "We ain't cool! Fuck you!"

I turned my back to him and walked to the conference room door, stopping briefly by Dave Mays.

"Told you this would happen," I said coldly, looking into his stunned eyes.

I strode from the room. Mays stumbled to his feet and followed me out into the hallway.

"Yo, chill, Sel. Come back," he pleaded.

I ignored him. As I walked my limbs trembled and tears of sheer rage coursed down my face. I smashed my fist repeatedly into the walls of the hallway and, upon reaching my own office, picked up a chair and hurled it into the wall. The dent is still there.

Dave Mays stood at the doorway, looking at me with a helpless expression. I pushed my way past him and walked out to the lobby. The hushed mutters of the junior editors trailed behind. I slammed the button to bring the elevator up. Before it arrived voices drew closer. I turned around.

"So what's up, Sel? You mad now? You think you just leaving?" E-Devious, one of the guys in Made Men, stood before me, his gaze direct and fixed. I didn't answer, not trusting myself to speak. Just hit the elevator button once again. Another voice spoke up.

"Just move away from him! Move away from him!" Marvette Britto, an intense, fiery woman, pushed her way through the other bodies gathering behind and around E. She grabbed my arm. I stiffened, then relaxed slightly.

"All of you just go back inside. Leave him with me," she ordered. The larger bodies obediently moved away. Britto turned to me, her hand firmly locked around my wrist.

"Listen, Selwyn, I know you're upset. What just happened in there was terrible. But I don't want you to leave. Just come back in with me, okay?"

I stood still for a moment longer, then nodded in assent. Britto led me back to the conference room. I took a chair away from the table, set back against the wall. Scott reentered the room from wherever he'd headed after his eruption. Neither he nor Mays looked at me. A rambling conversation began again, this time Smokey Fontaine did the bulk of the talking, getting into one snappy exchange with Scott, who again scoffed at the lack of "street credentials" possessed by The Source's editorial team. Scott had his temper back under latch, now he was just being patronizing. Mays still said very little, and when he did speak it was to parrot Scott's lines or eagerly second his suggestions on making the magazine more "street." You'd believe he was a member of Scott's group, not the publisher. I shook my head in disgust, especially after one exchange—Scott: "Y'all just need more money to hire people? Dave, they can get more money, right?" Mays: "Right!" I'd only been harassing Mays with meetings and memos for months on the same subject to no avail, relegated behind his focus on the upcoming Source Awards and the Made Men project. Mays's instant vacillation to Scott in front of my staff made me look like an inefficient advocate for their needs, or an impotent liar. I could not believe that this was the man with whom I'd worked so well over the past four years, the control freak who had grudgingly, then with vigor upon seeing positive results, handed over control of his magazine to a twenty-five-year-old relatively inexperienced kid. As the conversation ground down to sheer idiocy, I walked out again. No one said anything this time. I grabbed my briefcase and went home.

The long-awaited return of the Source Hip-Hop Music Awards was less than two weeks away in Los Angeles. I resolved to keep my game face on at least until then. I needed to give the anger from that meeting enough time to settle so I could make a decision about my future from a place of reason, not rage. The awards show came and went. Soon we were back in New York to close another issue, October, in which we planned to run the review of the Made Men album, *Classic Limited Edition*. After Mays had given us the record back in July, the music staff carefully listened to it, and assigned the album to a young writer from the Midwest, Miguel Burke, who carried no baggage from the earlier *Source*/RSO debacle. Burke sent us back a measured, solid review and a decent rating—3.5 mics out of a possible 5—that we agreed with. An evening late in the closing process rolled around. I left the office after midnight. As I walked down the darkened city streets my cell phone buzzed. It was Carlito Rodriguez.

"Yo, man, you not gon' believe what this dude [Mays] is doing," Rodriguez said, fatigue and exasperation coating his voice.

"What's going on?" I asked.

"He ain't happy with the Made Men review. Got me reediting it."

"How bad is it?"

"I don't know yet, he's looking at the last version I did." Mays had not yet returned from Los Angeles. We'd been mailing him final pages.

"All right. Call me when you get his response."

Rodriguez rang back an hour later.

"Yo, man, I'm just gon' tell dude to write the fucking review himself. This shit is totally different."

"Read it to me," I asked. Rodriguez complied. Mays wanted the review completely sanitized.

"And this is the good part," Rodriguez continued.

"What," I said wearily.

"He says he's changing the rating."

"To what?"

"Four and a half mics."

I laughed out loud: 4.5 mics was the de facto highest rating we ever gave out, since almost no one got a full 5. In one fell swoop Mays was voluntarily placing the magazine's credibility on the chopping board and loping its head off. As editors we often argued fiercely about ratings; and a passionately made case could nudge a rating down or up a half mic. But those albums deserved the bumps. This was not the case. Mays was unabashedly lying to our readers and trampling over editorial decision. I just could not understand why this otherwise smart, driven man would willingly plunge into stupidity's depths.

"Yo, Cee, on this one can't nobody tell him shit." I sighed. "He's too far gone. I'm not fucking with it anymore, man. Just get out of that office and go home. It's late enough."

"I'm gonna take Miguel's name off of this piece," Rodriguez replied. "It ain't what he wrote."

"All right."

I wrote a four-page resignation letter the next day. There's something to be said about mentally closing a door, for within a week Russell Simmons called with an offer to run his new Internet property, RS1W.com. After three weeks of negotiation with Simmons, I came into the office to deliver that letter to Mays. Turned out he was in Boston, staying at a hotel. But I was determined that he would see the letter that day. Had already spent too much damn time staring at it on my computer screen. I called him.

"Yo, Sel," he greeted me cheerily. We hadn't spoken much since the conference room.

"Listen, I'm faxing something to you. Call me back when you get it."

"Cool." He signed off. I sat back in my chair and stared around my office. It was done. No turning back now. Minutes later the phone rang. Mays.

"Hey." He sounded like he'd been kicked in the stomach.

"Did you get it?" I asked, struggling to keep my own emotion out of my voice.

"Yeah." He paused. "This is . . . this is just fucked up."

"Let's talk about it when you get back." I wanted to keep the conversation short.

As soon as I got off with Mays I buzzed my assistant, Felicia Williams. She came into the office, eyeing me carefully. Felicia was incredibly tuned into me, and was all too aware of the events of the past month or so—the furious meeting, my pensive moods, the phone calls from Russell Simmons. She'd been anticipating this moment.

"Can you ask the staff to come in, please?"

Without a word she went out to gather everyone. In short order they assembled in my office. This would be the hardest part, for I genuinely loved my staff. We had fought so hard together. Learned so much. And it didn't matter who was younger or older, senior or junior; they all felt like my kids. Now, I had to tell them I'd be leaving. I uttered the words with a lump in my throat. Few faces looked surprised. I only made scant reference to the infamous meeting. Told them that I'd grown tired, weary, and that I wanted to focus on my own writing. That I'd reached the editing burnout that any editor who writes eventually confronts. But I didn't tell them the overarching truth, that I no longer trusted Dave Mays, that I now realized that when push came to shove, he would toss all aside for Raymond Scott every time. And I could no longer work that way.

They just stared at me, so silent. Tracii McGregor's gaze bored right through, her eyes wide, head nodding slowly. I fought to keep tears back and watched faces before me moisten. They left then, a mournful file tapping out of my office. Tracii looked back. Head nodding slowly. Eyes wide open. Those eyes whispered understanding even as they screamed betrayal. The door eased shut and I sat alone, relief and guilt descending with equal, crushing weight atop my shoulders.

I was only marginally surprised when, some two years later, the FBI showed up at my door. The buzzer rang. I looked out of the second-floor window to see three unassuming white men clustered at the front door of the brownstone in which I lived. Figuring that they'd punched the wrong bell, I returned to my TV viewing. Minutes later the doorbell to my apartment clanged. I got up and opened the door to see the same three men gathered outside.

"Mr. Selwyn Hinds?" one of them asked.

"Yes," I replied, somewhat guardedly.

"We're with the FBI." He held out identification.

In one nanosecond varied possibilities rushed through my mind as I stared, disbelievingly, at the gold shield dangled beneath my nose—Do I owe back taxes? Did something happen to my brother? Then, in the very instant one of them voiced reassurance, "This isn't about anything you've done," I knew why they were there. Raymond Scott.

Later, as I watched them clump down the stairs, a wave of deep sadness washed through me. There was nothing I could tell them about guns, drugs, or the like. But if the feds had their sights set on Ray Scott there was little chance of *The Source* escaping the rounds that would eventually come down range. Not with Scott's inextricable attachment to Dave Mays, as well as his newly public position as having been co-owner of *The*

Source all along—either a marvelous piece of revisionist history, or the best kept secret in the world since it escaped those who worked there in the decade between 1990 and 2000.

I could visualize the media frenzy, the stories about the poor white guy from Harvard and his manipulative gangsta friend. All of it washing over the real story, the story of young people who spun substance from a vacuum, of young journalists who thrived in spite of adversity. In the *clip-clop* of the hard shoes of those FBI men I heard the cracking timbers of the house Dave Mays had built coming down about the heads of all whom had dwelled there. How horribly tragic. How utterly wasteful.

9

BULLETS OVER TINSELTOWN

Although I have written about him often, I only met Christopher Wallace, the Notorious B.I.G., one time. One moment of genuine, mutual acknowledgment, not the shallow, acquaintance dance that we in hip-hop circles practice far too often. The place was Daddy's House recording studios, the Times Square audio home of Bad Boy Entertainment honcho Puff Daddy. The time, a February evening late in the winter of 1997. Biggie's sophomore album, *Life After Death,* was due out in a couple of months and his label, Bad Boy, had organized a sneak preview for a select group of music journalists.

We were quite a handful: Nathan Bracket from *Rolling Stone;* Jeff Mao of *Ego Trip,* who at the time was writing a Biggie cover story for me at *The Source;* Smokey Fontaine from *Trace,* who'd later become my music editor; Elliot Wilson, then music editor of *The Source;* and a host of other opinionated scribes and editors, all downing the available liquor and finger food.

Biggie sat quietly in the back of the main studio's control room, shifting his contemplative lazy-eyed gaze between the yapping journalists and his thick, pudgy hands, which lay carefully clasped on a table surface before him. He wore a black suit, and had a large gold chain nestled against his chest. A pair of crutches leaned against the wall behind his chair. He'd been using them to rehabilitate a broken leg, the result of an accident some months before. But there was no infirmity about him whatsoever. Biggie looked secure and confident, certain that the dreaded sophomore album jinx would hold no sway over him.

A publicist from Arista Records, Bad Boy's parent label, took me over to him to make the introduction. Biggie nodded.

"Wassup, duke," he drawled in that husky tone made famous on vinyl and CD.

I murmured a reply and we shook hands firmly. A photographer contracted to snap photos of Biggie with the journalists in attendance drifted over, lens raised. I eased off. Always disliked staged photo moments with artists. In retrospect, I should have taken that one.

Sufficient food and liquor consumed, the journalists were gathered up from the nooks and crannies of Daddy's House and ushered into the main control room by Bad Boy exec Jeff Burroughs. At some point Puff had come in, unbeknownst to most. Now he stepped to the fore to talk briefly about Biggie's new music. The man himself still sat in the back of the room, occasionally grinning and mouthing words to his main cohort, D-Roc.

Preamble complete, Puff motioned to an engineer type and the music began. Now-famous selections from *Life After Death* rushed out of the speakers, knocking the dour expressions from journalists legendary for poker faces at listening sessions. Song after song saw the increase of the head-bob rate. Biggie just took it all in with a satisfied smile.

Then the moment came upon us. "Kick In the Door," the album's DJ Premier–produced, hardcore sonic romp, exploded into the air. We sat spellbound. And when the last strains faded away, the roomful of highly critical types exploded into spontaneous, enthusiastic applause. I had never seen such a reaction before, or since.

Biggie nodded.

Every spring the movers and shakers of the hip-hop and R&B industry gather in Los Angeles for the annual Soul Train Music Awards and 1997 was no exception. But there was a distinct sense of unease on the part of many New Yorkers who would be traveling out to Los Angeles that year. It had only been a few months since Tupac Shakur's murder in Las Vegas and the air in hip-hop still felt tainted, still felt fraught with menace. The ugly war of words that had crackled between Bad Boy and Tupac's Death Row label for months before Pac's killing lay simmering—waiting for a spark to ignite. Although no evidence had been unearthed, speculation in the streets about Tupac's murder ran wild: Biggie and Puff did it; Crips who were working for Biggie and Puff did it; Death Row kingpin Suge Knight did it so Tupac wouldn't leave the label. It didn't take an overactive imagination to wonder if L.A. in March of 1997 was such a smart place to be.

Ironically enough, it was Biggie and Puff whose actions seemed to pooh-pooh that sentiment. In the weeks leading up to Soul Train the two spent considerable time in Los Angeles doing promotional stuff for Biggie's *Life After Death*, including filming the video for his lead single, "Hypnotized." By many accounts, Biggie enjoyed his time in La-La Land, despite an initial reluctance to go. He was moving in Hollywood circles and people were lobbing exciting opportunities his way. For a player looking to up the ante and stay sharp, this was just another level of the game. Plus, Suge Knight was now tapping his toes behind bars, tossed for violating parole by taking part in a scuffle between Tupac and the man the media would eventually label as the prime suspect in the volatile star's murder—the now deceased Orlando Anderson, himself a victim of murder in 1998.

With Suge off the streets, danger may have sunk into the realm of low probability for the Bad Boy crew. I didn't see Biggie until that fateful Saturday night. But Puff was highly visible. Thursday night he sauntered into the House of Blues' pre-awards bash, looking sharp with gray suit and white sneakers. And the next night, following the show, he chatted animatedly and openly with all manner of folk on Sunset Boulevard, just outside Hollywood's celebrity watering hole, the Mondrian Hotel.

I didn't go to the show. Caught a bit of a bug. Figured I may as well rest up for the big *Vibe* party Saturday evening at the Peterson Automotive Museum. People had been rumbling about this party all week so it promised to be major.

The Peterson Museum sits on the corner of Fairfax and Wilshire. It's an impressive structure. Shells of cars jut out from the walls at odd angles in pure defiance of gravity.

"How'd they hook up the party in this joint?" I muttered to my man Sean, who was with me. He shrugged.

We parked and followed the stream of partygoers into the building, passing through a lobby area, eventually coming to a bank of escalators that led up to the floor on which the party would take place.

Sean and I rode the escalator up, peering at the faces of

those beside and behind us. The entertainment industry had come out in full force—music artists and executives, Hollywood players, fashion mavens. We stumbled across the likes of Russell Simmons, talking it up on his ever-present cell phone, and Chris Tucker, standing quietly in one corner, quite the contrast to his manic screen persona. I had to admit *Vibe* had done good, though the admission was grudging given the intense rivalry between that magazine and my own *Source*.

Biggie strolled in midway through the party. Puffy and a handful of associates were with him. He had a relaxed air. His walk was one of ease. The crutches that had hobbled him since the September car accident were gone, replaced by a black cane. He and Puff settled into chairs around a table at the edge of the dance floor. Biggie seemed in good humor. His smiles came quick and often, glinting like the familiar gold piece he wore against a black sweater.

The party slid on, its passage well-lubricated by free alcohol and chest-pounding music. Twice, the DJ played the first single from Biggie's forthcoming *Life After Death*, the dance floor mover "Hypnotize." Twice, the crowd roared its approval. At one point I noticed Biggie's estranged wife, singer Faith Evans, dancing alone, ignoring her husband's presence while she, too, grooved to his music. The Bad Boy royalty nodded its appreciation, greeting the well-wishers who continually strode up to their table with laughs and firm handshakes.

The music ended abruptly, just short of midnight. A mass groan went up. Later reports will attribute the stoppage to L.A. fire marshals, concerned about overcrowding. Reluctantly, the crowd began to shuffle toward the exits.

"Yo, party at Steve Stoute's place," someone yelled. People began repeating the refrain. Soon enough the L.A. residence of the New York music executive—manager of Nas, Track Masters, and others—appeared the destination of choice.

Sean and I ambled into the parking lot and got into our car, a nondescript Toyota Camry. As before, I drove and Sean settled into the passenger side. A great number of people milled around the parking lot, some getting into vehicles, others walking out to the sidewalk, so progress was slow. We pulled the car into the exit lane and after several minutes managed to leave the cover of the garage and turn into the nighttime buzz. Then the night split. Firecrackers and car backfires can sound like gunshots on the street, but the reverse, strangely enough, is seldom true. Sean and I reacted instinctively, ducking our heads beneath the dashboard of the car. As the reports faded away I raised my head and witnessed a chaotic scene. Seven or eight cars ahead of us, right at the intersection of Fairfax and Wilshire, sat a large SUV with its doors splayed upon. Several figures raced in and around the vehicle, limbs moving with a frantic energy that shouted panic. One man appeared to be running in a circle, his head and arms jerking spastically.

"I think somebody caught one," Sean said, peering at the commotion.

"Yeah, think you're right," I replied. We stared for several seconds.

"Let's get out of here."

I jerked the wheel to the left, pulling the car into the lane heading away from the intersection. Several other vehicles mirrored that action.

"That was a fucked-up way to end the party. Wonder who that was?" I mused.

"Yeah, I know . . . let's see what else we can get into," Sean replied.

Little did we realize.

The phone woke me around 7:00 A.M. It was Dave Mays.

"Yo, man, Biggie got shot last night. He's dead."

The words didn't penetrate.

"Wha . . . ?"

"That party last night, the *Vibe* joint. Turn on MTV, the news is all out here in New York."

Still dazed, I pointed the remote control at the TV and selected MTV. Sure enough, MTV News was all over the fact: Rapper Notorious B.I.G. shot dead. I mumbled something else to Dave then hung the phone up in shock. I called Sean at his hotel.

"That drama last night . . . it was Biggie who got shot. He's dead, man."

Sean was silent for several heartbeats.

"Oh shit, man, that's just foul, real foul."

That first day, Sunday, passed in a blur. Two other *Source* staffers were staying at the hotel—fashion editor Mimi Valdés and photo editor Janene Outlaw, in L.A. for photo shoots, including a Wu-Tang Clan cover—and I went to see if they had heard the news. They had. Mimi, who'd had personal ties to Biggie, was especially broken up, weeping uncontrollably.

Like an automaton I began to revert to journalist mode. Dave and I spoke again. Our May issue, with Scarface on the cover, was already at the printer. Obviously we'd have to hold the issue. We decided that I'd stay in L.A. to help coordinate an editorial package, and do the reporting for that package's central piece. Additionally, we realized that L.A. would become ground zero for press reporting on the murder, and given both my attendance at the party and the fact that Big was on the *current* cover of the magazine, *The Source* stood to receive a great deal of notice from the media.

Didn't take long. The next morning MSNBC sent a Town Car to pick me up at 5:00 A.M. Somewhat groggily—I'd hardly slept a wink since Dave's phone call—I entered the long, black vehicle and the driver set out for Burbank, site of the NBC studios. Ed Gordon, the former BET newsman, hosted a morning news program on MSNBC and I was slated as one of his guests. Once we reached the studio I was swiftly ushered to the taping venue: a newsroom in the midst of which stood a solitary chair set among lights, monitors, and cameras.

Gingerly I settled into the chair. The techs quickly attached a microphone to my lapel and directed my attention to the monitors before me. The show was originating out of New York and I was linked in via satellite. I envied Gordon and the other guests their extra three hours and hoped weariness wasn't stamped too deeply on my face.

An audio playback crackled in my ear. The faces of Gordon and the show's other guests flashed up on the monitors arrayed before me. I noticed one of them was Keith Clinkscales, CEO of *Vibe*. He looked fairly composed, although some remnants of shock still sat on his brow. At that moment I truly felt for him.

"Good morning, gentlemen," Gordon greeted us all.

We murmured our replies. The conversation proceeded on automatic pilot. Ed Gordon asked the relevant questions. We all expressed our shock and dismay. He closed the program with a somber parting word. I rose from the chair, disengaged the microphone, and returned to the waiting Town Car.

A FedEx package awaited me at the hotel. I took it to my room and shook the contents upon the bed. A cassette tape fell out. It was an advance copy of Biggie's album *Life After Death*, the only copy that existed outside of Bad Boy. The prior week Mays and I had cajoled Puff into giving us the tape for review purposes. Elliot Wilson had then mailed it from New York on Friday, never dreaming that it would arrive on Monday morning like some dire, final testament.

Later that day I drove around L.A. with Allan Gordon, a former *Source* staffer now at Larry Flynt's *Rap Pages*. We listened to *Life After Death*, marveling at Biggie's craftsmanship, wincing at the cruel irony of the album's final song, "You're Nobody Till Somebody Kills You." The car remained quiet long after the music drained away.

The rest of the week ached by as the mainstream press ate up my time. As we had predicted, I became a magnet for media organs looking for commentary on Biggie's shooting. It quickly became burdensome. Every day, sometimes twice a day, crews would turn up at my hotel or I would be directed to some network location. CNN, FOX, ABC; I even ended up on *America's Most Wanted*. Everyone was chasing the story. *The Source*'s able publicist corralled each opportunity like some savvy media cowhand, and then funneled them my way. Things got so hectic that I ached to avoid her. When her number came up on the caller ID of my cell phone I would take a deep breath before opening it to receive the next instruction.

It was a deeply ambivalent moment. Clearly I needed to be a representative that could offer some informed commentary beyond the generalized hatchet jobs that otherwise prevail when the mainstream media tackles the subject of violence in hip-hop. Yet, I grew increasingly uneasy at being a participant, no matter my spin, in the media circus that must have been sickening for Biggie's family, a circus that sought to reduce him to a crack dealer turned gangsta rapper who had surely received his just rewards, a circus from which *The Source* benefited, no matter how noble our intentions.

By Friday it was a relief to head to the Wu-Tang shoot with Mimi and Janene, to lose myself in something besides Biggie's death. The members of the Clan were late, as they usually are, entering en masse around midnight for a shoot that had been scheduled since early afternoon.

"Yo, yo, we here, let's do this!" someone called out.

I sat quietly in my car. Listening again to Biggie's album. Raekwon and Ghostface ambled over. Raekwon got in the passenger seat. Ghostface poked his head in the door. I let the tape run. Both carefully checked out the work of their deceased peer. Chuckling at lyrics every now and then. Then Raekwon broke into a wide, appreciative smile upon hearing the irreverent "Loving You Tonight," featuring R. Kelly.

"Hear that, son, hear that?" He motioned at Ghostface. Ghost tipped his chin in reply.

Other members of the Clan drifted by the car. Masta Killa stood a few feet back from the doors. Method Man inclined his head. All listening.

The tape ran to a stop. I ejected it. Raekwon nodded slowly.

"Son was about to eat real good, man," he said, sorrowful note in his voice. "Real good."

10

STREETS IS WATCHING

Jay-Z looks okay when he walks in to Q-Tip's album release party. It's a cold Wednesday night in November of '99. Jay wears a Prada skullie pulled low on his head. Black joint with a red stripe up the middle. I nod at him. Reach out. He smiles and nods back. Gives me the strong black man greeting—left arm around shoulder to pat on back, right hands firmly clasped in between chests—before moving deeper into New York's Kit Kat Club, heading to the VIP area, entourage trailing. Some time passes. Then a scuffle breaks out in the VIP section. In short order Jay-Z passes by on the left, an angry expression contorting his face, stiff-arming people on his way to the exit. Later I find out Lance "Un" Rivera—head of Undeas Records, recording home of Lil' Kim, and business partner and friend of the deceased Notorious B.I.G.—had been stabbed, not fatally, in the back and shoulder, allegedly by Jay.

On Friday I'm handing my two cents to Kurt Loder on MTV. Jay-Z's the news of the week. Turned himself in to the police earlier only to be swiftly released on bail. Loder asks the right questions, I give the right answers. The exchange is quite journalistically proper—measured, restrained, objective. And too damn familiar: A hip-hop star as the recipient, alleged perpetrator, or supposed cause of violence.

Later that night I'm riding with my boys up New York's FDR Drive. Radio blaring. Jay-Z and crew are guests of Funkmaster Flex's Street Jams on Hot 97. Jay sounds cool as usual. Cocky. Confident. Amped up like a man about to drop the most anticipated hip-hop album of the year. And, maybe, just a bit too blasé about the swirling allegations. Joking about them even. Everyone on the show has a good chuckle about the stabbing. It's either the height of arrogance, the security of innocence, or some murky, distinctly hip-hop combination of both.

"If he gets away with this, cats ain't gon' be able to tell him shit!" someone exclaims.

Heads nod around the car. Boy, we've come a long way, huh? Now violence, alleged or actual, is a joke.

Wasn't so funny in 1995. That year the debate over violence in hip-hop was in full uproar. The target was gangsta rap, and the people aiming rifles were powerful. Senator Carol Mosley-Braun convened hearings in Congress; Bill Bennett chimed in from a distant bully pulpit; and an elderly black woman named C. Delores Tucker led a strident vocal campaign in the media, purportedly against the excesses of gangsta rap and the role of large corporate entities in "polluting the minds" of youth, black youth in particular.

In early 1996 I had the good fortune of meeting Dr. Tucker on FOX's *Hannity and Colmes*, a *Crossfire* kind of show where two hosts and two guests debate controversial issues. Dr. Tucker came representing the forces of light; I was the kid defending the evil hip-hop smut. I was also a rookie at this type of television. Sean Hannity's soundbite-oriented tirades and Dr. Tucker's finger waving blew my wig back; I got my ass thoroughly kicked. See, you just can't call a woman old enough to be your grandmother a bloody idiot on live TV. And what can you do except sit there flabbergasted when said woman reveals herself to be a canny media manipulator, holding up graphic pieces of artwork and reading song lyrics guaranteed, in that context, to sound like dispatches from depravity?

Tell you one thing, though, the experience made me get good at live TV in a hurry, and it sharpened my own thoughts on violence and graphic imagery in hip-hop. I rushed home that night and penned a letter to Dr. Tucker. It ran as an editorial in *The Source* a month later, a scathing piece of prose, full of piss and vinegar.

I read that piece again in 2000 as I prepared material for this book and realized that the old adage was never truer than in the case of hip-hop: the more things change the more they stay the same. Tupac Shakur, Dr. Tucker's favorite target at the time, was now dead. So was the Notorious B.I.G. At one time the killings, which occurred within six months of each other, seemed capable of shocking the hip-hop nation straight, as it were. Yet, after an appropriate period of mournful soul searching, hip-hop in 2000 seemed just as beset by the lurking specter of violence. Puff Daddy and his latest protégé Shyne were staring at the prospect of years in prison stemming from a wild night at Manhattan's Club New York that saw Shyne fire gunshots in response to some threat or insult to Puff, wounding three patrons in the process. Jay-Z waited to confront the New York City DA over the alleged stabbing at Q-Tip's party. And hip-hop poster boy of the moment, Eminem, faced gun possession charges of his own. It's enough to make a lover of the music and culture wince in agony, and provide a critical cynic with ammunition for yet more darts, for incidents like these always play as indictments against the culture at large, and not merely as individual transgressions. Blame a mainstream media that profits by reducing debate and conflict to "us versus them" and reading any complexity right out. And a hip-hop machine that keeps feeding them fodder.

Understanding the violence that too often clutches hip-hop's artists by the throat is not a simple undertaking. Many forces are at play, elements that combine in a combustible mix: the economic demands of the hip-hop market, urban social realities, youthful machismo and ego and outright gangsterism, to name a few. First, consider a hip-hop record market grown fat on hardcore gangsta narratives, and the economic reasoning that assures the continuance of such, as long as it stays profitable. Although hip-hop is a notoriously fickle and cyclical form, the hardcore element, since its commercial introduction, has never fallen very far from primacy, and always seems to reassert its sway when another trend loses currency. The Compton group N.W.A—Dr. Dre, Ice Cube, MC Ren, and Eazy-E—is generally acknowledged as having introduced gangsta rap with their seminal first disc, 1988's *Straight Outta Compton,* although 1987's *Saturday Night* by Philadelphia rapper Schooly D and *Criminal Minded* by New York's Boogie Down Productions are also cited as records whose explicit treatment of inner-city violence helped lay the prototype for gangsta rap. But it is clearly N.W.A., the other California artists who came in their wake, and the region-specific narratives that they unveiled—gangbanging, drive-by shootings, corrupt police—that thrust the gangsta aesthetic into the light of day. An aesthetic developed further by Suge Knight and Dr. Dre's Death Row Records. The Los Angeles-based label's lurid tales of street violence and sex ruled the charts in the early and midnineties, along with the likes of Wu-Tang Clan and the Notorious B.I.G., who, with the now classic *Ready to Die*, finally provided a New York-centric version of the street lore mantra and put New York hip-hop back on the commercial map after years of being pummeled, saleswise, by music coming from the West Coast. After Biggie's death and for much of the latter nineties, the pendulum drifted more to the feel-good, living-large party aesthetic popularized by Puff Daddy and Mase. But today it has swung back to the hardcore, thanks to the efforts of DMX, Jay-Z, Cash Money, Eminem, and others. Trafficking in narratives that spring from urban pathologies—crime, drugs, etc.—is profitable, perhaps more than ever. Everybody loves a bad guy, a thing as true for hip-hop as for most other fields of popular entertainment.

Then consider the larger social tangles that wrap up the inner-city youth populace who represent the emotional and narrative foundation of hip-hop. Despite the drop in violent crime over the last decade, young black men continue to die in outsize numbers in cities all across America. If crime and gunplay are statistically more likely to visit themselves upon the person of a minority male, that statistical factor does not readily decrease because said male enters the house of hip-hop. But it should, one may protest. Surely he or she can now leave those social ills at the door, exchanging them for the trappings of music business celebrity. You don't see Garth Brooks worrying about being shot. Well, it is not that simple, for many reasons. And most of those are encapsulated by two words—*the streets.*

In Frank Herbert's classic science fiction novel *Dune,* Duke Leto Atreides warns his son Paul that they will need desert power if they are to survive and thrive upon their new home, the desert planet Arrakis, a place that makes the Gobi look like a vacation spot. If Duke Leto were to take up residence on planet hip-hop he would need to rephrase that admonishment to Paul: to survive and thrive in hip-hop you need street power. What are the streets? They're a hallowed entity in hip-hop, a subject with its own distinct lore. The streets are the people and places from which an MC springs. The streets birth you. Certify and validate you. Protect you. Crucify you. They can also kill you.

Hip-hop's visceral connection to the streets is its power, as well as its Achilles' heel. That connection gives the best hip-hop it's narrative strength, like early Ice Cube on 1990's *AmeriKKKa's Most Wanted* and 1991's *Death Certificate,* articulate, sophisticated records that generated their fair share of deserved controversy but served as psychic road maps to the problems in Los Angeles that would flare up during the riots after the Rodney King verdict in 1992. That connection gives hip-hop its astonishing grassroots support, the homegrown, around-the-way feel of the artists, the just-like-any-one-of-us factor. But that connection also keeps hip-hop artists, even the most successful ones, tethered to the darker manifestations of the streets: jealously, exploitation, worse. Hollywood stars exist in rarified air, on some plane removed from the rest of us. But hip-hop, particularly hardcore gangsta and its requirement that one stays close and true to the streets, renders its stars far more touchable. A hardcore artist may grow rich and move from the old neighborhood, but he—it is almost never she—must still come back around the way; still frequent places most other entertainment celebrities would not; still roll with friends from the old 'hood who, not having the record contract to jeopardize, remain quite capable of starting anything, anywhere; still, at times, run up against others all too willing to poke holes in carefully crafted tough-guy images.

Nor is it just the superstars, the Biggies and Tupacs of the world, who have fallen victim. One need look no further than the tragic slayings of Big L and Freaky Tah from the Lost Boys in 1998 and 1999. Both were moderately successful rappers largely unknown to the pop mainstream, both murdered in their respective neighborhoods of Harlem and Queens. Today we have largely debunked the once-popular myth of hip-hop, gangsta or otherwise, being the sole product of the ghetto or working-class youth. Far too many folk in hip-hop possess middle-class credentials. But the fact remains, the great majority of the successful practitioners of hardcore hip-hop today come from the environments of which they speak—the likes of Jay-Z, DMX, Eminem, Master P—and all must navigate that dance with the streets; all, despite their economic success, have strayed only so far from the statistical reality that circumscribes the fate of many young men in the streets from which they sprang.

Ultimately, though, it is the perception of violence *in* hip-hop narratives, more than the occasional flare-up of violence around specific artists, that has generated much of the debate. Incidents like Puffy's and Shayne's recent trail and the unsolved killings of Tupac and Biggie serve as giant exclamation points in a long-running text. In actuality the hand-wringing over violence in hip-hop lyrics is merely one component of a larger debate on how the lyrics and images of hip-hop exploit or influence urban pathologies, how hip-hop's lyrics and image present an unhealthy, some say unholy, view of a large component of the African-American community. The truth of the matter is that contemporary hip-hop stands guilty of overdosing on sexist imagery, and has descended too far into abject materialism. But the charge of hip-hop peddling nihilistic violence through music is as grossly untrue and unfair as the clichéd defense that others adopt to make hip-hop's case that rappers are only "reporting what they see." Nonsense. Perhaps that was once true in the days of early N.W.A. But hardcore rap these days is lurid, entertainment fare. Today's rappers construct narratives as expansive and creatively embellished, even if they spring from a kernel of truth, as a giant Hollywood action flick. These are not documentaries. Nobody *believes* this stuff anymore, even the impressionable teen market on whose behalf most of hip-hop's critics presume to speak. It's all big business and hip-hop's fans have always been sophisticated enough to discern that, although they are seldom given the credit. Ironically enough, it is the artists themselves, flying too close to the sun source of urban myth, who too often fall prey to the fate of the true believer.

Critics of hip-hop must tread carefully to avoid their own hypocrisy. By all means, call exploitation and excess by their true names. Rhyming about, and profiting from, the fact that we're living in shit don't help the situation none. But no scouring brush applied to the mouths of rappers will clean up the truly profane conditions of America's inner cities. Nor will they dispel the violence, patriarchy, and sexism this society has long thrived on. Those conditions existed ages before hip-hop spun into being and will exist long after, unless we apply meaningful change. And I don't mean hiding the dirty laundry behind closet doors.

The year 2000 inched by and each of the big hip-hop guns under a cloud of violence came to his day of reckoning. In March of 2001 I went down to the New York courtroom where the trail of Puff Daddy and Shyne was set to wrap up. As I stood in line to enter the court, Shyne, clad in a loose-fitting gray suit, red baseball cap perched on his head with brim low, Bible clutched in one hand, walked through the narrow hallway leading to the courtroom. He caught my eye, nodded quickly, and shook my hand. I would never have imagined this fate for the young man I'd met almost two years prior, a young man tagging behind Puff in the California sun, calm, collected, and most ungangstalike in his demeanor and dress. Puff arrived some moments later, he, too ,clad in sharp-fitting designer suit. Pale in color. He moved purposefully. Our eyes briefly met as he drew closer.

"'Sup, Sean," I murmured.

He gave a slight smile. His chest rose slightly and he pushed breath out through tightened lips, like a man preparing for a major effort. Then he entered the courtroom.

The trial wrapped up in a few days. Puff got off. Shyne got ten years. Eminem plead to his charge and escaped with probation. Over the summer I'd see Jay-Z at the gym we both go to, dancing around the boxing ring, getting in fighting shape for the release of a new album in the fall of 2001. By year's end he, too, would plead guilty and be hit with probation, three years in his case.

Not that long ago I saw Puff for the first time since his trial. Short months later he would re-christen himself P. Diddy. On that day he served as a panelist at a hip-hop conference organized by Russell Simmons, a conference meant to discuss progressive change from within the hip-hop community. Puff sat at a table with Russell and several other executives. He wore a white fisherman's hat that hung low over his face. He was quiet, humble. In this closed-door session of music business peers he could be frank. And he was. Talking ruefully about the lessons learned in copping to an untrue image, and the simple points he now stresses to his young, eager artists: you can't be mad all the time, nobody wakes up on the same side of bed every day, and if you put it out there, someone, somewhere will call you on it.

11

RETURN OF PREACHER SON

Wyclef Jean can run. His strides are jerked and uneven, yet swift. Maniacal grin plastered on his face. He scampers across the green expanse of lawn that surrounds Haiti's Presidential Palace. In his wake comes a throng of security personnel, all looking slightly annoyed at the unpredictable antics of this expatriate turned cultural hero.

"We love you, Wyclef!" The subjects of Clef's attention scream out their greeting as he reaches the green wrought-iron fence that separates the masses from the pristine halls of power. Another roar goes up as the crowd catches sight of Lauryn making her own way toward them. Impending motherhood seems to have bestowed an extra level of grace to the divine Ms. Hill. Her careful, measured glide brings a breath of calm to the frenetic excitement of the moment.

"Laureeen, Laureeen, I love you, Laureeen," one little boy cries out, tears streaming from his eyes. Wyclef pauses his mad dash and runs back to grab Lauryn's hand. Together, the two stride toward the people, while the third member of the trio, Pras, angles in from the far right. They all hit the fence at about the same time, breaking into distinct meet-and-greet modes. Wyclef sprints off to the left, shaking hands as fast as they're offered; Lauryn holds down the center, smiling angelically and trying to touch as many people as possible; Pras slides off to the right, slapping hands and nodding at those he cannot reach. The poor masses of Port-au-Prince bask in all the attention. For a people of little material wealth, this spring day of 1997 must be priceless. Finally, the Fugees have come home.

Upon landing at Haiti's airport one immediately notices the white UN observation posts along the side of the runway. The structures are a visible reminder of this country's complicated past and delicate future. Those thoughts can't help but bubble in the mind as our group of weary journalist types emerges from a silver-plated American Airlines jet into Haiti's golden sunshine. With nary a wasted moment, we collect our things and get whisked through the airport with the swiftness accorded American media piggybacking on the fame of an international act like the Fugees.

Haiti is a damnably hot country. That evidence blasts us in the face as we step from the relatively cool confines of the airport, along with the first clear indicator of the economic deprivation that has made this island notorious: a crowd of dark-skinned, poorly tattered, hungrily staring young boys lined up along the wire fence that sets the airport off from the road.

"American?" one asks hopefully upon catching sight of our party entering a jeep.

"Fugees!" another says firmly.

"American . . . Fugees!" The words bounce from mouth to mouth, mixed with a smattering of rapidly spoken Creole as they thrust eager hands in our direction.

"One dollar . . . one dollar." The entire crew takes up that litany as our jeep tries to navigate through the massed flesh. Finally, we break free as a chorus of despondent howls arises. One brave soul chases our jeep and leaps upon the passenger-side running board, face pressed against the window, mouth uttering the magic words: "One dollar?"

"Hold up," one of our party, Neil Strauss from *The New York Times,* says irritably as the driver guns the engine. The driver slows down slightly. Strauss rolls the window down and hands the kid a dollar bill. A smile splits the child's face and he hops off the running board of a jeep speeding along at thirty-five mph.

"*Merci. . . .*"

His thank-you comes floating back on the air, settling uneasily on a bunch of disturbed Americans.

"So many beautiful little children, so many beautiful little boys," Lauryn Hill murmurs quietly as she reaches over to accept a kiss on the cheek from yet another child. The stage is the swanky Le Ritz Hotel in Haiti's upper-class suburb of Petionville. The occasion, a reception for the Fugees thrown by the corporate backers of this weekend's benefit concert.

The people here, particularly the children, stand in marked contrast to the Haitians we encountered at the airport. There are boys dashing around in European sport jackets with ascots around their necks, beautiful young girls who look like they could have stepped from the pages of any high-fashion magazine. One can see the residue of colonialism all throughout the black diaspora. Even in America we have our own historical dynamic between darker and lighter-skinned blacks. But I have never seen color and class divisions as rigid as those in Haiti. There may as well be two nations here.

"It's kinda ill, right?" Lauryn comments wryly, catching sight of my bemused expression. Ill doesn't even begin to describe it. What's really ill is Wyclef. Clef's a child of Haiti's poor—a dark-skinned, unabashed representative of the people. Yet here he stands, holding court with the denizens of Haiti's upper class. A group of about twenty surround him, listening intently as he conducts interviews with the local press. In fact, if you didn't know better, you'd swear he was a candidate for office. But don't tell Clef that. "I'm not into politics," he'll insist if pressed, lips curling in disdain. Yet nearly every move he'll make here will be political. Like Haiti, Wyclef reeks of his politics, despite himself.

The evening passes swiftly. The Fugees smile graciously and chitchat with their admirers. Then Haitian Minister of Culture Raoul Peck begins the official proceedings, moving up to a poolside podium to welcome the group to the tune of thunderous applause. Seventeen-year-old Rosalee and eighteen-year-old Anouk squeal with excitement when the Fugees themselves step up to the mic to offer thanks. The two girls are clearly children of privilege. And they are quite proud of the Fugees and what they represent, touting them as representations of Haitian pride. Yet, for them, there's still a degree of class complication in Haitians' appreciation of that representation.

"In Haiti there are two social classes, higher and lower. We have television, we travel, etc., so the lower classes really don't get exposed [to the Fugees] as much," sighs Anouk, eyes fixed on Pras. "The Fugees are more popular with the higher class."

But the next few days will give me more than enough

evidence to contend that assertion. For now I can only nod and watch two teenage girls struggle with their perception of themselves and the world they occupy.

"It's an important issue [the Haitian poor]," Rosalee continues. "It's very sad that we can't do anything. The differences are so big. The poor dating and mingling with upper class? Not at all . . ."

Wyclef's closing comments suddenly jump out, momentarily breaking our conversation. " . . . and to the kids, you guys are the future to Haiti. I'm getting old right now. You can accomplish anything that you want in the world. God bless you." The attendees break into enthusiastic cheers, yelling out the group members' names and clapping loudly. Anouk, Rosalee, and their friends beam brightly before uttering their final thought: "You just don't have poor people in the U.S. like we have in Haiti."

Haiti's Presidential Palace is a grand structure. Built by Americans during the occupation earlier this century, the imposing white building gives off more than a few echoes of Washington, D.C.'s government buildings. A green iron fence rings the palace in some parts; white stone encircles the remainder. Politically inspired graffiti dots nearly every white portion of the fence. It's an odd sight. After all, one wouldn't expect to see tags coating the outskirts of the White House.

It's Friday morning and all of Port-au-Prince is abuzz. This is the day that the Fugees will receive medals of honor from the government. On the street that borders the palace's side entrance, the local populace mutters excitedly as they await their heroes' arrival. Grim-faced security men stalk everywhere, openly touting a variety of arms. A few American personnel are scattered among the security folk, their sweaty red faces clearly marking them apart. "Hurry up, move it," one screams at us as the journalists emerge from a van. His walkie-talkie waves excitedly. Eyes flash over the crowd.

A squeal of brakes, a sudden rush of motion, and a throaty roar mark the entrance of the man of the moment. Inexplicably, Wyclef arrives on the back of a motorcycle. Apparently he refused to ride in the jeep with his bodyguards, preferring to greet his people openly. And they love it. Hands reach out to pound Clef on his back, shake his hand, or just offer a thumbs-up. For a brief moment I'm afraid that he'll be pulled from the bike. But the love is communicated in a respectful manner. No one's trying to snatch a piece of Wyclef's clothing as a keepsake. Maybe it's the multitude of watchful eyes and cocked Uzis. But I doubt that. These people aren't rabid fans; they're celebrating the return of a native son.

The inside of the palace looks as grand as its exterior. Busts of Haitian heroes and leaders past surround the central foyer, a huge, open space. Ornate chandeliers hang from thirty-foot ceilings. On the stage at the head of the room rest six gilded chairs, one of them distinctly thronelike. Haiti is a land large on ceremonial appearance, at least in the case of the elite.

The fifty or so neatly arranged chairs within the foyer area contain a mixed bag of press, Haitian political and business leaders, and other luminaries, all gazing expectantly toward the head of the room. The recipients of the collective eyeballing occupy three of the seats onstage. Wyclef, in a black Armani suit and tie, slumps sideways in his chair, a decidedly irreverent expression on his grill.

Pras, the very picture of informality in jeans, T-shirt, and Timberland boots, lounges to Clef's left. Lauryn, wearing dark shades and a bright-colored, dashiki-inspired outfit, sits to the right. The other chairs are taken up by Haiti's minister of culture, the prime minister, and in the larger, fancier number, the president, Rene Preval.

Events proceed in a fashion quite similar to last night's reception. The minister of culture sets the proceedings off. President Preval himself, then each of the Fugees, quickly follows him. The group members look well aware of the gravity and significance of the situation. Nonetheless, Pras doesn't miss an opportunity to keep things real, offering the president a pair of high-fashion sunglasses and suggesting he procure a pair of Tims. Many words are said over the course of the twenty-minute ceremony; but Clef's seem the most significant:

"I'm the kid that stands behind the palace that cannot come in here today to see the Fugees; that's who I am. It's all good that the media is here and the press, but none of that really matters to the Fugees because if we didn't sell the millions of records that we did, we wouldn't even be here. I wouldn't be able to get inside the palace to make this speech . . ."

The attendees applaud enthusiastically, Clef's implicit criticism having sailed right by. And with a flourish of beams from the president and scowls from the security heavies, the stage party is ushered from the foyer. Fifteen minutes finds Lauryn on the palace's second-floor balcony, eyes directed across the lawn at the people pressed against the fence. Clef's words must still be buzzing in her head. Half-tentatively, she raises a hand. A dull cry goes up in response. Lauryn grins.

"That was really heavy," she says very quietly, a slight

note of awe in her tone. "My life has not been remotely close to what I might have imagined. If I could've sat down and planned it, then I would've finished college, got a job and met a man, and got married. But it didn't. I don't really try to understand God; I just try to accept His will and performance the best way possible. It's very easy to disassociate your success with God. You think like, 'If I didn't make that beat phat,' etc. I recognized that it's not even me, man. It's not even me, 'cause as easy as it could've been me, it could've been someone else. It could've been any one of those kids out there . . ."

Wyclef Jean is tired. He has every right to be. Just keeping up with the frenetic pace that he's set since arriving in Haiti has me exhausted. This Friday night promises to be no exception. We're at Club Med, believe it or not, lounging on an air-conditioned patio surrounded by pampered European tourists and gun-toting guards. It's just another one of those weird dynamics that makes Haiti such a difficult place to pin down. But for now, Clef's just catching a quick moment, preparing for the show the crew came here to perform. Tonight's one hundred-dollar-a-head shindig is just a precursor for the real deal tomorrow night. It's also supplying a fair bit of the cash to subsidize Saturday's benefit. Clef eats quietly. His gaze seeks out the stage where the band's equipment is being erected.

"Hey."

He turns his red-rimmed eyes toward me.

"How in the hell did you put this together?"

"Just a lot of hard work," he replies, eyes occasionally flicking back to the stage. "You can't do anything big in this country without getting support from the government. Just like we can't do anything in Jamaica, Cuba, and other islands. Islands have certain conflicts. We felt we had a good chance to make a statement. I was just flying back and forth, keeping it real low. Coming in to see the president and being at the cabinet meetings, arguing with them pricks."

Clef offers one of his infectious grins and it suddenly occurs to me how little we really know about this man. Sure, he's recognized as the guitar-strumming, occasionally singing dude in the Fugees. But there're layers to Clef—artistically and personally—that have yet to be realized on a large scale.

"Ever since I was three years old I've been into music. Growing up in Haiti you can't really grab a guitar or bass, I was the less fortunate. I would beat on bottles and make drumbeats, and sing songs just to go with the drums. It's deep, 'cause now I'm like twenty-six, but I play [several] different instruments. And I just conducted my first hip-hop symphony, and it tripped them [the New York Philharmonic] out. 'Cause they was like, 'And the conductor is?' They were like, 'Wow, what a beautiful piece of music. Where's the conductor? Can he conduct it?'"

Flipping expectations on the head. That could be Wyclef Jean's mantra. Sometimes we take the significance of what he's accomplished, of what the Fugees have accomplished, for granted. And it's taken a first-hand visit to the environment that bore Clef for me to realize that. As a kid, Clef didn't live too far from Club Med. And he couldn't dream of even getting within smelling distance. It's an irony that he's all too aware of, leaning over so he can be heard above the din of the tourists.

"I mean, even while I was in the White House, I told them, 'Don't be mistaken. Put the money aside and all that shit aside and I'm the same nigga that's outside the palace. That's what y'all gotta understand, so they're the ones you gotta help. Don't be bringing me here to make things look good when they're not.' So everyone respects that and they respect the Fugees on all levels."

It might be respect back in the United States, but here it's nothing short of love. Aside from reel footage of Chinese girls fainting at the sight of Michael Jackson and vintage Beatlemania, I've never seen such a heartfelt outpouring of affection toward a musician. Typically enough, Clef downplays his end of the equation, preferring to big up the people.

"The whole thing is that they know I'm really from here. I went to school down here, so it's like you could tell the perpetrator and you can tell the real person, and these people got soul. They can call a bluff, they know who's supposed to be in power and they know who're the bullshitters. All they do is beg for money, but when they want somebody out of power, they get down. And what they see in me is simplicity. I think what they see in the Fugees is simplicity. The Fugees ain't hiding in a room, under the lights when we go onstage. I think that's what makes people respect the Fugees more."

"Simplicity? That's the Fugees' key?"

"It's just something we're doing naturally. With this next album, *Carnival*, I'm taking it there. It's thug related, that's the first thing. It's something we're doing subconsciously. At a carnival anything could happen. There was a cousin of mine who they assassinated at the carnival here in Haiti. So then I started working on the album while I was on tour. But subconsciously we've been all around the world. So it's bugged, 'cause the album sounds like some thug shit, but it's trippy 'cause it's not the ordinary sampling you're used to listening to. You'll be like, 'Damn, this shit is crazy. Where's he get that loop from?' I think it's just being in different parts of the world, you'll inquire more. And I think for us the way it used to be, the Smokeys, the James Browns, cats used to travel, son. Go around the world. We just stayin' in this fifty-state thing. They think a fifty-state radius is something, but all the music is staying in one place. Hip-hop is the only form of music that can do this to people. And that's all the kids are listening to and they're convincing the older people who don't have a clue to what's going on."

Saturday. The carnival has come to Haiti tonight, manifested through the power of the Fugees. In order to grasp what's going on here, you must process it with the senses. Smell the dockside air and the wafts of ganja hanging pungent like scented mist; listen to the crash of music and the ebbs and swells of seventy-five thousand black voices; see the sea of dark skin spreading out from the stage, standing, sitting in treetops, perched on top of buses, on the edge of nearby balconies, rhythmically waving their hands in the air. Even then you'll only have a poor man's approximation of the beauty unfolding tonight.

The stage on which the show takes place is a monstrous affair. Canadian and American work crews spent all day assembling the structure, as well as light and sound gear. The rear of the stage looks out upon the Port-au-Prince waterfront. To the left lies the backstage area, chock-full of scurrying bodies. The stage is large enough that a group of us cluster at the rear, practically invisible to the crowd, but well able to witness all that transpires onstage.

It's well into the night before the Fugees emerge. The wait has been eventful. The local acts that precede Wyclef and company, several of whom perform hip-hop infused with a distinctly Haitian flavor, are vibrant and compelling. But even they can't top a sudden, dramatic appearance from President Preval. A flicker of movement tugs at the corner of my eye. I glance toward the backstage area to see khaki-clad men with Uzis heading toward the stage. Several men. Moving swiftly. Uzis held with menacing, businesslike purpose. The entire group at the rear of the stage takes a collective step back. Then, in the midst of the armament, I catch a glimpse of Preval's face. Okay, the mini-army must be his bodyguards. We relax.

The crowd roars as the Fugees finally take the stage. The proceedings may have been long but the swelling, appreciative bellow from seventy-five thousand pairs of lungs holds no note of frustration. The group rewards the crowd's patience, launching into the freewheeling mix of sound and energy that characterizes their shows. Lauryn moves from side to side, exhorting the crowd, a large T-shirt barely concealing her all too pregnant belly, soft fisherman's hat pressing her nascent locks against her scalp. On these trips to the wings of the stage she criss-crosses with Pras, cool as always in his ever-present shades. Wyclef mans the center, guitar attached to his hand, excitement plastered on his face. At one point he strips his shirt off, wraps his body with the Haitian flag, douses his dreadlocks with water and shakes them furiously. The main stage light locks on him and a nimbus of white envelopes his body, turning the little pellets of water shooting from his head into gleaming projectiles.

A catwalk extends from the stage into the heart of the crowd. Every so often one of the group, usually Lauryn, will make a mad dash down that walkway. Then scores of brown hands reach longingly toward the scampering legs, screams redouble, and on more than a single face, tears stream. When Lauryn does this a security person, her uncle, actually, trots right behind her, concern stretching his features. But the hands never pull, the group never stops, and the wave of sound and emotion never crests.

3:30 A.M. The concertgoers are tramping in the streets, blowing away on those unique horns that give *rara*—a Haitian carnival music—its particular feel. Somewhere in that mass of gliding limbs is Wyclef Jean. Lauryn and Pras have long retired to their respective jeeps. But Clef can't let this moment go. And I don't think he should, at least not abruptly. The joy that's been created this night has to be lowered slowly into the soul, lest it drops too swiftly and all opportunity to savor it vanishes.

But if sixteen-year-old Stanley Bloy is any indication, that joy will be around for some time. He's a young Haitian teen, hopping excitedly by the side of our van. His English is quite good so we strike up a conversation.

"Wyclef is my life," he says excitedly as the marchers pass by. I look at him curiously, like the jaded New Yorker I am. *Your life?*

"I don't want anything to touch him because he's doing something for my country. I can't explain how much love I've got for this guy. He's a leader. When he plays the music, I'm so happy I cry. It's the first time a Haitian plays music like this in Creole that everybody can understand and appreciate."

175

Damn.

It occurs to me that we don't give ourselves enough credit. You know, what America fucked up—namely, the black diaspora—through the export of destabilizing politics, it now has the capacity to connect through its latest cultural export, hip-hop. We just need a little carnival to bring it all together.

I can finally see Clef. Someone's wrapped a flag of sorts around his shoulders. He looks tired but buoyant on the energy that's been generated tonight. For once, the security dudes are unobtrusive. It's just Clef and his people. Tramping gently off into the night, blowing on them horns.

12

COMING HOME

Day 1: Tuesday, December 29, 1998. 10:30 P.M.
I'm here. Back in Guyana. Remember telling Clef last year in Haiti that I longed to return to my own Caribbean home. Now the moment arrives.

Bit nervous aboard the airline because I had to check my bag. That's always a risky proposition when traveling to Guyana. Forced myself to relax and have faith. Arrived at Timerhi Airport, now renamed Cheddi Jagan International in honor of the recently deceased founder and leader of the PPP, or People's Progressive Party, one of Guyana's two major political parties. My bag was there.

Emotionally, it's a bit of a balancing act. Always thought I'd make this trip with T, my ex-girl. We'd planned it for a year. Then the breakup shattered those plans. Now excitement is tempered by a tinge of regret, a yearning to share my elation with the woman I still love.

My memories race the speeding car into town, the former straining to match the pace of the latter. We fly down the East Bank Road. I catch occasional glimpses of familiar sights: the water of the Demerara River winking in the moonlight off to the left, the signs announcing the towns of Golden Grove and Covent Garden. But it is the sounds and smells that let me know I'm in Guyana: the wafting aroma of burnt sugar as we pass the distilleries, the inexorable chirp of crickets. After eleven years, I'm finally home.

Day 2: Wednesday, December 30

I rise rather early—8:00 A.M. to be exact. Ten o'clock pickup by my Guyana Defense Force contact, Lt. Col. "Banks" Reynolds. At first it feels awkward to be driven around by such a senior officer. But Banks is cool.

Daytime reveals that the place has changed. Overgrown drains. Ruined roads. The once-pristine stretches of green where I played cricket and football now overrun by high grass, flooding, cows, and goats.

Seeing Queens College, my old school, breaks my heart. This was the pinnacle of secondary school education in Guyana. Now it's recovering from a bout with arson. The entire middle section of the building is gone, along with all records and tons of irreplaceable memories. I so wanted to walk the floors of the old auditorium, trace long-ago steps on the badminton courts, imagine the smell of food wafting out of the cafeteria, what we called the "tuck shop."

Things seem less awesome, but I still feel a deep, abiding love, muted by a touch of sadness. Paradise has lost its innocence for me. Nowhere is that clearer than in the constant talk I hear of the crime wave sweeping the country. Merchants gunned down. Residents robbed at home in broad daylight. This is not the Guyana I remember.

Banks drives me by my grandparents' house on 41 Dadanawa Street. Mama's house, where I grew up. The sight of it has much the same affect on me as Queens College. Windows over the stairwell are smashed. The pale, yellow fence is discolored. Stone Avenue, the street

overlooked from the front of the house, lays torn and tattered, a far cry from the smooth asphalt of childhood
memory.

My escort tells me that infrastructure improvement
has only been taking place in areas populated by Indo-
Guyanese and other supporters of the majority Indo-
Guyanese government. Don't know if that's true, but it's
a mind-boggling idea that puts a name to the fumes I've
been sniffing—the fumes of politicized, racial antago-
nism. When I was younger I had no idea such divides
existed between Guyana's blacks and Indians. And having had my race calibrations set by fourteen years in the
United States, seeing the ugly, local variant depresses
me immensely.

I grew up under Forbes Burnham—the long-deceased
founder and leader of the black-dominated PNC, or
People's National Congress, which ran the country for
nearly three decades after independence in 1966.
Burnham's Guyana bore little resemblance to the nation
now rolling before my eyes. Admittedly, I grew up black
and middle class, or what constituted middle class in
Guyana. Many of my schoolmates were the sons and
daughters of PNC ministers, military officers, and stal-
warts from the private sector. Privilege seemed a
birthright—chauffer-driven cars, the best schools, and
money for junkets to America. Guyana in the late seventies and early eighties was a cocoon for us. For the most
part we rollicked through childhood in comfort and security, troubled by little, even the inflation creeping through
the country that deepened the burden of the poor. The
horror of Jonestown in 1978 was a blip on our radar, mentioned only in whispered gossip sparked by the thump-
thump of American choppers passing overhead, heading

to the country's interior to collect the bodies of Jim Jones and his followers. Our social studies classes extolled the achievements of our glorious leader and the party. Nowhere was there any inkling of the crisis and violence that had accompanied the founding of the modern nation in the early sixties, when blacks and Indians had tussled with the British, then each other, for political control. As for Cheddi Jagan and the PPP, they were bogeymen, though ineffectual. Shrill phantoms at the margin of the nation's discourse. Acknowledged but ignored.

Night comes quick in Guyana. I forgot how different the evening here seems from its cousin in New york. When night comes in Guyana, the air smells wet, like sweat from the dance of tiny moleules borne in from the Atlantic Ocean, or the Demerara River. When night comes in Guyana, the ear grasps a more primal hubbub, a mix of sounds derived from man—the growl of cars, the bark of laughter—and nature—the yip-yipping of dogs, the droning buzz of mosquitoes. When night comes in Guyana, the tapestry above winks like a field of diamonds set in deep indigo.

I go back to my hotel, the Pegasus, to change clothes for the evening. Take a cab, alone, to a club called the Library. The cabdriver, an older man, directs one look at my obviously foreign self and bids me a cautious farewell. Going into the club I realize that this is a novel situation. I know no one here. What if drama breaks out? The place is dark and dank with the smell of sweat and alcohol. Young people grind against each other on the small dance floor. Small packs of men hover on the periphery, or congregate at the bar. Several of them eye me curiously as I walk in. Wedge myself into a corner. Try to look unobtrusive. Brick by brick, the wall of my

New York arrogance begins to crumble. Parties in the States have conditioned me to treat groups of youngsters with alcohol at hand with wariness. Now I begin to regret the rash decision to come without my friends. Paranoia starts to gnaw. I self-consciously finger my expensive watch and diamond earrings. Mama's urgings to not wear such things come back to mind. As do my gentle assurances to her that I'd be fine. *Mama, I'm Guyanese. Plus, I live in Brooklyn. What's going to happen to me?* In the darkened smoke fest inside the Library unpleasant possibilities rush up to answer that question.

I stand with my back to the bar, feeling strangely alien. The irony shocks me. Take a sip of beer. To relax I focus on the crowd. It's a mixed bag. Some older. Most younger. In American clubs they'd embody the thug aesthetic. Hip-hop holds much sway here, especially Will Smith, believe it or not. "Getting Jiggy" bumps out from the speakers, setting the dance floor rocking.

Eventually I head back to the club's open-air patio, still waiting. Still a tad anxious. Then they start flooding in. My schoolmates: Kym Backer. Roger Benn. Tycho Fung. Richard James. The night now begins.

Day 3: Thursday, December 31

New Year's Eve. Lay in bed most of the day. Make a couple of phone calls to set up the night. By early evening Kym and Karen come by to pick me up. Kym's an expatriate now living in Brooklyn. Known her since I was six, since rough-and-tumble childhood days at St. Gabriel's Primary School. Karen's her American roommate. She's becoming an honorary Guyanese. Caribbean culture will do that to you.

They marvel at the hotel's room. Rich, natural wood furnishings. A balcony that looks over the Seawall, the Dutch construction that keeps the Atlantic Ocean from washing away Guyana's coast. From this vantage point the ocean looks gray and murky, not the pristine blue-green water that surrounds our island neighbors to the north.

Leave hotel for Kym's house. On the way catch sight of things not yet seen—the large statue of Cuffy, Guyana's Nat Turner; the Residence, Guyana's White House; and the Cultural Center; Guyana's Lincoln Center—along with things new and never seen: the National Gym, for instance.

Two hours later finds me in my hotel bed again. Waiting to head out to party. Listening to time creep by. I pass the moments before midnight looking at a local television show, some sort of countdown. Then the midnight bell tolls and the new year sashays in. Don't think the dawning of a new year has ever found me alone. Impossible to keep thoughts of T from flooding my mind.

Eventually get picked up by Kym and Karen. Head to party at Sidewalk Cafe. First impression: tons of gorgeous women. Never knew Guyana had it like this. I shake my head at what I've been missing all these years. Rum and Cokes—which may as well be the country's national drink—flow, along with the sweet, sweaty strains of calypso and dancehall reggae.

Never been particularly aggressive when it comes to women in clubs. Not my style to grab a girl by the arm. Even the thought of leaning deep into a woman's personal space to shout, "Wanna dance?" always seems clumsy and invasive. But the music, drinks, and women here combine to do a number on my inhibitions. Especially her. Standing a few feet down from me at the bar. Tall and slim-figured. Light caramel complexion with penetrating eyes and a cool smile. Long hair lays flat against her skull in a cornrow style. Beautiful. But oh so imperious.

Funny how the liquor stokes manly courage, and quenches the voice that tells me, even though we've broken up, somehow I'm betraying T. I down my rum and Coke, catch this other woman's eye and smile. She smiles back. Kym, standing to one side and observing with interest, nudges me forward. I half stumble, half glide toward the girl fixated in my scope, and, in one motion, gently take her hand and walk to the dance floor. She levels a brief, incredulous, "I don't believe you that bold" look at me, and then comes along. Hello 1999.

Day 4: Friday, January 1, 1999

James, the foreman on my father's chicken farm, calls me. Wants to pick me up to go to the farm. Promised Dad I'd check on things while I'm here. Wait for James down in lobby. Not long until he arrives. I see him come into the hotel, a slim, dark-featured man, and I am drawn to him right away. Despite the slight bend of trepidation on his brow, this son of Guyana's lower class walks into this upper-class enclave with quiet humility and confidence.

James drives me into town. He's an intelligent guy and measured talker. Learn much about the current political situation, from his perspective, of course: the tension between the majority Indian government and the majority black police and army, the resulting downsizing of the latter two by a nervous government, the subsequent inability of the police and the army to combat the brutal crime wave sweeping the country, the ease with which corruption can and has taken hold.

James and I drive into town. As we motor along, I lean out of the window, filming the images flashing past with a little Sony camcorder. Then we turn down a pothole-filled side street. I angle the camera toward a little boy running alongside the car. He can be no more than eight. Gliding blissfully down the street in shoeless feet, oblivious to the holes and gravel beneath. His little, bare chest heaving with deep breaths.

We reach our destination—a police station. Walk inside to wait for a cop friend of James. Incongruous juxtaposition as Puff Daddy and Aaliyah wail from a small transistor radio, filling the stark, grimy interior of the station with the praises of American pop materialism. James's friend sits upstairs, taking statements from witnesses to a murder last night. A murder that took place at the Library, the same club that made me so uneasy. Guyana is a dangerous place now. Can't allow myself to forget that.

Day 5: Saturday, January 2

I know it's a worn, even cliché sentiment, but nothing puts things in perspective like witnessing the lot of the less fortunate. My father owns a chicken farm on Guyana's East Coast. To get here from the city of Georgetown you must traverse a road that mutates from paved highway to cattle-choked, dirt-laden thruway. The farm itself is a trio of small buildings on one acre of ragged greenery—two larger buildings in which the chickens are housed along with the smaller main house. There is no toilet on the farm. Simply a battered, wooden outhouse only accessible by a sodden, muddy grass trail. To use the bathroom I must gingerly pick my way along this path, careful not to place my Nike sandals in clots of mud or still water. Feel a twinge of guilt at my middle-class, Americanized finickiness, especially when I watch the two young farm laborers steadfastly working under the hot sun—barefoot, barechested, tattered pants cut off at the knees.

Come back from the toilet and relax on the porch. James's wife comes outside; insists that I eat. Although breakfast still fills me, it would be impolite to refuse. So I sit at the small kitchen table of the main house while she brings a huge lunch for me. Work my way through it with focus and determination.

Later on, back in town at a small shop owned by aunt of good friend Virgil Granger; like Kym, he's another chum from six-year-old days at St. Gabriel's: stern teachers with flashing eyes and flashing wild canes to deliver cutting licks to mischievous backsides; screaming, hollering kids in khaki-and-white uniforms; fun antics and furious fights in a sand-covered school lot.

Virgil, like most of these guys I've not seen in years, is now huge, towering above me in height and girth. And I thought American food made you grow. Many of my old friends from St. Gabriel's and Queens College are here: irascible, cynical Andre Griffith, cool-ass Roger Benn, and good old Randolph Skeete, now a captain in the GDF, a far cry from the wild kid we used to call "Eyedolph" 'cause of his wandering left eyeball.

The instant, natural return to camaraderie astonishes me. Folk say you can always go home again, but we jaded American city-dwellers always wave that off as sentimental drivel. I've kept very little contact with this place and these people over the last decade. They'd be well within their rights to remain distant. But my friends will hear none of it. We gather on the cobbled road in front of the shop, the early evening breeze starting to pick up, and we drink. And if there's one thing Guyanese can do exceptionally well, it's drink. So the rounds keep flowing.

Eventually stagger back to hotel. Pissy drunk. Flop on

bed. Then, in an impulsive inebriated fit, pick up the phone and call T back in New York. To wish her happy new year? To just say, "Hi, I miss you"? Don't know. What I do know, two hours and three hundred dollars later, is that you never, ever make a drunken call to your ex from a foreign country. I place the phone back in the receiver and lay on the bed. Sad and flat. All the air let out by an emotional pinprick.

Day 6: Sunday, January 3

Only got one more day here. Figure I better take advantage of the hotel a bit more. Head down to the pool for a brief swim, then a quick workout in the gym. Strange. Maybe it's leftover melancholy from last night, or predeparture blues, but I feel remarkably lonely.

Walk out through the hotel's palm-shaded lobby. Out front, white taxis sit. The drivers fan themselves slowly in the still, hot air. Not much breeze coming in from the ocean on this early afternoon. Nod at the first driver who hops out to open a door for me. Today is the day: I'm going to see the house, Mama's house. Banks and I drove by the first day I was here, but I hadn't the nerve to go inside.

The car pulls up before the house. Get out slowly. Walk to the gate and raise and lower the latch so that it clangs, a reverberating *dong-dong-dong* that makes me cringe slightly. The serious-seeming young man staying here as caretaker eventually pokes his head out of the door and smiles once I introduce myself. I enter.

The house seems rundown inside, too. My actions are hurried, as if slow movement would allow the memories to catch up. An onslaught of feeling wells. To hold it back I try to maintain a detached distance, even as the house cries out for my attention. Even as I ease up the wooden stairwell and sit on the open verandah so loved by Mama. Even as I peer cautiously into the main bedroom, the room where my granddad died. Even as I walk back downstairs and outside, to stand on the stone patio that played tolerant host to all my boyhood adventures.

Finally, with a quick, muttered word, I bid farewell to the young man living in my home and swiftly depart.

Day 7: Monday, January 4

Time to go. Gather up my bags and walk from my room. Lingering smiles of farewell from the older women of the domestic staff, all of whom seem to have adopted me as a long-gone son. The younger ones just smile coyly.

Banks meets me in the lobby. Along with an uncle of my father's, a small man, dried and stretched by the Guyana sun like old, faithful leather. I've never met him before. But he wants to make sure he sees me before I go. The two of them bundle my bags into the car and we make the long drive back to Timerhi Airport. In daylight this time.

At the airport the line of Guyanese returning to New York is huge and heaving, like some impatient organism. I'm daunted initially, but let it swallow me nonetheless. Banks and my uncle help me drag my bags over; but they cannot stay long, as they're not traveling. Banks tries to cajole the security official, flashes some military ID. No dice. He turns to me and shrugs. They have to leave. Just then my uncle leans closer and whispers conspiratorlike.

"Listen. Yu think yu got some footwear yu could lef' fi' me?"

I smile sadly and shake my head. Then I reach out to grip his small wrist.

"When I come back next year."

13

THE SWEETEST THING [OBSERVATION]

In the spring of 1997, months prior to the birth of her first child, Zion, Lauryn Hill stood on a quiet beach in Haiti. She was quite a sight. Slim legs protruded from oversize khaki shorts. Toes curled into pink sand. And thin brown fingers gently lay atop a distended belly. I remember looking at her with something akin to wonder. Here stood a woman whose maturity, wit, and sheer humanness belied her twenty-two years. Plus, she would soon birth a child. Little wonder I became her creature then and there.

But that moment was really the culminating point on a line that stretched from 1994. Back then I was a Princeton student and occasional *Village Voice* writer, and she was a key member of an eclectic hip-hop outfit called the Fugees. One Sunday afternoon Lauryn breezed into a studio facility on Princeton's Nassau Road where a group of friends, including Lauryn's older brother Malaney, were discussing arcane matters of music and technology.

"This is my sister, Lauryn." Malaney said. Needlessly, of course.

The rest of us just smiled. Lauryn beamed back. She

was a mere sprite of a thing at the time. A small, delicately formed teenager. Fragile even. Until she opened her mouth.

"Okay, see, I'm here because I love my brother. And I believe in what he's doing. And this is how we're gonna do it . . ."

The rest of us looked on with bemused expressions as this little nineteen year old with the big mind proceeded to dominate the conversation.

That was the beginning, but I would run into that mind over and over again as the years unfurled: lecturing me on the social implications of *The Source* not awarding the Fugees' sophomore album, *The Score*, a classic mic-rating of 5 (would you believe that girl cussed me out? But it was the nicest, most intellectual cussing out I've ever received); discussing God and geopolitics on the balcony of Haiti's Presidential Palace; and musing about what she wanted to do on her first solo foray while sitting in a cold photo studio in London.

That solo effort, '98's *The Miseducation of Lauryn Hill,* thrust her to full-out fame. It pushed her relationship with the members of the Fugees, particularly Wyclef Jean, into full display. And it publicly threw the group's future into questionable territory.

How things got to that point is a fascinating story in itself. We have to go back to the so-so reception of the group's '94 debut, *Blunted On Reality.* The buying public largely ignored the record while the critics latched onto Lauryn, calling her the trio's saving grace and initiating the mumbles about her going solo. Those mumbles became a roar after the blinding success of the '96 follow-up, *The Score.* While the critical reaction to Pras and Clef grew a great deal warmer with that record, L-Boogie was still the acknowledged darling, and folk continued to salivate about that Lauryn solo disc.

"Everyone knew Lauryn would go solo, but it was just a matter of when and how," Pras, the enigmatic third member of the trio, told *The Source* in 1998. "But I have to give it to her, 'cause she was getting offers from some of the top producers in the world and she didn't go. She had all the hype and she stuck with us."

Then Wyclef's acclaimed solo record, *Carnival,* caught everyone by surprise, including the group.

"While we were on the road in '97, Clef got up and said he was going to do a solo album," Pras continued. "Me and Lauryn looked at each other and were like, 'Wow, that's deep. Where'd that come from?'"

And if you don't think all the talk about the two "bums" weighing Lauryn down didn't propel Clef, well, think again. *Carnival* was a smash. It sold over a million copies and the critics lauded the record's diverse mix of musical aesthetics—hip-hop grooves, sultry reggae, Latin rhythms, hip-rolling calypso, and Clef's native Creole melodies—all topped by irreverent and compelling narratives. Now the onetime "bum" was being hailed as a genius by the fickle press.

Lauryn felt that keenly. Her resolve and boundaries began to firm up. I spent much of the spring of '97 on an extended trip with the Fugees, going to Haiti and London. All that time Lauryn talked and thought about what she was going to do with a solo record. By that summer, while *Carnival* was in full swing, she was actively looking for partners to help implement her musical ideas. This would be her project in mind, body, and soul. No Fugees. No Pras. And especially, no Clef.

Those two had a complicated relationship. Both have

flirted with genius. Both are driven to take the lead. They have shared love—as friends, as artistic collaborators, and more. It is the conflict and fracture in those relationships that helped give *The Miseducation of Lauryn Hill* its impetus, its urgency. Lauryn poured herself out on that record. Cleansed her soul. And America, to the tune of several million, picked up the mops and brooms right along with her.

The Grammy Awards ceremony possesses a certain splendor and majesty, even during rehearsal. It is early in the afternoon of February 25, 1999. Tonight, L.A.'s Shrine Auditorium shall play host to the Grammys and the expected coronation of Lauryn Hill as pop music's queen. As for right now, those thoughts must be the furthest thing from the minds of the hordes rushing around backstage at the Shrine, trying to bring all the diverse elements of the coming show into line.

I, however, am not rushing anywhere. I'm stuck. Standing with Miguel Baguer, Lauryn's able publicist, as two security types prevent our access to the auditorium to witness the rehearsal.

"I'm telling you, she's my artist," an exasperated Miguel huffs at the looming Neanderthals.

Big Guy Number One shrugs noncommittally. Big Guy Number Two nods knowingly. They've been told to look for orange passes and we only have blue. So the color-deficient civilians stay put. And Lauryn's rehearsal time inches closer.

Not to be outdone, Miguel pops out a list of phone numbers, dialing them at the touch of a speed button. Finally, he reaches the right person and procures the right colors. We glide past the human roadblocks with nary a word.

Inside the auditorium things are in full swing. A jocular Rosie O'Donnell stands to one side of the stage, fussing with her microphone, while Celine Dion, with full orchestral accompaniment, belts out her show number. It's a surreal moment, made all the more so when a jean-clad Eric Clapton and a relaxed-looking B.B. King go through their set before presenting the award for Best New Artist: "And the winner is . . . Lauryn Hill!"

I'm slightly confused, especially when a young black woman in the front row bounds up onstage and accepts the award: "Oh, I wanna thank my producers, my label . . ."

Belatedly, I realize that this, too, is merely practice for tonight, so the production crew can get the timing down pat. But does it mean that Lauryn will win that award later? The members of her band seated right behind me seem to think so, hooting and hollering with appreciative abandon.

The rehearsal trudges on, but things are behind schedule. Onstage, a parade of casually dressed celebs makes its way on and off: a sweatsuit-wearing Pavarotti with towels wrapped around his throat; George Lucas; John Williams. Behind me, a somewhat morose-looking Puff Daddy winds his way around the seats. Rumor says it took some serious campaigning on the part of manager Benny Medina, an intense power broker type, to get Puff on the show. Seems no one wanted to present with him. And they damn sure weren't having him perform. The scuttlebut has Medina pleading with NARAS head Michael Green—the guy who runs the Grammys—to give Puff a presenter's slot. Green relented.

I can't help but wonder: Is this the end of Puff's pop moment, and does the same near-inevitable, cult-of-celebrity backlash await Lauryn?

Finally, the lady of the hour gets up onstage. She's attired simply enough. Jean jacket and skirt. Sandals. Shades. Hair covered, calves exposed. And for a moment, she's almost indistinct among the members of her crew—the band members, comanagers Jason Jackson and Suzette Williams. Indistinct, that is, until she steps into the lights with a microphone in her hands. A barely audible, collective sigh goes up from the assorted folk in the auditorium seats.

Slowly, unhurriedly, she begins to sing "Zion," the song dedicated to her son. The venerable Carlos Santana stands to her right, plucking away at the guitar that has made him a legend. The band grooves behind them, riding the song through its ebbs and flows. They close. But Lauryn seems faintly dissatisfied with the performance, and wants to do it again. But the worker bees of the production crew are already dismantling the set, even as she makes her case to some official-looking type. No can do. Things are running late, and the precast begins in a couple hours. So Lauryn makes her way off the stage. The coronation awaits.

I tend to be early for few things these days, and even the Grammys proves no exception. By the time I take the wrong exit, navigate the confounding orange cones set up by the LAPD to channel traffic around the Shrine, and dodge through the knot of spectators clogging the area, the precast is long over and Lauryn's already won three awards.

The backstage press area is a bit of a nuthouse, but it's a hell of a lot more interesting than the sterile show proceeding onstage. Out there, the lack of hip-hop and R&B performers makes the proceedings a tad bland. Back here, the knot of reporters, foreign and domestic, flashing cameras, and dashing TV crews creates a rather lively, albeit hectic, mix. Monitors beam the show from most corners. And all of us press types walk around with *Star Trek*-ish headphone devices that allow us to tune into audio feed from the show, or from the microphones set up on elevated platforms in the press area. One by one the winners are led back to these platforms to utter a soundbite or two: the still-funny Mel Brooks, the always funny Will Smith, and the gorgeous, decidedly unfunny, Madonna.

It's all very well and good, but my attention is riveted on Lauryn's progress, and locating one other individual. Suddenly, he pops up on the monitors. I wince; Wyclef Jean looks uncomfortable at best, downright pissed at worst. I can hear the rumormongers now: Did you see Clef? He looked mad 'cause Lauryn was winning! Of course they couldn't know that Clef got into a huge fight with his wife before the show, and that he is a man who wears his emotions on his sleeve. Under the most benign set of circumstances this would still be a delicate night for Clef. In his current mood, well, his expression speaks volumes. I can only imagine what must be going through his mind.

The evening rolls on. As rehearsed, Lauryn cops the Grammy for Best New Artist. Later, she performs "Zion." Outfitted in flowing white, which bounces beautifully off of her dark skin, she strides the stage like she owns it. Imploring. Revealing. Emoting. It is a riveting performance. Yet, it seems a touch vocally restrained, a bit physically controlled. As if she were loathe to push Grammy boundaries too far. Nevertheless, it is the perfect precursor to the night's biggest moment—Album of the Year. Lauryn's competition is stiff—Madonna, Shania Twain, Sheryl Crow—and the fists of quite a few back-stage patrons are clenched in nail-biting anticipation. When the call rings through—"And the winner is . . . Lauryn Hill!"—shrieks and triumphant arms fling into the air. It's remarkable how many have adopted our beloved L-Boogie. And if their adulation needs further cementing, she surely gets it after gliding onstage and reading from the Bible, giving thanks with humble, earnest sincerity.

Later, Sony music celebrates their big Grammy night with a party at Jimmy's Restaurant, off Santa Monica Boulevard. Lauryn sits in a corner with her parents and friends. Her boo, Rohan Marley, lounges right beside her, his eyes shining with pride. Security types ring the group. Even this collection of well-heeled, well-connected revelers can't just walk up on Ms. Hill. Of course, the rules don't apply to some, like Sony Music head Tommy Mottola, producer extraordinaire Quincy Jones, and Atlantic Records honcho Arhmet Ertegun. After greeting Lauryn warmly, the three of them hug each other and cackle over some joke or the other, lookin' all the world like three geezers with too much dough.

I manage to squeeze through the various bodies and Miguel drags me over to Lauryn. Beaming, she gets up to give me a hug. With the possible exception of the first time I saw her with Zion, I've never seen L this happy, this buoyant. Her eyes are lit and her spirit seems like it's dancing lightly above our heads. Clearly, this is her night.

Neither Wyclef nor Pras come to the party . . .

14

HOME OF THE BEAST

Let me tell you a story. It's set in the Northeast. A town that occupies a weighty place in our nation's history. This town is called Boston.

What do you know of Boston? You may know that it was once the center of the abolitionist movement that fought against slavery. You may know that a great man named Frederick Douglas once called it home. You might call Boston a significant force in the progress of American racial affairs. And you'd be right.

What else do you know of Boston? Well, you may know that it was a site for ugly racial confrontations in the seventies over court-ordered busing. You may also know that during the eighties, a middle-class white man named Stuart murdered his wife and blamed it on some fictional black youth—a familiar litany, that one—sending the Boston Police into an abusive tizzy. You may have even heard that the Boston Police have had a troublesome relationship with the black youth in their city. Indeed, you might call Boston a test tube for the problems of class, race, and crime that bedevil our cities. And you'd be right.

I went to Boston in cold January of '99. A party was

being given in honor of *The Source*'s ten-year anniversary and several staffers flew up to attend. We arrived at the club, some twenty of us stepping from cars into the cool Boston night. Right off I could see that it was a mad-house, and a potentially dangerous mix: far too many people, far too little security, and antsy, aggressive Boston police officers.

Two black cops stood before the door of the club.

"That's it. No one else is getting in," screamed the heavier set of the two, arms flashing out belligerently to push back the crowd. I approached his calmer partner and quietly told him who my group was. He shrugged.

"I understand your situation, brother, but we've got orders to close it down. Too many people." I nodded my own understanding, thanked him, and pulled my people away from the door and some distance from the club to wait for our rides to pick us up.

Then *he* rolled up. A new cop. White. Red-faced. And charged with a game day energy. Like a linebacker itch-ing for a sack. He strode toward us.

"Off the sidewalk, everybody move!" he barked.

Undeterred, I slid up to him, intent on explaining the nature of my twenty-person group and seeking permis-sion to remain where we were while our cars circled back. I opened my mouth . . .

"Not one fucking word, I don't wanna hear a fucking word," he snapped, eyes glaring down at me.

Momentarily taken aback, I stared at him. Maybe I hadn't heard right. I began again.

"I just need to ask you something—"

"I said not a fucking word. You people always have a goddamned story."

You people?

Perhaps I got angry. Perhaps my own arrogant faith in my ability with words, the capacity to talk things through, refused to let me back off. In retrospect, maybe I should have employed ghetto survival tactics. Then I would have muttered, "Yes sir, Mr. Officer, sir," and meekly moved aside. But I just wanted to ask a question.

So I kept coming at him. Again and again. Asking to be heard. I don't know how many times I opened my mouth, or blurted a word or two. I don't know how many times he cursed me. It may have been seconds or minutes. I do know that finally, angrily, he shoved me out of his way with a stiff-arm.

I stumbled back. And a curious thing happened. My mind raced along the paths of possibilities, calculating all the outcomes that could spiral from this moment. I could react. And get arrested. Shot. Beaten. Anything. Then the incredulous outcry, wondering how the hell the editor of a successful national magazine got into this mess in the first place. I could react . . .

But a hand grabbed me from behind.

"Come on, Selwyn. There's no talking to them like this."

Then other voices erupted around me. My editors. Screaming. Cursing.

"Fuck you, godamned pig!"

"Yeah, fuck you, too," he leered back.

I shook my head in frustration. Why had it reached this point? I was only trying to make what I thought was a reasonable request. I tugged against the hand holding me and stubbornly opened my mouth again. The cop just yanked a bottle of pepper spray from his belt. Seeing that, I lurched away. Leaving him standing on the sidewalk. A sick scowl of triumph twisting his face.

Back in front of the club things had denigrated completely. Unhappy with the speed of the egress, the nervous cop initiated a pepper spray barrage into the eyes of the standing patrons. Screams and cries split the ear as young people clutched their eyes and ran away.

I looked on helplessly. Astonishment mingled with rage coursing through me. I don't know which pissed me off more. The Boston cops' attitudes or the matter-of-fact way the black youth out there accepted it.

"That's just the way they are. It could have been worse," one kid said, shrugging.

Well, I don't accept it. I can't. I've dealt with asshole cops in NYC, L.A., Miami, other places; it's part of the package deal when you sign up to be a young black man in America. But I have never felt such a disavowal of my humanity. Never seen such ignorance. Have a nice life, my fine cop friend. Still have your badge number.

15

THE MAKER

You look amused, listening to the nutty photographer explain the concept behind this shoot. But you're clearly enjoying yourself. Grinning. Chuckling. Ripping to shreds the stiff characters that we've become familiar with throughout the years.

Your energy and focus are startling. Perhaps that should cause no surprise. You are a pro, a vet for most of two decades. Yet the picture we have of you is of a much more laconic, even unapproachable man. Not this dynamo of unbridled energy and enthusiasm continually sprinting and leaping for the camera.

You may have uttered the words *been there, done that* a few years ago, but today that phrase has even greater meaning. You've been Mr. N.W.A. Been the angry assailant of Dee Barnes. Been the architect of the Death Row sound. And been the wiser, jaded artist of the post-Death Row days, shaking your head at your own youthful shenanigans.

A complex man you are. And those complexities certainly remain part and parcel of you. Today you are/were/shall be each of them, and more. You are simply enough, Andre Young. And Andre Young, more than anything else, makes things. Image. Music. Money. Perfect sense. Stars. Gangsta shit. Hits. You craft, carve, shape things from your own personal ether, some cosmic stuff available to genius, invisible to the rest of us. This is what makes you a maker. This is what drives your twin-pronged purpose: continue the weave of Andre Young's life; stoke the fire of Dr. Dre's second coming.

You are Andre Young. And, at times, you make out-landish things happen. One afternoon, you drive down LaCienega Boulevard in Los Angeles, on your way to a favorite restaurant, when two excitable young women spot you. *Oh Lord.* One leaps out the car at the red light and does an excited jig on the roadside. You look over and smile pleasantly. They speed along beside you, beg-ging, pleading for you to pull over. You figure you'd bet-ter. Before somebody has an accident. So you oblige, pulling your silver BMW 750iL to the curb and signing a couple autographs. The two young women drive away. Ecstatic. You've made someone's day. Month. Year, even.

But this does not make you trip on some, as they say, "star shit." You seem almost humbled by it, remarking wryly, hopefully, that, "there go two more people who may buy the album." This response seems far too nor-mal. Far too *regular*. Not jibing with your long-estab-lished, aloof caricatures. Surely, you are not a man of the people. Then you wonder aloud, only half in jest, if the incident looks like you set it up to make the story inter-esting. And you laugh. Uproariously.

However, you do make things interesting, albeit not in the manner you just implied. Minutes later, you swing into the parking lot of the restaurant that's your destina-tion, the Stinking Rose. You acknowledge the smiles and half nods from the largely Mexican valet attendants lounging around in the Cali sun. This is familiar territory, the watering hole you've run to after many a studio session.

You ease out of your car, and a familiarity of another sort accosts you, in the form of a random white cat with heavy beard and glasses.

"Dre!" the dude intones with knowing enthusiasm. Shakes your hand with gusto. Like he knows you. But he doesn't. Then, inexplicably, he urges you to come over to his ride, a beaten-up black thing, and listen to some music. Perhaps now the caricatures will take life. Surely you will brush this cat off with a menacing frown. But no. You oblige. Heading over to his car and carefully wedging your wide shoulders through the driver's side door.

Dude sits in the driver's seat. Cranks the sounds up. Births an awful audio mishmash, an industrial rock kind of thing.

Maybe now is when you'll hit him with the condescending nod, the pat on the back, the (wink-wink) keep-up-the-good-work line seasoned pros seem obliged to deliver to hapless amateurs.

Not quite. You pull your shoulders out of his car. Mutter a few words. Then you gesture in the direction of your own ride before leading the way toward it, the excited grin of a kid with some hot, new toy splitting your face.

Hello? You are *not* about to play *him* some of *your* music? You cannot be planning to hook this clown with an impromptu listening session any hip-hop head would die for, not to mention the folks at your own record label? Wrong again.

"Yo, check some of my shit out," you say. Then you lay one into him, a track festooned with snapping snares, punishing kicks, grumbling bass, and—lo and behold—the silky voice of Snoop Dogg. Even on the BMW's factory system it sounds like a hip-hop revolt-in-waiting. Another opportunity to apply cleansing fire to hip-hop's pop excess and stultifying mimicry.

Like you've always done. In '89 you thrust the gangsta form to prominence with N.W.A. In '92, *The Chronic* put the West over the top. Now in '99, you look to cap a decade, a millennium, with *2001*.

Dude listens carefully. Strokes his beard with gravity. Nods like a knowing peer.

Bullshit. Don't this fool realize he's been blessed?

You are Andre Young. And you make history. But we knew little about yours. You grew up in Compton, that infamous mini-city in Los Angeles that would come to occupy a grim place in hip-hop and urban lore. In 1980 you were a student at Compton's Centennial High. Back then you were all about Grand Master Flash & the Furious Five. In fact, it was Flash's mesmerizing cutting and scratching on one song, 1981's "The Adventures of Grand Master Flash on the Wheels of Steel," that motivated you to become a DJ. That song seeped its way into your gut, commanded you to do something with the inspiration.

And you did, getting down with the glam funk of that era's block-party hip-hop. You'd frequent a club in Compton called the Penthouse. All of the hip-hop stars of the time performed there. One night Kurtis Blow came through with his DJ, Davie D. And D's antics were the first time you'd seen someone cut live. Now you could put sight and sound together. Flash on record. Davie D in the flesh. Your evolution had begun.

It was only a matter of time, or fate, until you realized you wanted to make your own records. The club had a little four-track studio, complete with drum machine. So you decided to experiment, copying the instrumental sections of songs you liked so that you could have a rhythm track to rock. From that point the urge naturally mutated into a desire to make original stuff.

Remarkable, this growth of yours. There were no music programs in school; no piano lessons; not even a musical mentor in the family. But your folks were musical in their own right. The house you grew up in was filled with sound, day and night. It was the house that all the neighborhood kids grew up in. The one on the block from which laughter constantly pealed, mixed with sweet melodies off the stereo.

Your moms was cool like that. Maybe it's because she had you at sixteen, still a child herself, forced to age at the rapid pace that grips all things urban and colored in this country. But she was real cool, though.

Yep. Family is real important to you. You had a big one. We know about baby stepbrother Warren G, but you had another brother who was killed. Tyree. That haunts you still. And your sisters. Seven of them. Three of 'em stepsisters. All of you, coming up in Compton.

Man, listen, Compton was a wild place to come up in the early eighties. Not as bad as it would become, granted. But even then it possessed that mix of danger, intrigue, and temptation that lures young men. It was fun, too, though. You used to leave school, anxious to catch a glimpse of the lowriders hoppin' by in procession. And, of course, you lived for the parties. Right behind your house was a park, Kelly Park. It had a lil' venue that folks called the Hut. Everyone had parties there. Matter of fact that's how you and Eazy-E, a short, Jheri-curled street cat, hooked up. Every year there was a big block party. And you would come out with the DJ equipment you'd gotten through scraping and scrapping. One year, on the Fourth of July, a party was in full swing and the police shut it down. They just drowned the block. But it was still early in the evening. So folks headed over to Eazy's backyard.

From there N.W.A, your seminal gangsta group, was a veritable hop, skip, and jump away. You knew what you wanted to do. And Eazy had, ah, some funds to invest. Circumstances just completed the equation. You were flirting with mechanical drafting at the time, 'round '84. And you were supposed to go for an interview, land a job, get a tangible, ol'-school hustle, not this wispy music thing. But, as any screenwriter would pen it, you fronted and went to DJ a party instead. Well, cool as Moms was, that shit would not fly. She put you out on your ass. And you went to stay with an aunt, who just happened to live near some kid named Ice Cube.

Cube had a rep as a good writer, so you asked him to lace this joint for some cats from New York you were messing with. You liked how they flowed, but not their lyrics. Eazy was gonna pay for the studio time. You had the whole shit covered. Only thing, them New York niggas wasn't tryin' to say that Cube shit, that Compton shit. They were like, "Fuck that shit," and broke out. So you said, "Fuck it. Eazy, you do it." And that's how "Boyz-N-tha Hood," Eazy's first song, was born.

We know your history a bit more from here. You got

with Eazy, Cube, Ren, an intense lyricist from Compton, and DJ Yella, who'd been in an earlier group with you (World Class Wreckin' Cru). N.W.A was born. Niggas with Attitudes. One badass group of mufuckas dressed in black. Took that pissed-off Compton aesthetic and branded it on wax, creating the whole Cali gangsta chamber in the process. Damn, those memories must be something else. Something good—and bad.

Good, like your record going so big, and all the attention you got. Even the hoopla the FBI raised about "Fuck tha Police" was cool. You were really touching people. Folk were listening. Seeing your record go number one on the pop charts, and all of you being able to go out on tour. That's all you ever wanted: get paid for doing the shit you really liked to do.

Bad, like when the beast of finance reared up. When everyone started to pay attention to what was going on with the loot and realized that stuff wasn't kosher. You drop much of the blame on the shoulders of Eazy's long-time crony, manager Jerry Heller. But now, unlike the venom-laced, "fuck Eazy and Jerry" *Chronic* days, you don't think he was a snake.

You just think he took advantage of your youth, inexperience, and naiveté about the record business. Though Eazy and Heller disputed it, you were in a contract that only gave you two points, and you were a producer of a platinum album. A producer of that status, you shoulda been getting four points at least. Once you were making money, maybe Heller shoulda stepped in, offered to renegotiate the miserly terms of your early contract. But he was like, "Fuck that." Just gave you crumbs. And took care of Eazy, so he could keep the other niggas in line.

Cube was the first to break. But you, too, could not tolerate the bullshit indefinitely. You gave Eazy an ultimatum: "Get rid of Jerry and I'll stay." But he chose Jerry. So you went your way. Things were tense for a minute after that. The infamous, alleged strong-arming to get you out your contract to Ruthless, Eazy's label. The videos lampooning Eazy. The records. The back-and-forth disses. It was bad.

But that Compton bond must have been way strong. You could drift away, not apart. The two of you talked again. Even talked about doing another album. Couple of phone calls. Seen each other at video shoots. It was all good. Until you started complaining about Jerry; and he started complaining about your new partner, Suge Knight. More drift. Then resolve on your part.

"Forget all that," you told him. "Let's just me and you work it out because we're much stronger together."

But the Devil gets between resolve. Twists it up. Eazy died.

You are Andre Young. And you must make your mark, again. For this hip-hop ocean, along with those who swim in it, can swiftly become an unforgiving tsunami. Sweeping over hero, villain, and spectator alike. Dispassionately. Inexorably.

You have swum in this ocean for some time. Plumbed its depths in triumph—from N.W.A, through the heady, hectic days of Death Row, to the birth of Aftermath, after you'd grown disgusted and disenchanted with life on the Row. But you have been gone a while. Resting on some private island. Now you must swim once more. Or sink.

"Even now people are saying, 'Is Dre fallin' off?'" you murmur. "And, 'Is his next album going to be just as good, or is he even going to be able to make another album people are going to be interested in?'"

Of course, you have the answers for them.

"I'm doing one of two things: Either I'm not paying attention to it, or I'm using it as fuel. But all in all, I'm just staying focused and keeping an eye on my goals. Even before the Dr. Dre album, I always wanted to complete something I started. I feel like everybody has a plan, but only the smart people are prepared to execute their plan and make it work for them."

And your plan begins with a new album. A tome you wanted to call *The Chronic 2000*. But you must distinguish it from *Chronic 2000*, put out by your former colleagues at the Row. This bold-faced audacity on their part irks you, but you accept it. Deal with it. Thus, the new title of your album—*2001*.

Today, you sit at a table in a low-lit corner of the Stinking Rose. In here, too, people approach and look. The manager inquiring to your needs. The occasional bug-eyed patron. The chummy banter from the waitstaff. You respond much the same to all. With grace. Confidence. Composure. Like a man about to push the red button.

And you certainly look the part. Stress has fled your brow. Any excess weight has dropped off, leaving behind hollow cheeks, clear eyes, and rippling muscle tone. Indeed, while most of the TV-dwelling denizens of celebrityland seem shrunken in person, less significant, you appear larger. The energy in you is palpable and contagious.

Completing this new record has been a road that appeared endless. It taxed your confidence at first. You'd done over one hundred songs. Now you can see the horizon. See the thing taking shape. You look up from the darkened corner. Return a passerby's nod before murmuring a thought.

"I have to be honest and say for the first five or six months I was like a little nervous, but I know me and I know I'm not gonna present it until it was ready, so I feel real good about it now."

It has been some time getting back to this plateau of confidence. The last record, *The Aftermath,* was supposed to bring you here. But it didn't quite make it up the hill. The spiritual fallout from splitting with Death Row clogged the intakes. The corporate-type stress of trying to run a boutique label slowed the wheels. The crazy moment that was your life in that instance seized all forward momentum and refused to let go. People appreciated *The Aftermath*'s lead single, "Been There, Done That"—the reflective sentiment, the tango number in the video, the thump of the track. But they wanted more. This you now know.

"Most of the feedback I got from 'Been There, Done That' was, 'That shit was nice, now let's hear some [dope] shit.' And they were totally right. I have to get back into what I do, what made me who I am. And that's just straight-up hardcore hip-hop—that gritty shit. When people go to the record shops and they buy a Dr. Dre record they wanna hear that hardcore grimy shit, and I had to sit down and really realize that.

"So the two-year period that I went through making the records I did, like *The Aftermath,* was just a period in my life," you continue, tearing into the garlic-laced food from which the Stinking Rose derives its name. "And I was getting kinda dissed from the hardcore hip-hop community because they wanted to hear Dre be Dre and it was crazy to me, but it was real. I do need to do the shit that I really know how to do, and the shit that I know is hardcore hip-hop."

And you are doing hardcore hip-hop again. And it excites you. Which is good, because not much has excited you of late. You like Jay-Z and DMX, but nobody's made you get out of bed and run to the record store. The way you did when you heard Eric B. & Rakim for the first time.

You are Andre Young. And you always make things good. Mostly anyways. Sometime they go bad, though. Like Death Row. It became so much. Yet, it could have been so much more. If only . . . well.

It starts with you. And him: Suge Knight. You knew him a long time before you did business together. He lived on the other side of Compton. Ended up doing some security work for D.O.C. This was before D.O.C. lost his voice in that fucked-up accident, when he was a star on the come-up.

One day, you remember, D.O.C. asked Suge for some money. And Suge grew curious, like, "You selling all these records, where's your money?"

So Suge got hold of D.O.C.'s contract and had someone look over it. Sure enough, it didn't look right. So the two of them, Suge and D.O.C., stepped to you. Urged you to look at your own contract. Down crashed the first domino. And the whole Eazy/Ruthless/N.W.A. construct fell. Then you and Suge took this idea you had: harness your creativity with his bulldog acumen, and build something special.

And it was. You envisioned something like Motown. A label that had everything internally: artists, a production staff, writers. You don't step out of your camp for anything. You don't put your artists on anyone else's albums. You don't write or produce for anyone. When you sign someone, accept him or her into this paradigm, stardom was the natural, indeed, the logical expectation. That was how you planned it. And that was the way it went down. For a minute.

Then the Money came into it. Millions flooded in and eroded the bonds. And cats stopped chillin' together. Like when you made *The Chronic* album, everyone was at the studio everyday. And everyone threw their little piece into the pie. When it was time for Snoop's album, it wasn't quite the same. The vibe grew more relaxed. People would drift in late. And you started seeing a lot of new cars pulling up.

And the violence. The senseless, frighteningly regular violence. Beating up engineers. Beating up people on tour. These things dampen the spirit. Even today, you don't like to talk about it too much. You just know, deep in the core that knows, that it could have been the most powerful label that ever existed.

You left. You had to leave. They made it hard. Questioned your manhood. Hinted at violence. But the one thing that stuck in your craw, the one thing that fucked you up, were the comments about you not pro-ducing the records you did. The records that have your name on them.

But you know the proof is self-evident because when you left the sound left with you. "I never put my name on one song that I didn't work on or didn't produce," you say emphatically. "I never would put 'produced by Dr. Dre' if Dr. Dre didn't produce it or coproduce it. If I had somebody in there producing the song with me, their name was on the song with me."

Death Row may be in your past. But it can never be past. Even now you wish things were different, could be different.

"Me and Snoop was just talking recently," you explain, a tinge of regret in your voice, "saying if everybody was just on some cool shit we [could help] them with some of the records, making sure that the shit we helped build doesn't just crumble. But it's like, right now it's just so much negativity we can't even begin to try to fix that shit; we can't begin to have anything to do with it. [When] somebody starts to show some positivity or something, maybe we can get together and do something, but the way it is now, I'm just thinking about whoever is down with me."

Even now, the clang from "Stranded On Death Row"—that defiant, Death Row-celebrating posse cut on *The Chronic*—must ring in your head.

You are Andre Young. And often when you make music, you plug your fingers into your ears, filtering the sounds floating in the studio, humming notes to yourself. On this afternoon, at Burbank, California's Encore Music Studio, you search for a string melody to lay atop one of your album's more sinister numbers, a nightmarish affair you currently refer to as "Murderer" (all your songs have working titles till you decide their fate). It features the haunting piano melody from *Halloween* and the captivating vocals of Hitman, a short, stocky, intense member of the crew you've assembled this time around.

And what a crew it is: the jovial and irreverent MelMan, your creative production partner; Ms. Rock, a wild-spirited hard rock of a female lyricist; the quiet, contemplative Knockturnal; and the aforementioned Hitman. Aside from your new protégés, you've also enlisted the talents of Eminem, Snoop, Xzibit, and Kurupt.

Almost all of them float through this place on a daily basis. It is your office. A workplace as productive and potent as any Pentagon lab. And it comes replete with equally arcane, powerful equipment: the SSL board you prefer; stacks of outboard gear; keyboard and sound modules, including MelMan's Korg, which he massages consistently in his quest for sounds, any sounds. Through it all drifts that buffer between thought and electrodes—the engineers. Nerdy-lookin' dudes upon whom your crew bestow funny-ass handles. One, baptized Seinfeld, remains the continuous butt of MelMan's cracks: "That nigga was out of control last night, right? *Who?* This dick, nigga!"

You keep working. Chuckling on occasion. Your attention to detail and focus is remarkable. Fingers fly over the board. Testing. Turning. Nodding in appreciation. This is all part of your process. One that's as fluid and diverse as your approach to music.

"It might start out with somebody comin' in with a hook," you explain. "I might just use some music that fits that, or I might just sit there and tap out some shit on the drum machine, and we always have musicians in the studio on deck waiting. We might have a drumbeat and a bass line would come to mind, and I might hum it to the bass player and be like, 'Play this.' Or MelMan would come in and be like, 'I got some shit'; come in with a drum track or just a rhythm track or something. And I'm like, 'I got a keyboard track to match that.' We all just get in there and put our heads together and try to make something that is exciting."

Sounds simple. But it isn't. Look at the way you finally hum the right violin part. Then call in your resident composing whiz who interprets your hums on the Korg keyboard. Scribbles the notes out. Calls in a six-piece string crew who attempt to match their academy-trained violin and cello skills to your urgent beats. The sight of these middle-aged, lily-white individuals strugglin' to rock to your shit is, well, more than a tad surreal.

"That's the only problem I have with these mufuckas—rhythm," you sigh in feigned exasperation.

Then they get it. Or enough of it for you to sample, at any rate. Just like that, this song slips into your "good record" category. A record that sounds like somebody really put some time and thought into it. And when that person is you, when you feel that certainty, you have made something good.

16

ME, MACHINE: THE CURIOUS CASE OF A MAN CALLED SEAN

Lock this moment in a capsule. Before Daddy became Diddy. Maybe we should start here:

"Do you think evil chases you?"

Sean "Puff Daddy" Combs pauses for the merest of moments to consider my question. Then he answers. In a blur.

"I don't know if it's some kind of evil that's chasing me, [but] you know how people say, like, you're going through pain 'cause you're getting prepared for something greater in the future? I be like, 'Damn, how much more painful is it gonna be in the future?' I'm such a strong human being it's to the point to where I get afraid 'cause I don't want to be cold, you know? So it's like I get hit and I get so many shots that bounce up off me, you want to be bulletproof and have that armor. But, at the same time, you want to be able to sometimes express your feelings—to yell or scream or do something."

Or here:

The church that Sean "Puff Daddy" Combs calls home sits on Liberty Avenue in East New York, Brooklyn, between Bradford and Miller. It is known as the Love

Fellowship Tabernacle. Puff Daddy is not with me. But I stand on this street nonetheless, staring at his church. I have come here to make sense of Puff Daddy. Or Sean Combs. And Sean Combs. It is not an easy undertaking. And after weeks and days with him on this story, not to mention a couple years of casual acquaintanceship, I still find myself wracked by the *inexactness* of it all. The lingering, conflicting questions. What the hell makes him tick? How can he be, by turn, so thoughtful and so tyrannical? How does he separate Sean, the man, from the machinelike, all-consuming drive of Puff Daddy? And why does he do it, still?

Murky answers. So I stand here on a Brooklyn corner in the sweltering mid-July humidity. Staring. I don't really expect the stone veneer of this place to give me clarity. But maybe I'll find small clues by sheer proximity. The church that Sean "Puff Daddy" Combs calls home sits on Liberty Avenue in East New York, Brooklyn, between Bradford and Miller.

No. Here:

It is a steamy Sunday afternoon in New York City, June 13th, 1999, and I am looking for Puff Daddy's soul. No. That's not quite right. I am looking *at* Puff Daddy looking for his soul. He does this quite often these days. Sometimes it seems a conscious act. Him groping among the far too few rest moments in his life, seeking balance, searching for happiness. But most often the soul search stays in passive mode, just an unconscious addendum to his talented and tortured trek through life.

Today he will be trekking along New York's Fifth Avenue. Not quite yet, though. For this afternoon plays host to the Puerto Rican Day Parade and the P-Diddy float isn't ready to move. It sits amidst controlled madness: the cordoned-off Bad Boy area on Forty-fourth Street between Madison and Fifth. The float itself is a grayish, titanium-looking thing. Three ascending, circular platforms set atop a flatbed. From this stage Puff will roll into the heart of the New York Puerto Rican community's annual celebration, filming scenes for the Spanish (yes, Spanish) version of the video for his first single, "PE 2000," a remake of the Public Enemy classic "Public Enemy No. 1."

However, the filming will have to wait a moment, at least until the peculiar chaos that often affects Bad Boy productions reluctantly slouches aside in favor of order. Appropriately enough, the trailer that houses Puff sits in the heart of it all: frantic video crew, security hulks, visiting celebs, label personnel, and the like. It is the nerve center of this organism, and it's protected as such. One zealous security guy sticks out a meaty arm to bar Puff's high-powered manager, Benny Medina, from entering the trailer, earning himself a look of incredulous venom and a few whispered, heated words. Unabashed, the guy lets Medina in, looks around, and shrugs his shoulders. Refusing to apologize for doing his job.

The trailer door creaks open one more time and Puff himself emerges, instantly generating a roiling wave of security, associates, camera-snapping types, and sundry others, all seeking attention. It is a phenomenon that never ceases to intrigue me, no matter how many times I've seen it swirl around him. But for Puff, the wave is part and parcel of being the guru of hip-hop's cult of celebrity, an electric current snaking its way through the unstoppable Puff Daddy Machine.

After some twenty minutes, amplified voices ring out.

"Clear the street. Everybody clear the street!" the security chief keeps screaming. Someone from the video crew takes up the effort and, eventually, a different security guy. They're trying valiantly to clear unnecessary folks from the immediate vicinity of Puff's float so things can, well, start.

Soon, chaos grudgingly begins to give way to order and the machine begins to hum. Puff carefully climbs to the top of the float. Instantly, a group of little kids standing to one side begin clamoring for him.

"Puffy! Hey, Puffy!" one determined little fellow hollers. Puff's attention is elsewhere. So the kid shouts again, insistently. This time Puff swivels his head left and down, spying the group of kids, waving. They react predictably enough. Wide grins. Open eyes.

Puff returns his attention to the business at hand, eyes intently surveying the scene fifteen feet below him. He's quite a sight up there with his white pants, sleeveless leather vest festooned with the colors of the Puerto Rican flag, and the obligatory iced platinum. He wears a lot of it, from the truck chains jangling around his neck to the sweatband-size diamond bracelet on his right wrist. The entire collection winks madly in the high-afternoon sun.

Slowly, the procession rolls out. The float moves first. On it stands Hurricane G, who does the Flavor Flav-type intro for "PE 2000," Flavor Flav himself, as manic at forty as he was a decade ago, Daymon John, CEO of FUBU, radio host Ed Lover, several Bad Boy staffers, the video crew, and, of course, Puff himself. To either side of the float marches a line of security men clothed in white uniforms. Just behind rolls a silver Lincoln Navigator, transporting Puff's main men, Bad Boy President Andre Harrell and Executive Vice President Jeff Burroughs, in air-conditioned comfort. Smart guys. And bringing up the rear are, literally, dozens of New York's finest on mopeds.

The screams come suddenly. And at shocking volume. The Puerto Ricans lining Fifth Avenue have just caught sight of Puff Daddy, rocking the colors of their flag no less. And rhyming to them in Spanish over the ol'-schoolish percussion of "PE 2000."

"Puerto Rico, Puerto Rico!" Puff shouts out.

And they scream right back. As I walk by the side of the float, a scant twelve feet or so from the sidewalk, the consistent roar buffets me with its sheer volume. Then I catch sight of the teenage girls. Three of them. They stand at the curb; somehow they've slipped in front of the blue police barricades that pen most of the spectators in. And, between screams, they gaze at Puff with pure rapture on their faces. Almost on cue, all three begin to cry. Big, heaving sobs, all the while fixing those wide-open eyes on Puff. One little girl just stands there in shock, her left hand covering her mouth. Her right, the one holding the flag, hangs limply by her side. A friend grabs the dangling hand and raises it in the air so the flag can be displayed. But, as soon as the neighbor removes the supporting hand, the little girl's right arm plummets back down. And the tears keep falling.

What do you know of Puff Daddy? Probably a lot. You know the oft-repeated tale of his professional arc, his own pauper-to-prince fable. The way he used to break out of Howard University to come to New York for his internship at Andre Harrell's Uptown Records. The way he went from intern to A&R whiz kid in mere months, shaping the careers of acts like Jodeci and Mary J. Blige, birthing that whole R&B/bad boy/urban swagger thing. The way his frenetic youth and ambition eventually played him out at Uptown, causing his boss and mentor Harrell to put him—and his fledgling Bad Boy idea—out on the sidewalk. The way he walked into Clive Davis's Arista conference room, boldly outlining his plan for a label called Bad Boy Entertainment and a rapper named Biggie Smalls. The way he proceeded to tear up the urban music market, becoming a top-flight CEO, producer, and, eventually, artist.

You know how controversy and tragedy have dogged his every step, from the 1991 concert he promoted at the City University of New York that left nine people dead after a stampede, to the still-unsolved '97 slaying of the Notorious B.I.G., to his own headline-grabbing assault of music bigwig Steve Stoute.

You know he's a lightning rod for polarized opinions. Hate. Love. Adulation. Disgust. He's a brilliant producer and talent spotter. Or an unabashed rip-off artist and manipulator. He's an inspiration for hard-working, entrepreneurial folks everywhere. Or the chief proponent of a glitzy lifestyle so out of reach and over the top for most adherents of hip-hop, it ceases any pretense at aspiration and becomes debilitating, hollow, and soulless.

What do you know of Puff Daddy? Probably not enough. You may admire his position, his status. But what did it take for him to get there? And what does it cost him to remain there? Those are the thousand-dollar questions. To even begin to answer them you must understand one simple thing about Puff: He wants to win. More than me. More than you. And more than most anyone you know. I asked several of Puff's associates and friends to put that idea in context. All of them gave fascinating anecdotes and observations, but Ron Gillyard, Bad Boy's VP of marketing and a man who has known Puff since Howard, put it most succinctly.

"He's driven, and he's focused. He's clear about what it is he wants; he has a clear understanding of getting there and nothing is going to stop him from getting there, short of death."

Gillyard really meant that. And I think he's right. Puff's been talkin' about "he won't stop" on records for years. And most of us have danced and sung right along, never regarding those words as anything more significant than trite, pop music utterances, a cute little refrain. But they were true. Though probably not as true as my own little remix of that phrase: "He *can't* stop." Put it this way: He's like Jordan in the fourth quarter—all day. Ever read Peter Benchly's *Jaws?* Remember how the great white shark only died when it stopped moving, when the cessation of motion kept precious oxygen from sloshing through its gills?

But that type of obsessive-compulsive focus—and I would hazard a guess that most hypersuccessful people share the trait—does not come free of charge. Bill Gates must pay it. Oprah probably pays it. Puff pays it. And few people are in a better position to even begin to estimate that bill than Andre Harrell, his longtime friend and mentor.

"I think when a person is driven by achievement in that way, a certain part of their own inner peace is always at risk," Harrell told me one afternoon in late June, sitting behind his desk at Bad Boy's new offices in the BMG building in Times Square. "'Cause there's no time out to think about [certain] things; moments that happen every day and how to appreciate and take advantage of those moments. Those moments at his age in life might be in the way of what he thinks his goals

221

are. And maybe, in his mind, he'll get to those moments after he's achieved his goal."

Maybe.

Los Angeles. June 16. The Whiskey Bar. One of those "L.A. places," populated by a certain high-society element culled from music and film. White. Black. Others. Nightcrawlers all at this 1:00 A.M. hour. Leaning over drinks, flashing pearly whites and the occasional intoxicated leer. There's sex here. Money. Hollywood intrigue of the most banal sort.

Puff Daddy is here, too. And he wants to talk. He really wants to talk. Chalk it up to the challenging year he's had. Or, better yet, attribute it to this particular place he's at. Not simply the eve of an album release, his sophomore project, *Forever,* but that soul-search moment. That nanosecond where he can pull away from the machine and find his soul. Of course the machine isn't just connected to him, doesn't just surround him—he is the machine—but he must try regardless.

So he sits with me in the Whiskey Bar. We're on a couch set off from the main area of hubbub, slouched down, staring at the patrons. MC Lyte is over there. And a few other folk of note. All of whom want to chat with Puff. He smiles. Makes quick small talk when someone breezes by. But he's much more interested in unloading. The need is palpable. So we talk.

"Tell me about this year."

He doesn't even pause.

"This year has really been crazy. It's been blow after blow. I look back on my shit [and] I be like, 'This has been so fucking dramatic, just constant twists and turns, like a saga.' This year was like so much personal life stuff, having a baby; working so hard to keep everything afloat business-wise, more than afloat, to keep everything successful, to that successful peak that everyone expects when you sell as many records as a label like Bad Boy has sold. Your personal life suffers a lot. That right there hurts you. You be getting pulled this way and that way, like, 'Damn, what I'm supposed to do?'"

"How did the label do, anyway?"

He sighs.

"The label has done better with the acts [whose] albums have sold more this time than they sold the previous time. It's just that when you up there in the ranks and you on a streak, people are trying to knock it. People are trying to compare the sales of Biggie, Mase, and myself to the sales of Mase [second album], Total, and Faith. It's ridiculous, it's like apples and oranges. You can't put out Biggie, Mase, and Puffy in the same year all the time."

"So what about Mase, him leaving you?"

"I got a call one day that Mase didn't want to rap no more. I was like, 'What the fuck? Where did that come from?' He just renegotiated our deal; we had just finished an album. Me and Mase, we never really had bad times. The shit just came out of nowhere, and then he was on the radio like, 'Yeah I'm retiring.' I'm like, 'Oh shit,' and I felt confused, I felt like, damn, like I put in a lot of time, the label—everyone put in a lot of time—and we wish we could have talked about it. But it was a situation where God told him this, and I would never second guess that or judge him against that.

"Honestly, it kinda, like, hurt me. I never went and like pressured him or offered him money or told him to do anything that went against his feelings. I just let it be, but also there was a point where I understood, too. Sometimes

I feel like taking a break from this. Sometimes it feels over-whelming. I feel like he definitely had his calling from God, but also it could have got overwhelming for him."

"You gonna let him out of his contract? Doesn't he owe you a bunch of records?"

"I'm not going to force him to make a record. I'm not going to sue him. I'm supportive of him, if that's what he wants to do. If he wants to make records, then we have a contract; it's just business."

We both stop for a minute. Perhaps to reflect on what's been said. To anticipate where it may go. To peer around the room again. To humor the drunken girl now planted before us, profusely apologizing for breaking our cipher, stubbornly refusing to move until she's told Puff how dope he is. He thanks her graciously, and with just a touch of amusement. I glance at him. Then at her. Increasingly mortified, but still trying to make some obscure point, she hops from hip to hip, drink sloshing around, until, at last, she moves on.

"Since you mention God, how are you doing spiritu-ally these days?"

"Spiritually I am as strong as I have ever been," he replies in that steady, yet animated tone of his. "Going through a certain amount of pain just makes you stronger. I made a lot of mistakes in my life, and I've had a lot of successes, and I've learned from both sides of it. I've nothing else to turn to. I chose the life that I was going to lead. It took a lot of sacrifices: I wasn't able to give people a lot of time; I wasn't able to hold a relation-ship with a woman; I wasn't able to be a good friend to somebody; I wasn't able to give that time. The only per-son I had after all was said and done, after losing my girl, after not being able to keep certain friends, was God.

[I'm] trying to just be a better person every day; watch the way I talk to people, watch the way I make people feel, try to control my emotions. Sometimes I slip off the horse, [but] I gotta get back up no matter what."

Speaking of slipping off the horse . . .

"So how do you feel now about the Steve Stoute incident?"

"I feel like I played myself. But it gets to a point where you get tired of putting up with the bullshit. What made me upset was that it was emotional for me. It was my religion that was involved. I was not trying to portray Jesus, but when I saw it I felt like it [looked that way] and I don't feel comfortable with that. And that's the only thing that I got. Money gonna come and go. Women gonna come and go. Friends, some of them, are gonna come and go. God will always be there. He gonna love me no matter what. And that had me so scared to death, 'cause no matter what I do, I can always go to church. If I disrespect God and make a mockery of God, I can't even go to church."

The typical day of a machine begins, appropriately enough perhaps, in the workout room. But Puff's trainer has his job cut out for him today. His client's mind is elsewhere. And he's just a tad irritated. Nevertheless, the machine that houses the soul of Sean Combs does not quit for anything, or anyone. He plows through the workout.

Afterward, he walks slowly along the outdoor path that leads to his private bungalow at the Beverly Hills Hotel. Blue Sean John pants and sleeveless white T drape his frame. His omnipresent phone sits in one hand, the connecting wire with the mic and earpiece lodged in his ear. From afar, it looks like he's talking into thin air. His bodyguard leads him by several feet, and members of his entourage trail him: Shyne, his next big thing, whose first order of business is to remain attached to Puff's hip and observe; D-Mac, his road manager; and Ari, his bespectacled trainer.

Up ahead, in the bungalow proper, rests the actress and singer Jennifer Lopez, all the more alluring in the simple bathrobe draped upon her shoulders. Recent rumor called these two an item. Yesterday innuendo slipped into fact when Puff directed his tour bus to LAX. This had not been on the schedule.

"I gotta pick somebody up," he grunted by way of explanation.

Then she floated aboard and into his embrace. Tanned. Beautiful. White outfit painted on like a second skin. She will be a cooing, supportive presence for him over the next few days.

Later, the machine will run to Universal Studios where scenes for the "PE 2000" video will be shot. There are already tons of people milling about the studio lot. Bad Boy staffers. Members of the video crew. All of them minute levers in the machine, aiding its progress.

Puff drifts over to an adjoining parking area, a place he will consistently head to when the day's phone conversations get intense, as they so often do. Mere distance, however, provides no buffer from the workings of the machine. He still has to flip gears rapidly: from the hustler cajoling or browbeating over the phone, to the artist approving wardrobe choices, to the CEO shooting down budget questions.

A machine's day unfolds with agonizing slowness— from without. From within it obeys its own rhythm. Herky jerk one moment, lightning fast the next, all according to the dictates of Puff. I do my best to maintain an observer's distance, but the machine, Puff the entity, Puff the phe-nomenon, will suck you up if you enter its sphere. So even I find myself taking a message for Puff, letting Puff know the director's calling him. Like everyone else, I'm subject to the machine's charisma, its maddening drive.

The day of a machine ends at SRI studios, just before midnight. Well, it doesn't really end. More like it shifts into a different drive. For this is dance rehearsal time. Puff has to master the choreography for his special dance sequence that will be filmed tomorrow. And master it he does. For near two hours, he pushes himself harder and harder. Until the sweat pours from his body, thoroughly soaking the gray tank top he wears. Leaning against a back wall, I have to fight to keep my eyes open. Not because the length of the day is unusual, but because hanging with Puff, trailing in his wake, can drain you in a way I find inexplicable. Even his trainer is mystified by Puff's ability to tap into energy. A week later, Andre Harrell will attempt to explain this internal fuel to me:

"I think in his mind he's gonna work twice as hard as anybody else so he can be ahead of the game. Most peo-ple think about eight hours, some people think of it as a ten-hour [day]; but, for him, he thinks of it as a sixteen-hour workday. He's driven by tasks. He puts things in front of him that he wants to complete. I think he gets ful-fillment out of that."

Tonight, however, all I can think about is *external* fuel. The things that the machine sucks up and uses to power itself. I visualize one particular, giant-size tank: The Notorious B.I.G. Whether you ascribe to the cynical viewpoint that says Puff launched his own career on the back of his dead friend, or take the more benign angle whereby the senseless tragedy of B.I.G.'s murder simply pushes Puff on, the fact remains: B.I.G. is fuel for the machine, perhaps the most potent one available.

Later that night, after the dance rehearsal, after the trip back to the hotel, I ask Puff about it.

"Talk to me about Big."

He sits back in a chair in the master bedroom of his bungalow. With his plain black T-shirt, white shorts, and no phone, he is clearly in a rest moment. A moment when the machine recedes, and Sean ascends.

"I still can't believe it," he answers. For the first time in our conversations, I actually hear weariness in his tone.

"I still see how depressed the whole family still is. Speaking to his mother, seeing his kids grow up. The shit is just so senseless and it's also so scary. Somebody could just die 'cause mufuckas is jealous. That's the reason he died. He didn't die 'cause he did nothing to somebody. He didn't die 'cause he was East Coast. He got killed 'cause he was just the hottest mufucka. And niggas just couldn't take it."

"Has it been frustrating over the past two years with the case being open?"

He casts his eyes at the ceiling for a second.

"That part of it hasn't been frustrating for me as much as him not being here has been frustrating and painful. Like a couple of weeks ago, we was celebrating his birthday, and it just hurt so bad when you got to really face the reality. Like onstage, I get upset every time I rock onstage 'cause that's when I come to the realization that he's not there. We all try to block it out, [but] it still has not totally digested. He just got killed on some hate and shit. That shit is fucking foul. I could just go on and on about Biggie. Shit just ain't the same. It will never be what it could have been to me."

"Did it hurt you, the whispers that your becoming a star wouldn't have happened if Biggie was alive?"

"I think that I would have had a certain amount of success, but even that success was because of Biggie believing in me. [But] another part of the success of the album [*No Way Out*] could definitely be attributed to the unfortunate situation. I had to go on because there was nothing else for me to do. Either I was going to die or keep going."

Let's slip forward just a bit:

I haven't been to Howard University in, like, ten years. Not since I was a college freshman barreling down I-95 to go to the mythical Howard homecoming. I still carry a lot of impressions from those days: the flood of well-dressed black students; the parties; and the girls, of course. Today those impressions ring true. It's Saturday afternoon in Washington, D.C., June 26, several days since I've last seen Puff. Technically, I'm in D.C. for today's West Indian carnival. But since the carnival's route takes it along Georgia Avenue, smack dab into the middle of Howard, the reporter in me can't help but peek at this shaping crucible. Machines are assembled somewhere, after all.

The students walking in and out of Howard Towers on Sherman Avenue look much like their counterparts from a decade ago. And the parking lot of the McDonald's on the corner of Sherman and Georgia still resembles an auto show-meets-fashion spectacle. I wonder what Puff's legacy means to these students. How many of them aspire to be like the Pied Piper of Howard?

"What I noticed about [Puff] was the fact that he always had a lot of people around him," Ron Gillyard told me. "Everybody was just following him. He had a Gumby [hairstyle] back then [and] he danced in a Stacy

Lattisaw video, and people who had cable, they were treating him like the guy who danced in the videos. [One day] during our homecoming [he had] a party. He had a whole list of celebrities that was gonna be there, Slick Rick, Doug E. Fresh, Guy, Heavy D, and damn near all those people showed up. And ever since that first party everyone made it a point to go to Puff's parties."

Of course, the components of the Puff machine didn't simply spring into existence in college. Howard merely provided, for the first time, a full-size test venue, if you will. The shaping goes much further back, and much deeper, for Puff. One day, on the video set, I deliberately tried to catch him off guard after he had just watched footage for his album's promotional video—footage that included very intimate, and painful, family recollections—like his father's murder in 1973, four years after he was born.

"Tell me about your father."

He looked at me in disbelief.

"Oh my God! Not right now." He shook his head, a tad exasperated. "I be running from that. A lot of times I face all my tragedies, but then I try to not keep on facing it 'cause they hurt so much."

I steeled myself, because Puff can be unpredictably temperamental, and pressed him anyway.

"In what way? You don't talk about, don't think about them?"

He just sat in his little director's chair, eyes sweeping the set, hand clutching the tiny phone he carries everywhere. Then, almost imperceptibly, he seemed to relax a bit, answering quickly in tangents, but with wistful sincerity.

"I think about him. I don't talk about him. My pops, he was a hustler and I can be looking at a picture of myself and I say, 'Damn, I'm really starting to look like duke.' Lots of times I be looking in the mirror and I be like, 'I wonder if he acted this way or he did that.'"

"Do you remember him at all?"

"I remember him throwing me up in the air. That's one thing I do with my kids, I always throw my kids, I hold them up in the air."

"What about your mom, did she talk about him?"

"Nah, my mom, because he was killed, she hid that from me."

"How did you find out?"

"I found out when I went to Howard. I did some investigation. I looked in the paper around the time he died."

"So what did you think happened to him when you were younger?"

"She [his mom] had told me he had died in a car accident."

Let's slip back:

Los Angeles. June 18. I hadn't the energy to meet Puff on the video set for the 7:00 A.M. call. So I straggle onto the Universal lot around midday and head to his trailer, just in time to catch one of the most heated phone convos I've witnessed him have since I've been shadowing him.

"Dog, that little stunt ain't help matters at all," he snarls into his phone. Then, as if remembering he's not alone, he gets up, walks into the bedroom section of the trailer, and closes the door. His voice still creeps through. Minutes later, he opens the door and bounds out of the trailer.

"Ask me about that Lox shit; that'll be good for the story," he tosses over his shoulder. I stare after him curiously. This isn't the first time he's suggested themes or lines of direction to me. And I can't decide whether it's part of his impulse to control or his desire to open up.

So I dial a friend in New York to find out that the Lox, Bad Boy's only hardcore group, were on Hot 97 FM complaining about being on the label and asking Puff to let them go. I set off to find Puff, tracking him through rolling cameras that look like *Star Trek* weaponry, equipment-laden tech types, and visiting camera crews from MTV, BET, and *Entertainment Tonight*. No pinning him down now. I've got to bide my time.

Two hours later, he looks relatively free. I nod at him. He nods back. We move to the same parking lot that's served as conference call central. Puff's been turning up the charm for the press folk, but I can tell he's still brimming with anger and frustration. I figure I might as well be blunt and direct.

"So the Lox wanna be off the label. How did things get there?"

And, like before, the floodgates open:

"Basically, the Lox want to be rich and there is nothing wrong with that. [But] it takes time to get to that point. I build with all my artists a long-term career. I didn't make no money off the Lox in any way. [The Lox] basically Sound Scanned seven hundred fifty-thousand albums. We shot a couple of videos. We went on tour. It's profit and loss. Artists get a record deal, and they think that they gonna be rich overnight.

"Me, I'm a different story. I been working at this shit for ten years," he continues in exasperation. "A lot of times you have this big 'Puffy is worth sixty this-million dollars.' People don't understand that, at the end of day, a lot of that is hype. People can't understand your worth versus how much you have in the bank. I'm not just sitting there in my house with sixty million dollars floating around me."

"But isn't it more difficult being a fledgling artist like the Lox or Shyne on Bad Boy, and want to make that money because this is a place that champions the whole high life style?"

"Yeah. It's definitely harder. And maybe we set ourselves up for that [with] the stuff we put in our records and the lifestyle that we live and all that, but the lifestyle that I live, I got from working every day, twenty hours a day, for ten years. And I tell you, if you do that shit, you will be somebody."

He stands in the high afternoon sun. Shades just containing the flash in his eye. I'm not sure which has him more heated. The Lox demanding to be released from his label, or the fact that they did it so publicly. It's the same "laundry in the streets" thing that hurt him where Mase was concerned.

Of course, it's plenty ironic. 'Cause Puff's had his own shit in the street of late—the Steve Stoute incident. So if his artists aren't adopting his all-consuming drive, maybe they're picking up on other things. Or maybe that very drive is what entices then pushes them away. Lotsa people think they wanna be Puff. But few find the work—and cost—attractive. Perhaps it scares them.

And since this man's also a father twice over, I can't help wondering about his sons, his obvious love for them, and the cost they, too, pay for the machine that houses their father's soul.

"What about your sons? Have you thought about how you're going to not have them grow up with just the famous father who is never there?"

"To be honest, I'm still trying to figure that out," he replies. "I got a lot of shit within myself that I'm cleaning out. My mind is not on worrying about this, or the frustrations of that, as much as it is as, 'Yo, the way you han-dled that situation right there was cool. The way you made them people laugh and feel good; the way you didn't flip out; the way you took time and spent more time with your kids, the way you spent time with your mother; that time when you turned off your phone and said fuck the business.' I need more of that."

"Was there a trigger or a point that made you realize that you had to get on that path?"

"Yeah, I went through . . . during the end of the tour, dur-ing the end of the album, I just went through a massive state of depression. I was like, 'I ain't happy in this shit, I ain't got Biggie, they don't like me, they don't appreciate what I do.' Mufuckas don't understand me, like, 'I hate this shit right here, what the fuck am I doing in this shit?' It was like, 'I don't even like the way [I am] right now. I don't like the way I'm moving. I'm bringing everybody else down.' I have a certain type of energy that if I want to make you mad, I can make you and five thousand people mad right now. I can walk into a room and just fuck up the whole mood of the room just by the way I feel."

He's not kidding. I've seen that infamous temper of his in action. I've seen his employees walk on eggshells when he's in *that* mood. I've heard him yell out, "Make me happy, damn it, or I'll fuck everybody's day up," when the video crew ignored him while arguing among themselves.

Still, few of his traits can be boxed and labeled easily. Even his temper. Those tantrums often have reason beneath them, calculation even. And his good mood, his positive emotional largesse, is just as contagious.

I just have to recall those kids in New York at the parade. The grins won by his glance. The tears spurred by his passage.

• • •

Maybe we end here:

"... think evil chases you?"

Sean "Puff Daddy" Combs pauses for the merest of moments to consider my question. Then he answers. In a blur.

"It's like you keep getting stronger and stronger to a point where you get tired of getting stronger. And that's the point I've gotten to. Just as a person going through all that stuff, it makes you weary; it makes you pray that you don't have to go through none of it again. It makes you look at the mistakes. It makes you search for answers. At the end of the day some of the things aren't explainable, a lot of the things are God's will and you have to stay strong, no matter how tired you are, you have to keep doing it and you just have to wait to see what He has planned for you."

No. Here:

The church that Sean "Puff Daddy" Combs calls home sits on Liberty Avenue in East New York, Brooklyn, between Bradford and Miller. It is called the Love Fellowship Tabernacle. Puff Daddy is not with me. But I stand on this street nonetheless, staring at his church. It has a different air in the daytime. Its outline burns the retina more sharply, as if God's rays were not merely providing illumination, but searing cobwebs from the eye.

I still can't claim to see Sean Combs clearly. He's still a soul that hovers within a construct called Puff Daddy. Still a man subject, in part, to the demands of a phenomenon, a machine. I do not know if Sean can ever separate himself from that machine. I do not know, even in his obvious search for *something,* if he truly wants to.

17

SPIRIT DIARY

June 1996. **Source** *editorial. I am in spiritual hell.*
Monday morning. I noticed that the A train to Brooklyn
had a new edition to the plethora of glossy ads coating its
steel sides—a poster touting a new organization by the
seemingly oxymoronic name of Jews for Jesus.

Then I recalled a news broadcast from the night before
about that very organization. Needless to say, there were
hosts of frenzied folk from the Jewish community
screaming that such a thing was impossible and that
Jews couldn't be Christians. OK. I sank back into my
seat, satisfied at having made the mental connection.

Damn, I muttered to myself. These people take their
religion and shit real serious-like.

Moments of exterior analysis inevitably become
episodes of self-reflection—at least they do for me. And
on that morning I shone my gaze inward and searched
for the wellspring that would allow me to give a fuck
about Christianity in particular and religion in general. I
couldn't find it.

Thus, my current revelation: I'm a twenty-something,
educated, hip-hop living and breathing, intensely
driven, generally normal black male undergoing a seri-

ous spiritual crisis. You know, spiritual crisis isn't really about an inability to get with organized religion. After all, I'd long given up any sense of connection to the gospel of God as communicated through the twisted words of men. I reasoned that the pursuit of faith has to be a one-on-one thing between the self and whatever greater awareness exists out there. Therein rests my problem. You see, although I can intellectually acknowledge the existence of something greater, I struggle to find the capacity to connect with it. The inherently selfish process of survival and advancement in the good old American capital system consumes my internals. And even though I may achieve some successes and triumphs, the bitter fight to find meaning often outweighs those precious moments.

Moreover—and more frightening—are the reflections of my crisis that I see daily. I work in an industry that seems to have taken the most corrupt mores of corporate America to their highest extrapolation, an industry that places all too many of us—young, black or white, talented—on an exploitative, vicious cycle: "Chase the dollar, chase the dollar, earn a meager pittance, outmaneuver the next man or woman, chase a slightly larger dollar, earn a meager pittance and a half, do it all again tomorrow." And for what? When the day is up and my magazine has sold hundreds of thousands of copies, individual A's record has gone gold and individual B's just inked the ill production deal (even though he/she won't own the master recordings), then what? What will give our lives meaning beyond the dawn of another day in the dog-eat-dog world of American society?

Perhaps that's why the latest album from A Tribe Called Quest, *Beats, Rhymes and Life,* has impacted me so greatly. Q-Tip and I are about the same age. And I feel like I've grown up right alongside him. *People's Instinctive Travels* . . . marked my own teenage dalliance in Afrocentric bohemianism; *Low End Theory* seemed to mirror the increasing worldview and general growth of initial postcollege years. But Tribe's latest has hit a previously untouched zone. Tip's conversion to Islam has had an obvious and profound impact on him. Thus, I find myself listening to the evidence of his spiritual growth with amazement, elation, and no small bit of envy.

Islam isn't for everyone. Matter of fact, I'm pretty sure it's not for me. But there's a path that I have to locate. Shit, there's a road out there for every member of our drifting generation. Me, I just wanna find faith in something. There's gotta be more to life than the barking of Glocks (real and imagined), the clinking of cash registers, and the sweat-stained residue of casual sex.

June 1997. **Source** *editorial. I have left hell for heaven's road.*

A year ago, I wrote a piece called "Spiritual Hell." It was a very personal testament, but one that held relevance for the hip-hop generation as a whole. When I wrote that piece I was tired and lost, looking for something to give life deeper, more grounded meaning. My faith was a tattered thing and I had little care or concern for any hazy notions of religion. Yet I longed for something more substantial than the mundane, material existence I'd been leading.

Much has happened to us all since the summer of '96. I don't have to document what's transpired in hip-hop, the events that have severely tested the faith of any hip-hop adherent—the tragic deaths of Biggie and Tupac. But on the personal front, something wonderful took place, something that countered despair private and public: I got saved.

You know, I still can't tell you just how it happened, and I can't define exactly what it means. It was a Sunday, and I was just another skeptic in the congregation, watching my goddaughter's christening at a Long Island church, a place filled, despite its Northeast location, with the life, breath, and energy of the black American South. The Baptist preacher roared and rocked, his raspy voice stuttering along in practiced rhythm, the congregation's amens punctuating every measure. A strange thing happened; I found myself deeply moved. Mind you, with the exception of weddings and funerals, I hadn't been in a church for over ten years. All I know is that when that preacher called out for anyone who wanted to be saved, my body seemed to move of its own volition. Seconds later, I stood before him, head bowed; slightly confused but glowing with a marvelous warmth.

Now, I haven't flipped on some Rev. Do Right steelo. And I'm not gonna tell you that my path is for you. I still believe that good works speak for themselves. And I cannot accept that praying to Allah versus accepting Jesus Christ, or whomever else, is a decision that can condemn a soul that performs good works. My journey has led me to God's house. You have to let your steps lead where they will.

November 1999. Journal entry. This road has many turns.
The church that I attend, on those Sundays when I manage to roll my catatonic self out of bed, is called St. Paul's Baptist Church. It is in East New York, Brooklyn,

Hendriks Street to be exact, just off of busy Linden Boulevard.

Don't know if I'm going to attend this morning. I need to. Bit wary of this new media world I'm moving into. Seems like stepping of a cliff. Need my faith here and now to buoy me up. Need to hear Pastor Youngblood preach with his fiery self. Tired, though. Maybe just a bit more sleep.

Damn if that don't make me feel guilty as all hell. Funny, no one told me of the work that must continue. No one mentioned the doubt that keeps assailing the insides. Trusting in something so ethereal as faith runs counter to everything I've learned about getting off your ass and making it happen, about the pursuit of self-reliance. Every lesson drilled in me from college through career. I'm saved. I believe it. I know it. But is it all some benevolent, self-induced delusion? Is my still-forming religious faith naught but a Pavlovian response to adversity, our conditioning to believe in something, anything, greater than ourselves when times grow tough?

February 2001. Journal entry. Back again.
Hello, diary. Has it been that long since I checked in? Man, I had no idea. This last year moved so quickly; yet some of the events, some of the emotions, still creep through my mind like scarred molasses.

I didn't go to church too much in 2000, diary. I don't know why. Wasn't like I gave in to the despair of old. Wasn't like I lost faith. But maybe, perhaps, my job became church for me. You know how we overachieving types are, diary. You know the way we pump every vestige of our lifeblood into something. Far too often to the

240

exclusion of everything else. And the job was something, diary. Finally, a large-scale hip-hop entrant in the trek through dot.com wilderness. Maybe we were late. But we weren't going to be left behind. I came running. But I prayed on it first, diary. I really did. I asked the Big Guy for guidance, for strength. And he delivered. I might not have gone to church much in 2000, but I called on him plenty. Had to.

Called on him when things were good, like when my forty-member team was caught in the fast-paced, giddy throes of building an idea. We would gather in the small conference room of our ragged, yet homey, Chelsea loft. And we would pray, diary. Can you believe that? A bunch of jaded, too-cool Gen X and Yers. Praying. We'd crowd in that room. Shoulders bumping other shoulders. Backs pressed against walls and whiteboards. Hands clasped. We'd pray for strength. Patience. Folk would cry sometimes, diary. And even though our human relations guru, bless her heart, advised me to, we couldn't stop the prayer sessions. They were lifelines in an increasingly uncertain ocean.

Called on the Big Guy when things were bad, too. When the dream imploded. When the funding dried up and it became clear the company would have to be sold. And equally clear that not all of my trusting team would survive. I'm not sure which was worse. Walking around for weeks with the knowledge of who would go and who would stay, or actually, finally, telling them.

Haven't prayed since that October day, diary. The day I fired my friends. Well, I've called on the Big Guy in private, but not in the inspirational collective of old. I don't know why. Perhaps I feel sickened by the whole experience of leading a flock and guiding so many of them to the slaughterhouse. You think that makes me weak, diary? Unfit for hard-edged business leadership? Maybe it does. Don't know if that's what the Big Guy put me here for.

Diary, I remember when my search for spirituality had me reeling out of balance, when I stumbled through life's aimless purpose. Eventually, I found that balance. But that did little for the topsy-turvy world around me. The waves of bullshit still battered against my shores. So tell me, diary, when you find light within, does it make the dark without easier to deal with?

August 2001. Sunday recap. Keep on trucking.
Johnny Ray Youngblood pauses midsermon. Peers at us through spectacles hung upon the bridge of his nose.

"First God tells Gideon, 'The thirty-two thousand men you raised for the army, that's a good number. According to numbers you don't have enough men to win the battle, but there are still too many for My purpose.'"

Johnny Ray pauses again. We umm-humm and amen.

"God says, 'We gotta test them. I want you to say, "All who are afraid go home."' Gideon does as God asks. And twenty-two thousand men leave."

Ahhh, we murmur. A few fans flutter amongst our gaily-colored rows. Despite the air conditioner the church thrums with heat. Johnny Ray wipes his brow.

"Then God says to Gideon, 'Take the ten thousand men down to the river and have them drink from the water.'" He moves from behind the lectern.

"Three hundred of the men got down and drank this way."

Johnny Ray stoops near the front of the stage. He is an older man but still limber. He places his right knee on the ground. Right hand mimes a scooping motion. Eyes look about as if to convey alertness. Johnny Ray has long limbs. The black vestment he wears spreads behind him as he kneels, much like some dark train.

"The other ninety-seven hundred who went to the river drank this way."

Now he places both knees on the ground, bends low from the waist, and mimes scooping water with both hands, eyes clearly fixed on the ground. He rises.

"God tells Gideon to put those ninety-seven hundred to the other side. Then he says, 'Gideon, the first three hundred are all the men you need for the battle.' So why'd he pick those men?"

Dramatic pause. We inhale with expectation.

"'Cause you can't drink water down like this," he motions to both knees, "without taking your sword off. And in battle *you don't lay your weapon down!*"

He ends fiercely. We congregants exhale with appreciative revelation.

"Oh, teach it, doctor, teach it!" a fellow behind me chatters happily.

My preacher, Dr. Johnny Ray Youngblood, is a fierce man. A hard man. Hard on a world still stricken by racism. Hard on the vices that afflict too many inner-city communities: crime, drugs, alcohol. Hard on overly sanctimonious church folk who refuse to get off judgmental high horses and talk to real people with more than hell and eternal sin heating their words.

Johnny Ray is a passionate man, railing against the political establishment or black folk's stuck-in-the mud ways, cussing when the moment strikes, an occasional "shit" or "damn it" that never fails to crack within the walls of St. Paul's like some creaky bullwhip, aged yet biting.

Johnny Ray is a compassionate man. He lives to shepherd black men, not to the exclusion of sisters or other folk, mind you. But his ministry is for the brothers. Especially the down-trodden brother; the lurking brother on the street corner most fear; the brother with a jail record, now marked by society's modern scarlet letter; the brother fighting the demon twins drugs and alcohol. Johnny Ray arms them with God's word. Gives them strength, purpose, hope.

Johnny Ray is just a man. He wears his own flaws openly, honestly. Wounds can be clearly seen. Like when he makes an admonishing point to the sisters in the congregation, usually about how they treat their men, and stops midpoint to ruefully acknowledge what we all know, that he's "going through his own stuff" because of a divorce.

Johnny Ray is so hip-hop. Not because he cusses, welcomes brothers from the street with open arms, and wages his obvious battles with patriarchal attitudes. But because Johnny Ray plows forward. He works from within his own challenges, going on about his mission with a searing honesty. God lives in simple truths. Like those hip-hop once spoke. Like Johnny Ray utters on the Sunday mornings when I roll my catatonic self out of bed. And truth makes you believe.

It draws me closer to God to hear that my preacher, too, faces doubt and insecurity, that my preacher has his own fears to conquer, that my preacher, too, must turn eyes heavenward and wail out his confusion in a frank, questioning, *"Yo?!!"*

Answers do come. We plow on.

18

THE SWEETEST THING [RATIONALIZATION]

18 February 2001

Dear Lauryn,

You've been gone from us too long. I know that rings unfair, even presumptuous. Really, I do. After all, who are we to begrudge any artist retreating from our draining attention in order to spend time with self and family? And Lord knows we drained enough from you in the wake of 1998's *The Miseducation of Lauryn Hill.* But you can't blame us. Your impact, your influence on our collective music psyche, was such that your absence, for even a few short years, seems painful. With *Miseducation* you created an intimacy unlike any in short-term pop memory. You strode upon a public stage, letting your soul soar, cry, and shake with deeply personal emotion. And we shuddered along with you, not as spectators, but as participants in the cathartic dance you led. So when you left, Lauryn, when you retreated deep into your own space, when you pulled back from the media, when you disengaged from us, it did not feel like the typical down period between an artist's albums; it felt like abandonment.

In the meanwhile we get by with wispy fragments of you. Because that's all they are, even your albums, solo and group efforts, just fragments of your complex self. We all have our favorite wisps, the memories of you that have sustained us. Mine is not your music at all, but a moment. Do you remember spring of 1997? You, Wyclef, and Pras were in Haiti to put on a grand concert. That homecoming event was a key moment during the buildup to Clef's first solo effort, *Carnival,* as well as a pit stop on what would be the last stretch of the Fugee race.

You sat by the poolside of Le Ritz Hotel, a high-post establishment in the craggy hills outside of Port-au-Prince, the hotel where the Fugee crew was staying. You were pregnant with Zion at the time, and the bulge of your belly nudged the cotton shirt you wore. A hat shaded you from the afternoon rays of the Caribbean sun, and in your hands you gently cradled an acoustic guitar. I sat quiet nearby with reporter's tools in hand—pen, pad, tape recorder—listening to you strum the chords from "The Sweetest Thing," the Refugee Camp song, featuring your vocals, from the *Love Jones* sound track.

"Did Clef write that?" I asked.

You just looked at me. Not with anger, or even annoyance. Just a touch of wry, incredulous amusement.

"No."

Then you let me know how things worked. How you would come up with the underpinning of the idea and use more developed musicians to flesh it out. And how determined you were to learn and master an instrument yourself, so you could do your own damn fleshing out, thank you. Determined. And focused.

I glimpsed steel in you that afternoon. And a year later, as I listened to your solo debut and heard that steel echo throughout, no image burned clearer than that look in your eye on a hill in Haiti.

At first you had us fooled, Lauryn. 'Cause in the beginning things seemed more silk than steel. I well recall that '93 video for "Boof Baf," lead single from the Fugee debut *Blunted On Reality*. I remember the confusion that nettled my brow on observing the high-octane antics of the then-bald Wyclef and the heavily bearded Pras, and you, of course, with the close-knit cap, braided tresses, powerful vocal presence, and beatific features. Some knew that face from your adventures in acting—*General Hospital*, *Sister Act II*, etc.—but it was new to me, though I did remember catching sight of that smile dancing around MC Lyte in her 1990 video for "Poor Georgie."

Neither my confusion, nor the almost otherworldly quality of the aggressive, ragga-driven "Boof Baf," could mask the fact that the three of you made sense. Some hip-hop groups seem so poorly patched together they resemble nothing so much as the bastard children of some urban Dr. Frankenstein. But you three were organic, integrated, despite surface differences. You, a smart-as-nails Jersey girl from South Orange, Valerie Hill's Columbia-educated daughter; Wyclef and Pras, Haitian boys by way of Brooklyn. But the mix worked. In later years Clef would fondly tell me the story of how you three got signed, the story of your office performance for Chris Schwartz of RuffHouse Records. He painted quite the picture: him atop Chris's desk, doing his best Sly Stone act; Pras grooving with his usual effervescent cool; and you, singing, rhyming, performing with the assurance of a star born.

When I saw that "Boof Baf" video I marveled at the sight of a female MC holding equal opportunity mic status within a group. There'd been male hip-hop groups and female hip-hop groups, male soloists and female. But the integrated archetype had hardly been seen, nevermind well executed, since the days of Sha Rock in the Funky Four Plus One—except for Digable Planets, maybe—and even Sha required a special setting aside. No such mandate for you. It was the silken quality of your voice and presence that helped pull together the eclectic, disparate thoughts that ran wild on *Blunted On Reality.* You were the middling anchor between Wyclef's frenzy and Pras's slow burn. Perhaps it was a foregone conclusion, albeit an unfair and premature one, that the critical public would laud you as the group's saving grace. Thus, we shut the book on the Fugees' first album, pausing momentarily as we heard the 1994 remix for "Nappy Heads." The melodic sounds and straight-ahead drum programming of producer Salaam Remi was a harbinger of better things to come for the Fugees, and your strong vocal performance on the song portended the same for you as an individual.

Even so, I didn't expect the album that landed on my desk late in 1995. It was a simple TDK cassette, ninety minutes long. Someone at Columbia Records, your parent label, had scribbled the name of the album along the spine of the cassette's paper insert: *The Score.* Curious, I slipped the tape out of its case and placed it in the stereo system that serves as the heart of any music editor's office. The music glided out of the system, almost shocking in its near perfection. The record had personality, broad narratives, and poignant musicality. And each of you sounded significantly better, although you,

Lauryn, always had less of a hill to climb in most ears.

Still, the range and technique you exhibited on *The Score* were evidence of striking growth. On the one hand you could appropriate a vocal performance by a singing legend and make it your own—Roberta Flack's "Killing Me Softly"—on the other you hit the three zones of MC ability—tone, delivery, lyrical content—with a consistency that few could approach, male or female. When the folk at *The Source* magazine, my old professional home, heard your vicious battle lines from "How Many Mics" they were fit to be tied. Our favorite part was the section that included the lines:

> *Sold your soul to some secular*
> *Muzak that's wack*
> *Plus you use that*
> *Loop over and over*
> *Claiming that you got a new style*
> *Your attempts are futile*
> *Ooh chile you're puerile.*

As music editor it was my responsibility to choose the best verse of the moment for the magazine's rhyme of the month column. There was no question whose verse would be featured in the February '96 issue. But you came damn close to missing it, Lauryn. All because I couldn't decipher three words in your rhyme. And I'm pretty sure *puerile* was one of them. So I called your crib, left a message explaining the honor involved in being awarded rhyme of the month. Waited patiently for you to call back. You didn't. I called again, left a similar message accompanied by a bit more pleading. Waited for your call. No dice. By now grumbles sounded back at the ranch. The magazine had to go to press soon; time was precious. And we couldn't go with lyrics that weren't accurate. Maybe we'd have to pick another verse; though that was the last thing anyone wanted to do. So I called yet again, and got you this time.

"Hey, Lauryn?"

"Yes?"

Went on to explain what the magazine needed, and you gave it to me. No fuss. And you know what struck me, Lauryn? How much more impressed I was than you with the whole situation. Not that you weren't grateful and genuinely pleased. But here I was thinking that I'd made some giant step for womankind in hip-hop, while you acknowledged it as the matter of course that it was: You had the hottest verse at the time and you deserved the recognition.

The Score would go on to capture the music stage, to the tune of seventeen million records sold worldwide, an achievement largely driven by your hip-hop flip of "Killing Me Softly." Between the months spanning the moment I got that tape and the album's release, *The Score* became both a personal and staff favorite. In the March '96 issue *The Source* gave the album a rating of 4, an excellent mark just two rungs below the highest possible 5, a great mark by any standard. But oh, you guys didn't let me off that simply.

The publicist from Columbia was soon on the phone.

"Listen, I've got the Fugees on the line. They just want to talk to you about the rating, okay?"

"Well, um, sure," I replied curiously.

"Lauryn, Pras? Are you on? Okay, go ahead."

I admit it; y'all had me a touch anxious. Were you calling to thank the magazine for its support? Or to flip about the rating? Talking to an artist about a review they've received is always a nervy game. Usually I didn't bother. But you are near impossible to refuse.

"Um, hey, this is Sel."

Then y'all let me have it. Well, Pras mostly chimed in with affirmative grunts. As for you, Lauryn, you skewered me with your arguments: Yes, you were pleased *The Score* got a 4, but it really should have gotten a 4.5. Why? Leaving aside the merits of the record, a year ago, summer of '95, the magazine gave Raekwon's *Built for Cuban Linx* a 4.5 rating, in your eyes validating the entire street/criminology narrative with the hip-hop faithful. And if the Fugees album was to provide a more nuanced, more intelligent alternative, it should have been placed on equal footing.

I tried to disagree and make the point of judging records separately on their own merits, but that wasn't an argument I was gonna win with you. Didn't know it then. I'm too wise to try that again.

You remember 1985, Lauryn? Damn, I sure do. Especially summertime. The crawling heat that snaked through New York's still graf-covered subways. Nighttime, weekend radio battles between Mr. Magic and DJ Red Alert, fervently witnessed by teens sitting on stoops, clustered around radios. And the urgent music thumping from passing cars or boom boxes resting upon shoulders of sidewalk-strolling kids: Run-DMC, Doug E. Fresh, and Slick Rick.

Honestly, at that juncture I wasn't into female MCs; I did enjoy Roxanne Shanté's back-and-forth with U.T.F.O., but that seemed a novelty. Hip-hop in 1985 was still thoroughly male-dominated, and we reveled in it.

Then emerged these girls from Queens doing a take-off on "The Show" by Doug E. Fresh and Slick Rick. They were engaging, personable, and just sheer fun to listen to. They came to be known as Salt-N-Pepa. That was the moment when many of hip-hop's testosterone crowd etched out genuine room for women on the mic. The late eighties and early nineties would flesh out that moment with a steady stream of talented women laying their own claims—Queen Latifah, MC Lyte, Yo Yo, and my personal, one-song-having favorite, Antoinette, despite her evisceration by MC Lyte on the scalding "10 Percent Dis."

I thought about Antoinette the first time I heard "Lost Ones," the initial underground salvo from *Miseducation.* Not because I imagined there'd be some modern-day MC Lyte waiting to take you out. Heaven forbid. But because, in the words of contemporary hip-hop parlance, Antoinette was *spitting* on "I Got an Attitude." She sounded tough, capable, steely even. And that's exactly what came to mind the first time the chest-knocking strains of "Lost Ones" exploded around me. You'd always done a marvelous job of creating an identity outside the two-poled paradigm that this increasingly commercial and sexualized hip-hop industry has forced upon women MCs since those late eighties, early nineties days—hyper sex kitten or gangsta bitch, sometimes both. "Lost Ones" showed that you could still spit and be authentic and credible without falling into the clutches of either stereotype. And the underlying narrative of betrayal gave us a not-too-subtle indication of what would be in play on *Miseducation.*

Columbia sent me another tape in the spring of '98. Actually, they snuck it to me on the low. The tape had just four songs—"X-Factor," "To Zion," "Lost Ones," and "Doo Wop (That Thing)." I was struck by several points:

Your maturation as a singer and songwriter, your development as a producer, and the fact that your complex relationship with Wyclef might just have provided much of the emotional and narrative thrust of the album. I knew from whence "Ex-Factor" stemmed, and the stark honesty of the song made me squirm at its emotional nakedness (*"No one's hurt me more than you/And no one ever will"*), while marveling at the strength and steel it took to compose, never mind its technical perfection.

You know, Lauryn, before Wyclef talked about your one-time relationship in 1999 prior to releasing his *Ecleftic* album, before you sent speculation rampant with *Miseducation,* and even before Wyclef dropped hints of a sort on "To All the Girls I've Cheated On" from *Carnival,* some of us in the hip-hop press knew of the relationship between you two. But we never put it out there. Maybe we had too much hope for what the Fugees represented. Maybe we loved you too much. Maybe we fancied ourselves a hip-hop Washington press corps, covering up the peccadilloes of our own JFK. Maybe we were bad journalists who crossed the line between subject and friendship. Know this, though: I, for one, have no regrets.

It was no surprise that *Miseducation* launched you to the top of pop music, though the heights of that success—six million albums, five Grammys and sundry other awards—surpassed even the rosiest expectations. Not only did you make the most incredible record of the year, you redefined the core notion of what constitutes hip-hop performance. You rhymed and sang with such facility, such equal dexterity, that labels—"Is she an MC who sings? A singer who rhymes?"—were rendered useless. Your musical breadth may have surprised some, but you always knew the potential of the hip-hop form.

But the real surprise came with *Miseducation*'s after-math. I was dismayed by your separation from us, the demanding public that had learned to adore you. Dismayed by the moralists who tried to lambaste you as a hypocrite for touting God and morality in every breath while making no apologies for having two children prior to marriage. Dismayed by scattered reports in the press about discord and rupture between you and Rohan Marley. We all had been so tickled at the idea of you becoming a part of the legendary Marley clan, of you bearing Bob's grandchildren. And your joy was always so evident. I remember a rainy December night in Jamaica, a tribute concert for Bob in 1999. Backstage a reporter asked you about being part of the Marley legacy and your emotion flowed.

"Well, you know, since meeting Rohan and having our children, my love, admiration, and respect has just intensified and grown," you said. "The more I get to know about the man, the more I just love and the more I respect. And the more it teaches me about my craft and my career, and things to do and not to do."

I prayed that the rumblings of you and Rohan splitting up were not true. You don't deserve to have your heart shredded again, even if beautiful music flowers from such pain.

And I was especially dismayed by the lawsuit leveled against you in November of 1998 by Vada Nobles, Rasheem Pugh, and twin brothers Tejumold and Johari Newton of New-Ark Entertainment, the young producers who worked on your album, charging that they were cheated out of production and songwriting credit. Lord, I know that must have punctured your very spirit. The focused woman I remember strumming guitar strings in

Haiti had to have been stunned. The producer who did sterling work for Aretha Franklin and Mary J. Blige would have been dumbfounded. The artist who walked up to me at her birthday barbecue in a New Jersey park to say, "I'm looking for some young producers to do session work for my album" must have been floored by this turn of events.

So I was cheered to hear that the suit was settled in early February, though the lack of details in out-of-court settlements is always vexing to a journalist, and this one proved no different. But I was more cheered by finally talking to you two days past, after more than a year, to tell you about this piece. And to solicit your participation, even though I knew you were still in a quiet, contemplative mood.

"Hey, Selwyn," you said. Your voice sounded full, strong, unbent by the drama between *Miseducation* and the now. Then you listened. And gently told me that you were not ready to talk. I appreciated your honesty, Lauryn, your frankness. Even more, I appreciated the sounds of music filtering through the phone when I called that studio, the sound of your voice atop music once again, the sound of one of our greatest talents working her magic.

I know now that you will come back to us.

Yours,
Selwyn

19

RUSH HOUR

She just called me one day. Out of the blue. Suppose
that's how most things of consequence begin—simply. It
was late in August of 1999. The woman on the phone
was Leyla Turkkan, a close friend and associate of
Russell Simmons. Our conversation was quick, and cryp-
tic. Leyla speaks in crisp, hurried tones and she gave me
two points of information: Russell was doing something
on the Internet; he wanted to talk to me. I said little more
than "okay." Then hung the phone up, mystified, yet
intrigued.

Russell conducts much of his business from the head-
quarters of Phat Farm, the successful urban fashion
brand he launched in 1992. A building in Manhattan's
fashion district housed the fourteenth-floor offices.
Though I'd known Russell in passing for a few years,
I'd never had occasion to visit these offices. Upon entering, I looked around the stylishly laid-out loft with
curiosity. Designs for pending seasons adorned man-
nequin bodies scattered throughout the main space.
Phat Farm was just getting into the footwear end of the
business and several samples lay on tables, chairs, and
shelves jutting out from walls. Young staffers, distinctly

multicultural in their composition, scurried to and fro.

Russell's office sat on the far side. The main conference room lay just opposite. We went in this latter space. Me, Leyla, and Russell.

Just listening to Russell talk is an art in and of itself. If most people's conversation style is akin to a rolling stream, then Russell's is a white water river. His thoughts pour out in a rush. Often he'll skip two, even three subjects ahead, embarking on tributaries whenever the urge pushes him, before winding back to the river.

He looked at me. Eyes bright and energetic beneath the bill of the jauntily placed Phat Farm cap on his head, the topper of his all-Phat Farm outfit. Then he began to speak.

I don't remember specific dialog. Until you get used to Russell you can only recall his conversations in chunks. Huge topical swaths dominate my memory: the Internet; Russell's magazine, *One World*; his television show of the same name; RS1W.com; hip-hop branding and lifestyle; access and opportunity; synergy; advertising; Coca-Cola; fashion; and on and on.

"Okay, great, we'll talk." With that he bustled out to another meeting.

I looked at Leyla.

"So what exactly does he want me to do?"

She grinned knowingly.

"Well, we're starting this hip-hop site, RS1W, and Russell wants you to be the creative head."

"RS1W . . . that stand for Russell Simmons One World?"

She nodded.

"Is it an extension of the magazine and TV show?"

"Not exactly, but whatever you do with the site could reshape those things."

Leyla and I rapped some more. Then I thanked her and took my leave.

I sat quiet and contemplative in the taxi back to the *Source* offices on Park Avenue. It had been two weeks since the Source Awards. Four weeks since the confrontation over the Made Men and Raymond Scott. I'd already made my decision to leave. Already composed the resignation letter. Just hadn't figured out when to squeeze the trigger. Now I might have the ammunition. I pulled out my cell phone to call my best friend since college, Mark Hines, the person I knew with the firmest grasp on hip-hop and technology. Mark was both a music producer with a gold record to his credit—for Def Jam's sound track to the movie *Belly*—as well as a former technology officer with JP Morgan. If anyone could advise me on venturing into the terrain of new media via hip-hop, it would be him.

"So Russell just laid this shit on me," I explained further.

"Yo, Sel, this is exactly it, this is exactly that shit!" he exclaimed.

"You sure?" I said doubtfully, though the doubt stemmed less from any uncertainty about Russell's idea than a need to hear the notion approved from someone I trusted.

"Are you kidding?" Mark replied. "This is what you need to do right now."

With those three conversations I drifted into orbit around Planet Simmons.

Secret Service dudes stood thick outside Russell's apartment building. Dark suited, fit looking. They eyed me quickly and carefully as I leaned against the wall by the entrance. Waiting. After a few minutes Reverend Run walked out of the building. Heavier in limb and jowl since Run-DMC's glory days, but still a presence to be marked. Our eyes met.

"Hey, Run," I said.

"Selwyn," he acknowledged. "I hear you're going to be working with my brother."

"Yup."

"Good," he chuckled approvingly, easing his dark-clad frame into a waiting Bentley, "that's real good." The Bentley ghosted off into the night.

I waited a few more minutes then retraced Run's steps, entering the building lobby beneath the watchful eye of the Secret Service. The list guardians checked my name, then, with broad smiles, ushered me to the elevator. I pressed the button for Russell and his wife Kimora's penthouse apartment. Shortly thereafter, the doors hummed open. I stepped out, buzz of laughter and conversation instantly snatching at my ears. The scene before me displayed Russell at his best: a blend of power broker and ambassador, steadfastly pairing hip-hop with some new entity, guiding it down some new path.

On that night the path led to Hillary Clinton. She moved by Russell's side through the crowded apartment. Here hung the very picture of Russell's America: rappers, business executives, fashion mavens, politicians, white folk, black folk, the fabulous, the relatively ordinary, all here by Russell's invitation to meet this woman who might be senator. They made an odd couple. He, clad as usual in casual Phat Farm gear, buzzed about like a ball of energy as he made swift introductions. She, more conservative in dark-colored pantsuit, seemed glued to his shoulder, listening with silent, smiling eyes until he completed his preamble, then she would grip the hand of the introduced, level a measuring gaze, and utter a few sincere words before moving off again in Russell's wake.

He noticed me across the room. I drifted into their path. Russell motioned at me. Mrs. Clinton turned her eyes accordingly.

"And this is Selwyn Hinds," he said as they drew near. "He edits *The Source*, the most powerful magazine in hip-hop."

Mrs. Clinton nodded appreciatively, smiling. I extended my hand.

"It's a pleasure to meet you. I do hope you will be our next senator."

"Thank you," she replied, looking directly at me while grasping my hand. She possessed a firm handshake and an unflinching gaze. "I hope so, as well."

Hillary Clinton and Russell moved on.

I circulated through the room, murmuring greetings to friends and associates. Then I saw him, the person I'd been waiting on downstairs. Sean "Puff Daddy" Combs waved a hand in my direction. I walked over.

"I'm gonna leave in a few, you wanna talk in my car?"

"Cool," I said. Well, this should be interesting.

He'd called me a few days before at the *Source* offices. The news that I'd resigned had just broken.

"Hello?"

"Yo." People like Puff don't need to say who they are. "You know a fly cat like you needs a fly crib. You live in Brooklyn, right? I hear that penthouse in the Clock Tower is still available. You could fuck with some shit like that, right?"

"Uhhh . . ." Did Puff just imply he'd buy me an apartment? "Shit, no doubt."

We both laughed. He went on.

"For real, though, you know I got this magazine *Notorious,* plus I'm gonna do the Internet thing. I know you talking to people now, but just don't make no moves till you talk to me."

"Okay."

Puff and I clambered in the back of a silver Lincoln Navigator parked just outside of Russell's building, driver and security sat up front. Small talk flowed for a few minutes as the lights on the West Side Highway winked by. Then he gave brief detail on his still-emerging ideas for an online business under the auspices of the *Notorious* brand. I asked a few questions, but listened mostly. He peered at me from behind dark glasses.

"So you gonna work with Russell?"

"Most likely."

Puff considered that answer.

"Well, even if you do, maybe I can make your situation better, make you more expensive just by us talking. I don't mind doing that. Then, you know, one day maybe you can do something to help me out."

I nodded.

"Like I said, I haven't made a final decision. But I'll probably be doing something with Russell."

The Navigator pulled up before Puff's midtown studio, Daddy's House. He grasped my hand in parting then hopped out.

"Take him where he gotta go," Puff directed the driver before exiting the vehicle, a gliding figure in Sean John denim, already holding another conversation with attached cell phone earpiece.

• • •

I couldn't get going with Russell until the beginning of the new year. In mid-September I'd handed *Source* magazine owner Dave Mays my resignation and asked to be released from my contract. That agreement would expire in December. At first Mays seemed inclined to negotiate. Ed Young, erstwhile associate publisher, even flew in from semiretirement so the two of them could sit me down at breakfast to ask that I stay another six months.

"Listen," Young would assure me in private the day before the breakfast, "things will be different when I come back. See, without me Dave just has no ability to say no to Ray. Before I left he could always say, 'Well, Ed won't let me do that.' Now he can't."

I nodded carefully to Young's words. But they served little. I'd already decided upon my course of action.

Then, on October 6, Keith J. Kelly broke the news of my pending hookup with Russell Simmons in his *New York Post* media business column. Immediately, all bets fell off. *The Source* dug in its heels. No way I was getting out of the contract early. And once the agreement expired they intended to hold me to its noncompete clause, which essentially forbade anything to do with hip-hop media for one year. It was a broad, all-encompassing statute, so much so I was willing to take the chance that a New York court wouldn't enforce it if *The Source* pursued legal action. In the meantime I'd simply cool my heels and let them pay me through the end of the year.

Those months were well spent. I used the time to develop ideas for the site and to recruit a team. That had to be done quietly, since I was still under contract with *The Source* and all my actions had to take an inevitable lawsuit into consideration. Mark—whose inclusion I'd insisted on—and I spent many an evening huddled atop napkins, sheets of papers, laptop screens, any medium upon which we could jot our musings. Russell had laid on a big task: create the ultimate hip-hop destination. We needed a succinct way to meet that goal, and a team to bring it to life. The Castling Group, the consulting company brought on early in the process by Russell, largely handled the face-to-face recruitment. I'd hand them a name and phone number and they'd make the call. Executive Editor Sheena Lester, former editor of *Rap Pages* and *XXL,* managing editor Chris Kaye, who'd been doing content development of AOL, along with senior editors Kris Ex, articles editor at *The Source,* Yvette Russell, entertainment at *Essence,* music scribe Joseph Patel, and Jeff Chang, longtime political activist and managing editor of the Bay Area publication *Color Lines*—all departed their respective perches to form the core of the content team. Ola Kudu, a Web head since our early *Source* days, left his art director gig at Tommy Boy Records to head up the design component. They responded enthusiastically to the opportunity to work together, and to be part of something novel headed by Russell Simmons. By January 2000 we were ready.

A rugged, open loft in New York's west Chelsea neighborhood—favorite locale of dot.coms in those days—served as home. It seemed dauntingly grim at first sight. Entry to our abode could only be gained through a simple black door with the letters *RS1W* in bright red pasted upon it. The entryway stood on the left side of a three-story Portico furnishing outlet on Tenth Avenue. Our space sat one flight up, sandwiched between the bustle of the Portico store on the ground floor and their corporate office above. On entering the loft itself three large wooden panels on the rear wall, set in place of windows, leapt out at the eye. Plastic grew around the edges of these Frankenstein shutters, waging a vain fight to keep out the brisk winter air. There were no dot.com toys in our loft, no funky chairs, weird colors on the wall, or angular furniture. We made do with ordinary, utilitarian desks, stark white walls, and plain chairs.

But we possessed energy in abundance. Energy from the incessant hum of computers stacked upon those desks, row after row, filling the wooden floor. Energy from the sixty-odd souls gathered around those computers and desks, constantly hurling ideas, invective, and invigoration at each other. It was all wonderfully chaotic. The scene took some getting used to for those accustomed to more traditional office geometry. The consistent blast of music from the creative and marketing types practically drove the business folk to insanity's edge. Our poor CFO, Jeff Khur, would often throw harried, pleading glances from his station across the way. I'd shrug sympathetically, for even with my whispered word to the worst sonic offenders, forty stereos on low volume proved no less intrusive than one jammed up to level ten. Fortunately, Portico would later lease us an additional office upstairs where numbers could be examined without the pernicious thump of a DMX rhythm.

Those first few months were heady times. For most of my team it was creative utopia, a chance to paint dreams on broad, open canvases. Few of us had done anything like this before. Although there were a decent number of Internet vets among us, most of the content producers at RS1W hailed from the print world. Much like our counterparts in the general media, urban and hip-hop magazine folk had migrated to the beckoning dot.com world in droves, lured by a combination of economic opportunity and the chance to do something new and special. Building a website of the magnitude suggested by Russell's vision meant wildly creative days in front of white boards pondering the question, "So what shall we invent today?" My entire staff would crowd into our lone conference room, batting ideas back and forth for hours. It was an exhausting, exhilarating process. Then we'd run those embryonic visions through the gauntlet of the technical staff, the folk who'd be doing the building and maintenance of our oft-fanciful requests, to determine what could actually be implemented. After two months we gathered the slimmed-down results under a pithy banner—the 4/3 Theory.

The 4/3 Theory was our articulation of RS1W's content architecture, as well as its philosophical worldview, which positioned hip-hop as the lens through which we viewed the world. In truth, it was simply an evolution of my editorial mind-set at *The Source*. The 4 came from the main content pillars, or silos: *music:* reviews, features, exclusive downloads, and the like; *politics:* international and domestic affairs; *Lifestyle,* including fashion, film, TV, and other societal aspects permeated by hip-hop; and *culture,* the resting place for musings in and around hip-hop's artistic building blocks—MCing, DJing, graffiti art, and B-boying. The 3 derived from *commerce, community,* and broadband anticipants that we were, a sector we termed *broadcast.* In our architecture, those three elements cut horizontally through the four silos, meaning they'd be integrated and present in each distinct content realm. The entire structure suggested a broad, spherical, interactive world. From that conception came the new identity of the company—360hiphop.com. Russell had been looking for a new name and just had this loose notion that it had to contain a number along with the word *hip-hop.*

"A number and the word *hip-hop?"* I asked him incredulously.

"Yes, yes. Trust me, it'll work." He replied in enthusiastic, rapid-fire fashion. "I don't know, Hip Hop 100, Hip Hop 24/7. You guys think of something."

On the last day we had to come up with the new name, Kris Ex and I sat down, tossing about ideas. Soon, he threw his hands up in disgust.

"Maybe Hip-Hop 24 is the best option," he muttered, only half in jest. "Or Hip-Hop 365."

That sparked something.

"That's it," I said slowly.

"Hip-Hop 365?" he asked disbelievingly.

"No, 360hiphop! Instead of thinking in terms of time, think degrees. You know, full circle!"

Kris, never the most voluble of cats, just shrugged.

"Cool with me."

Folks loved to hear Mark and I kick the 360 4/3. We did it throughout that spring for a variety of people: reporters, investors, potential employees, and potential deal partners. We did it separately and as a tag team. We were both probably doing it in our sleep. Invariably, it would be a hit. Once, Edgar Bronfman Jr., honcho of Universal's corporate parent Seagram before selling to Vivendi, came to hear the story. Bronfman strode into the loft bright and early. From the impeccable tailoring stretched out over a tall frame, sharp grooming, and tanned glow, the man practically reeked of money. He stood quietly by the entrance, just on the periphery of our usual energetic hubbub. The CFO anxiously escorted him to the conference room, a few heads nervously tracking his passage. Inside the conference room, I stood in front of a large white board, marker in hand. Bronfman took a seat before me. I felt the slightest twinge of performance anxiety before shoving it away after a simple realization: Russell had had me bumping into rich and powerful people for months. By that reckoning, even Edgar Bronfman Jr. was just another statistic. I grinned at him and hopped right into it. Ten minutes later he grinned back.

"That was very cool."

But no one beat Russell Simmons and Andre Harrell—former president of Uptown Records, Motown Records, and longtime friend and confidant of Russell's—for first-time reaction, or enthusiasm. I'm not sure which one of them coined the term, but inevitably after they'd heard some creative idea from us, one or the other would break into a wide grin and exclaim, "Damn, these Princeton niggas!" It was a term laced with incredulity and pride. I think Russell and Andre viewed us as some new species, some combination of cultural and institutional attributes that they'd seldom, if ever, encountered. I never took it as some kind of black-bourgeois critique. We were new faces in the sweeping, expanding hip-hop generation for whom they'd long been ambassadors. Of course, when Russell was irritated with us, his "smart-ass Princeton niggas" would become "that damn Princeton Mafia," meaning we were sprinting down our own path with the creative team, wrapped in coded plans with little time devoted to folk outside the department, a mode totally contrary to the kind of inclusiveness Russell preached. When the "damn Princeton

Mafia" came floating through the atmosphere, it was a clear command to slow the fuck down and reach back out to people.

Andre Harrell had more than a small hand in both Mark and me coming to work for Russell. In late fall 1999, not long after that first meeting with Russell and Leyla Turkkan, I had lunch with him at 44, the restaurant off the lobby at the midtown Royalton Hotel. When I walked in Andre was already seated, perusing the menu. He sat with tailored designer suit and open-collar shirt, as was the wont. Spectacled glance lifted and he eyed my own getup.

"Any nigga that can pull off a pink shirt with a black suit is a cool mufucka," he announced by way of greeting. Andre speaks in colorful tones.

We shook hands. I sat. Briefly chatted. Then . . .

"You told Russell and them any ideas for what you wanna do with the site yet?" he asked pleasantly.

"Not really. You know we're still discussing contract details and stuff."

"Well," he took a sip from his glass as he continued, tone still pleasant, "if you want this job you're gonna have to tell me something."

I'd only barely begun the process with Mark that the entire content team would go through months later—translating sweeping ideas into realistic concepts for the Web. Fortunately, I had enough to hit Andre with some verbiage and leave him satisfied. I had another lunch with Andre a few weeks later, this time with Mark and another schoolmate Chris Young, who had just sold a Web venture he'd set up eighteen months prior. Mark and I wanted Chris to serve as RS1W's COO. Chris would assist for the first couple of months, but declined to come on full-time. The four of us sat around an open-

air table at Barolo restaurant in Soho, bathed by fall sunshine and crisp air. We regaled Andre with a sequence of
ideas before pausing for a breath. But Andre was still
puzzling his way through fact one.

"Hold up," he said, half-bemused, half-perplexed.
"All three of y'all niggas went to Princeton?"

Both men possessed a frank, enthusiastic air. They said
what came to mind and you knew where you stood with
them, particularly Russell. He was capable of deep loy-
alty and affection, and was self-deprecating to a fault.
Unlike most, Russell had no problem owning up to what
he knew and what he didn't, what he could do and what
he could not. There existed little trace of the outsize ego
common to someone of his accomplishments. Russell's
ego and pride was much more invested in the people he
found to fill those vacuums of knowledge about him,
people whose particular talents he could then wrap into
the marketing and salesmanship cyclone that, perhaps,
remains his true genius.

"Let me tell you something," he remarked to me on a late
January night at Moomba, the onetime New York City celeb
watering hole. We sat upstairs, in the crowded second-floor
lounge above the restaurant below. Swaying limbs wove to
and fro like emaciated palms caught in a Caribbean gale.
Bodies mashed up beside each other, wiggling for hip space
on leather sofas and stools. Music moaned low and insistent. Russell sat on my left, leaned in close.

"This is something David Geffen told me. He said,
'You've got to walk along and keep your eyes very close
to the ground. Always looking. Then you'll stumble
across someone who can take you and the success you
think you have to a completely different level.' That's all
I do, Selwyn, I look for those people."

• • •

The inevitable *Source* response eventually arrived on my desk in February, cloaked in the form of a brown manila envelope. Inside was a cease and desist order, demanding that I immediately stop working for RS1W.com. Do not pass Go. Do not collect two hundred dollars. Although I'd been expecting it, the lawsuit still came as a shock. I was furious that after all that had transpired with the Made Men crew, after the years I'd invested in building his pocket, Dave Mays and company expected me to, essentially, go unemployed for a year while *The Source* went along its merry way.

The lawsuit itself was largely anticlimactic, however. The most dramatic moment for me was the one and only time I saw the inside of a courtroom. A gray, windy morning found me trudging up the enormous, white marble steps of the New York Supreme Court. Felt like I'd dropped into an episode of *The Practice.* Inside, I met three lawyers: Susan Povich, head of legal at RS1W, Hillary Richard, who'd been retained for this case; and my lawyer, Marco Matterassi, who'd negotiated my employment agreement with RS1W. Opposing us were Neil Goldstein, *The Source*'s lawyer and a man I'd worked with for years, and one of his associates. Goldstein approached to deliver pleasantries. I gritted my teeth and returned them. He and Povich moved off for a light-hearted discussion, smiles and laughter punctuating. The lawyerly banter amazed me. I was too pissed, and anxious, to be social.

The courtroom looked, well, just like they do on television. The judge was a dour fellow. He sat up ahead. No jury. Lawyers arguing another case clustered about him as he issued occasional muttered pronouncements. We sat on the pews and waited for our case to come up. Just a short distance away huddled a group of perfectly blonde, perfectly fashionable Upper East Side girls, with Diane von Furstenberg in their midst. Apparently, she had a case of her own to deal with. One never knows what strange bedfellows one may stumble upon in a courtroom.

When our turn arose Goldstein and Richard approached the bench. Goldstein described the emergency action *The Source* was seeking, i.e., me immediately ceasing all work for RS1W. Judge asked why. Goldstein uttered something about trade secrets and secret ingredients. Richard said something dismissive. Judge agreed with Richard. Pulled out his datebook to set a date for the next stage. We exited the courtroom. Goldstein bid me a cordial farewell.

"So what happened?" I asked.

"We won the first round," Richard said cheerfully.

"So what now?"

"The fun stuff, we'll depose Mr. Mays and everyone else up there."

But things never got that far. *The Source* and RS1W settled the case, a side effect of a proposed merger that temporarily threatened to shake up the hip-hop media landscape—the union of Lyor Cohen, Russell Simmons, and Dave Mays. Lyor had long desired a merging of the company with a hard media asset; he was a huge fan of Dave Mays and *The Source*'s powerful branding. Russell, too, was a great fan of powerful brands and loved the idea of building a hip-hop analog to Martha Stewart's Omnimedia, which had a spectacular market value. The opportunity to merge all those assets and cultural capital into a giant Hip-Hop, Inc. covering the Web, print, television, fashion, and advertising/marketing was exciting to all involved. Osman Eralp, a brilliant, European-based rainmaker and longtime friend of Lyor and Russell, as well as a significant investor in RS1W, had agreed to serve as our interim CEO, specifically to shepherd RS1W through the minefield of capital raising and merger opportunities that littered the landscape. Eralp had been a successful investment banker before becoming a music executive, cutting his teeth under the legendary Ahmet Ertegun. He had a unique grasp of both the corporate and creative flows of a company. Eralp pulled me aside.

"If this happens I need to know if you could work for Dave Mays again," he asked me.

"Would I be working directly for him?"

"Well, you'll probably always report to Russell but Mays will certainly hold some significant authority. Can you deal with that?"

I lied through my teeth.

"Sure, Osman. Look, I'm down for whatever works best for the company."

So I swallowed my pride and went over to Dave Mays's Union Square loft to show him the 4/3. We shook hands carefully and sat over a table to look at my sketches. Later, Dave and one of his executives, Jeff Jones, who was in charge of *The Sources*'s new media efforts, came by the office to see some of the demos we'd built. Sufficiently intrigued, the deal went into the due diligence, "let's look at the books" stage. Settling my lawsuit was one condition.

Hip-Hop, Inc. never happened. Chalk it up to the usual failure to agree over money and control. Can't say that I was disappointed. But it was a fascinating notion while it lasted.

• • •

We planned to launch 360hiphop.com on June 20, right in the heat of summer. The weeks leading up to that date were marked by the mundane, the fabulous, and the inexplicable, like the short-lived crime spree that visited us. With the onset of warmer weather, we'd finally done away with the Frankenstein wood panels and replaced them with large glass windows. Imagine our consternation one morning in discovering that some intrepid soul had smashed one of those windows, entered the loft, and made off with sundry laptops and other computer supplies. Cursing fickle fate, we replaced the stolen material and kept it moving, until 4:00 A.M. a few weeks later, when Mark's call jerked me out of heavy sleep.

"Yo, the alarm company just called; the alarm at the office just went off. I'm heading down there."

"All right, give me a few minutes to wake up."

I struggled into the city from Brooklyn and met him at the office. We stood on the sidewalk, figuring we'd rather the responding police discover us out front instead of upstairs where two young black men might be mistaken for the perpetrators. Once the cops came, we moved upstairs and, lo and behold, more computers had trotted out the door. Next morning we ordered bars for the windows.

Fortunately, the runup to launch also occasioned visits by rather more pleasant circumstances. Like Halle Berry, who turned up one morning to give an interview to Yvette Russell and the lifestyle silo crew as part of the press campaign for the movie *X-Men.* Remarkably, on the day Berry was scheduled to arrive, the office was packed at an ungodly hour. Folk who'd never run into 9:00 A.M. outside of a warm bed were cheerily perched in front of computers, innocently pecking away at keyboards.

"She's here, she's here," a rapid whisper shot around the room as Russell's distinctive verbal patter could be heard easing up the stairs. He entered the office; immediately behind him came Halle Berry and a small entourage. Heads swiveled, and conversation ceased for several seconds. Russell led Berry over to where Ola Kudu and I were standing, by one of our demo stations. We did our damnedest not to ogle as she glided over. Berry cut a stunning presence, clad simply in form-fitting, low-slung pants, cropped top, and dark glasses. Had the guys seated around us stared any harder at their computer screens, eyeballs would have been emblazoned by computer code.

"Hello," she said, once Russell introduced us.

Kudu took her through the site demo, fighting to keep the shit-eating grin on his face from breaking out. She smiled sweetly and exclaimed with astonishment several times. I cut my eyes over at Russell and he returned a brief, knowing smile. Later, long after Berry and company had departed, folk in the office, particularly the men, walked around with dazed, beatific expressions—like they'd been touched by an angel, however briefly.

At that moment, we welcomed inspiration in any guise. Not that we weren't motivated enough. Simply living up to standards expected of a Russell Simmons enterprise was sufficient pressure in and of itself. But the field was crowded with entrants all trying to capitalize on the seemingly natural pairing of two irresistible media- and youth-market forces: hip-hop culture and the Internet. Russell, perpetual marketing machine that he was, naturally attracted a ton of media attention, and made no bones of the fact that he intended to cream the competition. Common wisdom said that if anyone stood to make the merger of hip-hop and new media work in grand fashion, it would be Russell. For the last five months we'd been driven by the need to live up to our own billing. And in the final days that pressure was boiling over.

On the morning of June 20, site launch was still twenty-four hours away, at best. Russell was due to swing by the office that afternoon accompanied by an ABC crew from *Nightline* that had been tagging behind him for a special on hip-hop, along with other assorted media—all arriving to witness the launch. Russell did know that the deadline, 6:00 P.M. that evening, was a soft target. But he didn't know how soft. Truth be told, neither did we. I pulled the main staffers together in the conference room.

"Look, we'll take Russell aside and let him know what's going on. Let's just be cool with all the lights and cameras." Heads nodded. In short order the pack bowled into the office. Russell lead the way, the others sprawled beside and behind him. I shook hands with the producers from ABC and CNN. Eagerness pumped through them.

"Hey," the ABC guy chirped happily, "can you wear this?" He held up a small mic attached to a belt clip.

The lights and cameras followed Russell around the office, peering over the shoulders of staffers determinedly going about their duties, trying to ignore miniscule distractions. I bustled about like a nervous father-to-be, occasionally voicing important-sounding declarations and words of encouragement, switching off the microphone power pack on my belt when the mutters veered toward "shit, damn, what is the problem with this motherfucker?!" The ABC producer cast occasional suspicious glances my way, and eventually wandered over to inquire if everything was going as planned. I made soothing noises and shooed him off. Navarrow Wright, head of technology, walked up after the guy departed.

"You got to get these people out of the office or this damn site will never get up," he said bluntly.

"I know, I know," I replied in exasperation.

Finally, I managed to separate Russell from his trailers, who stood unhappily outside the conference room as I shut the door in their faces. He and Osman Eralp looked at me. I got right to the point.

"It's not going to go up tonight; tomorrow morning at the best. And we gotta get these TV people out of here so our people can focus."

Russell took it well. He almost always took bad news well. I don't know if he has always been that way, or if that resiliency came about from his devotion to yoga in recent years. But it had a contagious effect. I'd discovered that side of Russell on the occasion of my first true cluster-fuck in my new job. Early in the year I'd flown a bunch of staffers out to the Soul Train Awards in Los Angeles—too expensive—decided to have a "meet 360hiphop" event that was poorly planned, executed, and attended—bad imaging—and, for the guests, commissioned the creation of 360hiphop.com T-shits inscribed with a slogan so horrible it shudders in the nether reaches of my memory, never to be excavated. The day after, Russell summoned me to his hotel room at the Beverly Hills Hotel to discuss this road kill of a trip. I knocked on his door with gallows enthusiasm. But he just nodded after listening to my rueful admission and uttered his trademark refrains: "Well, it's your wack juice. You spilled it. You gotta learn from it. Gotta learn to use your resources." Nevertheless, as Russell, Eralp, and I left the conference room on that June afternoon, I realized that if I didn't get this site up soon, there'd be a lot more than wack juice spilled.

We would have done the CIA proud, or SAG at any rate. The play-acting commenced with me clapping my hands in the middle of the office to announce that we would now launch the site. Grins broke out and the staff gathered about the designated computer where Russell sat. "Speech," someone yelled out. Russell grinned sheepishly and said how proud he was of us all, what a moment this was for hip-hop. He turned to me.

"What do I do now?"

I pointed at the enter button on the keyboard.

"Just hit that."

He tapped the keyboard and the site, which had been living quite fine on our internal server for two days, sprang into colorful, vibrant life. Whoops and applause broke out. The camera crews crowded closer. We broke out champagne and made maudlin speeches. It was a moment of delirium. We'd been working twenty-four-hour shifts for a week, and the giddy celebration allowed a moment to taste, to imagine the success that still lay just over the horizon. If the site dancing on sixty computer screens wasn't enough to complete the illusion, the genuine emotions certainly were. ABC and CNN departed, satisfied. Russell left, too.

"Okay guys, tomorrow."

The entire office stood still for a moment, transfixed by the whooshing departure of celebration, lights, cameras, and extraneous bodies.

"All right people," I called out after a moment. "Let's get this thing launched."

By 6:00 A.M. the next morning, we still couldn't get the Vignette technology that drove the content engine to work properly. We were down to four by that moment: Melanie, the number two in the tech department; Matt, our Vignette consultant; Ryan, one of the tech interns; and a dazed, semicoherent me, staring at the fingers flying on keyboards and the arcane spools of code. Suddenly, Matt threw his hands up and walked out. I looked at his departing back stupidly.

"Where's he going?" I asked Melanie.

"Smoke, probably." She scowled at the computer with grim determination.

Seven in the morning. Matt never comes back. Muttering to myself in half delusion. Seminuts. Mark bustles in. Relieves me. I hang around still. Bleary-eyed. Osman Eralp arrives. He's ticked. Has investors waiting to see the site. Big dogs. Muckety-mucks at AOL and such. Snaps: This is not good, gentlemen, not good. Never seen him pissed. Russell comes in. He's cool. Takes one look at me. Take him home, Kenny, he says to his driver. I sleep for three hours and dart back to the office. Site's up. Performance varies on different browsers, but it's working. I stare at the large monitor on the conference room. Dazed amazement. It's alive. Don't get off that easy though. Phone rings. Ignore it. Check message in a few minutes. It's an employee who recently quit, then tried to change her mind. We scoffed. Now she's left some words. Calm tone despite the message: I know why you fired me. You're a faggot. An abomination. You've probably been fucking that white boy who was my supervisor. Race traitor. Not angry with you because God will take care of you. You will burn in hell. Most evil thing I've ever heard. So cold, so matter-of-fact. Punches the air right out of me. After all the pressure and tension. Finally felled by simple words. Have to sit to steady myself. Mark and coworker Erika find me. Startled by facial expression. Relate message. Mark flabbergasted, Erika raging that she'll beat that bitch's ass. Gather myself. More lessons from 360hiphop: Hate is the underbelly of public effort.

By July the market was only three months past its April crash. Companies like our own, often caught in the middle of raising a new round of finance, saw offers of funding vanish almost as swiftly as they'd been proffered. 360hiphop had raised money in the neighborhood of eight million dollars the past fall. A decent sum, but nothing compared to what some of our competitors had drummed up. Now, some ten months later, that sum was shrinking. Russell, Lyor, and Osman all put money in, but it was clearly a short-term strategy. Lacking Paul Allen dough, no one wanted to toss too much of their personal assets down the Internet siphon. Institutional and venture capital was scant, leaving few funding options outside of a merger. Fortunately, we were still seen as the prettiest girl on the block.

So they came a-calling, those competitors or ours: The gargantuan and well-funded Urban Box Office, or UBO; Hookt.com, a hip-hop site predicated on commerce and content; and BET.com. At this juncture the Internet bubble was imploding and our business assumptions were all tumbling down with our dwindling finances. The ad market had nose-dived, and e-commerce was already proving untenable. Content syndication likewise. It was clear that we'd have to dance with some of our competitors. Russell never understood or agreed with the very concept of Urban Box Office, a loose amalgamation of entities grouped under the rubric of "urban." We couldn't grasp the clear, definable logic that connected the dots. Hookt.com proposed a merger that stayed on the table until the last minute. The owners of *Vibe* magazine even got into the mix, offering a deal that would have put our creative apparatus atop a combined print and web product, a scaled-down version of the old *Source* idea. The *Vibe* deal was attractive to Russell for a spell, but that too evaporated. Enter BET.com

By the time Osman Eralp brought Mark and I into his confidence with regard to the possible merger, we'd already been knee-deep in trying to make the site better for over a month. We knew that much of our content offerings were weighted too heavily to the once imagined broadband nirvana; the navigation was not as intuitive as we'd thought; and our focus on spellbinding graphics made the site too heavy for lowband users. The BET.com deal put that on hold—permanently.

At first the deal seemed to make sense. They were well capitalized and purportedly had good business discipline. We were running out of money but possessed deep cultural capital, access, and creative talent. They explicitly focused on the African-American audience. We chased the multicultural audience that called hip-hop home.

But as we spent the next month in quiet diligence, with me fighting to keep the assets needed to do my job, my hackles were already starting to rise. I suspected that this deal would prolong the life of the company—and the hope of the shareholders—but it would be devastating for the people. Although coated with the gentle concern of a suitor, our new partners from the outset demonstrated a tendency to read out nuance and function with creative people, to view them as slots and board pieces to be shifted about without real thought or consideration. I fought for every soul possible, caught between the oftimes competing drives of a corporate officer concerned about the bottom line, a humanistic boss concerned about the well-being of his staff, and an editorial and creative manager concerned with having the tools to get the job done. Finally, after much debate on procedure, Eralp and I had over half the company come in one morning while the rest stayed at home. We asked for their attention. Eralp stood and simply said that for everyone here, including him, the journey had come to an end. Some faces were shocked. Most nodded in knowing acceptance. For weeks I'd tried to give enough hints to cushion the blow. Folk knew a bloodletting was coming. They just hoped that the slick blade wouldn't touch them.

I gave the new regime time. I'd promised Russell and Eralp that I would stay on at least six months to honestly evaluate the situation. But the heart went out of me that August day. The heart went out of us all. Scott Mills, head honcho at BET.com, went from understanding suitor to tyrannical boss. As for Russell, the figure that'd once inspired our energy became remote. I still spoke to him, albeit a bit less. But the staff would often bitterly joke that Russell had abandoned them to their lot. Mills shelved the plans to continue our improvement of 360hiphop and truly develop it as a multicultural counterpoint to BET.com. Budgets and priorities were realigned, and in short order the brainpower of 360hiphop found itself serving as glorified consultants, tasked to improve BET.com while 360hiphop languished in a corner.

I couldn't dictate the direction of the company to Mills, but I could leave it, and after months of reasoning and cajoling I finally did. Russell stopped me once in January of 2001. I strode into his office at Phat Farm, flopped on the couch, and told him I had to go.

"No, no, you can't do that," he replied. "The minute you leave I lose all interest in this. What do I have to do?"

"Russell, the guys that are left already feel like you've lost interest. You've got to come talk to them, and Scott has to deliver on the promises he made when we did the deal."

Russell did come by. And he gave the frank, inspired kind of talk we'd come to expect. Perhaps a bit too inspired for Scott Mills, who winced when Russell said that BET was "covered in wack juice," and that we could inject much needed flavor. But it was a holding action at best. Russell, who was no fan of Scott Mills, remained distant. Mills continued his slow dismantling of 360hiphop. Finally, when he insisted that we chop yet more people in arbitrary fashion, the time for egress had come. I wrote a polite letter. He made a polite acceptance. The two of us were clearly tired of dancing around each other by that point. Mark, who had an even more testy relationship with Mills than I did, wrote his at the same time. We looked at each other and shrugged.

"Fuck it," he said cheerfully. "Gotta have faith."

I sent Russell a message via two-way pager, just before I gave Scott my resignation.

It's time, Rush. We have to leave now.

His reply shot back mere moments later.

Love you guys. What are we gonna do next?

20

FATHERS AND DAUGHTERS

Your Daddy won't always stress a lot. I promise you that. I know I do it too much right now. Sit and let little whirls wiggle deep into the skin of my forehead. Maybe Daddy thinks too much. Worrying after wisps of thought like a hound on the scent of a far-off fox.

I don't want to be so consumed when you come into my life, and since I've only got three more months, I'd better put those wisps behind me. Daddy wants to greet you with worry stricken from his soul, with concern put in its relative place, far beneath the joy generated by the very thought of you. My baby girl.

We have not named you as yet, your mom and I. So forgive me when you read this in some not too distant future. Do not think that Daddy was impersonal or lazy for not having a name to call you when he wrote this. For now names are just joined letters scribbled on paper. They will carry no weight until I can gaze into your eyes.

You come from good folk, baby girl. Your mother, she's an angel. Though she's definitely more warrior angel with sharp sword than cherub with harp. But you make her all melty inside. All soft. You should see her sitting there, perched on a bed or chair. She glows with the light you give her. And Daddy just stares in wonder, stumbling between abject fascination and incredulous disbelief. Peering at the caramel skin of her rounded belly. Looking for some sign from you.

Mommy's roots lie in the Caribbean and the American South. Her mother's family comes from the island of St. Kitts. Her father's folk hail from Dismal Swamp, North Carolina. Uh-huh, that's the same thing I said when I heard that name. But your grandfather is a special man and there is nothing dismal about him or the incredible legacy he's built in American music. You know, the first time Daddy saw him play it completely shattered my notion of what drums could do. I remember your mother and I resting on a green lawn, blanket pulled about us. It was a chill night on the grounds of Columbia University and our eyes locked on a large stage where your grandfather and the great pianist Cecil Taylor spurred each other on in a complex, two-part conversation. Drums and piano. Max and Cecil. Higher and higher. There is history in your grandfather. Inscribed on his very skin. I am so happy that he is still here to meet you. Still here to rub that history on your forehead with gnarled hands.

You come from good folk, baby girl. Unlike Mommy, Daddy's no angel. But I try hard. Used to be so nervous, so anxious about having a child. In the past Daddy put too much emphasis on *things,* too much pressure on *things* not being in the right alignment: money, house, job. Seeking to design the perfect moment without realizing that the Universe has no need for a scriptwriter. The best things script themselves. I need glance no further than the bulge of your elbow—or is it a knee?—moving across the roof of Mommy's stomach.

Daddy's people come from Guyana. I will take you there as soon as I can. To show you the still-captivating sight of the Seawall curving up the length of Georgetown's coast, holding back the persistent tide. To have your ears discover the early morning call of the Kiss-Ka-Dee bird, the distinctive *kee, kee, kee,* that woke Daddy up on so many long-ago days. But one thing of Guyana you will not see. My granddad, Wesley Simon. I do wish you could have met him. He and Mama were the best things about early childhood in Guyana. So much of Daddy's sense of who and what a father can be flow from him. Your great-granddad was a stoic man, not given to extraneous chatter. Still, when he spoke everyone listened, for he was clearly a man in charge. Husband and father of four children; self-sufficient businessman; stalwart brother; good friend. Responsibility from all those relationships lay on him but he carried it with grace. He'd rest in his easy chair in the living room on evenings after work, the cooling sea breeze stirring smoke from his pungent cigar. Most times he'd fall asleep right there, mouth open in a low-rumbling snore. Even then he looked the picture of strength.

I'd lose him eventually. Yet I give thanks that I was able to sit by his bedside during the last week of his battle with cancer. Until speech denied him. Until his only response to my gentle "I love you" was a brief brightening of the eyes and twitch of the cheek muscles. Then one afternoon they called me home from school. I rushed upstairs to his bedroom, expectation brick-heavy in my stomach. As I came in Mama smiled bravely, sadly, and told me that he'd left. That he was out of pain now. But her pain shone through, etched deep in her face. We both miss him so.

You come from good folk, baby girl. Never mind that Daddy and Mommy belong to an oft-maligned generation. We've caught it from every angle: lazy slackers; Generation Xers gorged on entitlement and dot.com excess; hip-hoppers married to empty, material pursuit, eschewing love and commitment. Name the charge and it's probably been leveled our way. Society wraps a great presumption around Mommy and Daddy's generation, a presumption that we *won't* do it right. A presumption borne of baggage between and within generations.

Mommy and Daddy are the children of the civil rights era. Integration babies. We were born in the early seventies. The marches had been trod. The struggles had been fought. Leaders had died. Legislation had passed. We were the inheritors of the movement. But something went awry. And by the time the eighties rolled around to serve up a vicious diet of Reaganomics and crack cocaine we were struggling with the ramifications of divorcing parents, fractured political and community leadership, and social rollbacks. Any legacy that once waited seemed hazy and indistinct. When the nineties came upon us that legacy was all but gone. Vanished like the notion of a central movement to push a common agenda. Lost in the incredibly selfish ethos of boom times and economic expansion, the scramble to get mine. We muttered that our parents and their generation had abdicated mentorship, that we had, in effect, raised ourselves. So as hip-hop exploded we took refuge in this thing of ours, crouching behind its walls, speaking its coded language. From this vantage point we could seek success and definition on our own terms, thumbing our noses at our elders, driving them away with our flaunting display of all the black pathologies they once sought to overcome, or hide. Parents and children adrift around lost promise and thwarted hope.

We haven't done much better behind those walls, either. Love, for one, has been hard to come by. Gone are the days when A Tribe Called Quest put shy questions of the heart to Bonita Applebum. Now we run from encounters with vulnerability—on and off hip-hop records. Our generation inhabits a too-cold landscape, a world that runs on selfish fuel even as it touts selflessness. Often we find ourselves walking alone, or unfulfilled. We cast for meaning in a river of two-dimensional caricatures, figments from some sociologist's nightmare—player, baller, chickenhead, wifey. If such be our definitions of man and woman, it sparks little wonder that we fall victim to the cruelty of plastic identity and dashed expectations.

And responsibility, too often, has gone missing. Just the other day Daddy read an account in the *New York Post* about one of my favorite rappers from the old days, the days when Daddy was just a fan—Chris Martin, one half of the duo Kid 'N Play. According to the article, life post-rap career had been difficult for Martin, and he'd essentially had no participation, economic and otherwise, in the life of his seven-year-old son. Even with the *Post*'s gleeful tendency for hyperbole the account of Martin's arrest for unpaid child support payments struck shamefully hard. And absentee fatherhood is not the exclusive terrain of down-on-their-luck rappers. Seems like everywhere I peer—newspapers, water-cooler conversations—I discover anecdotes or statistics about some "damn man who don't take care of his kids."

But Daddy's seen so much evidence to the contrary. Enough to grow a little hope. Some of my most tender hip-hop memories come from the incongruous juxtaposition of larger-than-life characters interacting with their all too precious children. I remember a photo shoot we did at *The Source* for Father's Day and the wonderful moments captured: Havoc, one half of the hardcore duo Mobb Deep, planting a kiss on the face of his baby boy; Method Man lovingly playing with his one-year-old son; Snoop Dogg slouched deep in a chair, his kids asleep on his chest. And the evidence doesn't just come from rap stars; it comes from Daddy's friends, as well. Many of them have children of their own. All are loving, responsible parents. And they've let Daddy practice the paternal touch. The postmeal upright or over-the-shoulder burp. The walk twenty times around the room with hand supporting back, gently tapping, in order to induce sleep. The careful, serious negotiation with a two year old to explain just why no means no. Yes, Daddy owes a great deal to these aunts and uncles of yours. They have shown me that we *can* do it right. And for your sake, we must.

Baby girl, you will never draw breath in this life without the warm assurance of your father's understanding, support, and presence in your world. You are all that I am and all that I have. I love you so. And even when the inevitable comes, when I must leave you as Granddad did me, I make you this promise. Daddy will always be there for you, baby girl.

21

PROPS GIVEN

When assembling thank-yous, one inevitably runs out of space or forgets someone important, often both. Therefore I ask forgiveness, and indulgence, in advance. A book, especially a first book, is an enormous undertaking. And I owe a debt of gratitude to an immense number of people. So in the most logical manner possible . . .

To the anonymous Guyanese cook or cooks who invented the rice dish we call cook-up, a blend of disparate ingredients that make perfect sense in the final tasting, and a fitting metaphor for the inpredictable bumb, grind, and resolution of life's rhythm.

To my lifelong pals from Guyana—Don, Roger, Skeete, Tycho, Derek, Fudgie, Virgil, and Kym—you remain the foundation. To Ron, Richard, and Sean, without whom Flatbush, Brooklyn, would have been a lonely place indeed. To Shelly, Sean, Jamel, Derek, Vick, Sunny, Mike B, Bow-legs, Jah-Mike, Ahmed, Jiggy Joe, Mr. and Mrs. Bazemore, and the rest of you Freeport folk too numerous to name. To Tamu, for whom I shall always thank Miami, and Erika, the best friend a guy could have. To John, Dale, G-Battle, Norm, Kulleni, Sheila, and my entire fam from a place called Princeton, especially Mark and Alicia, you embody love and friendship. To Guy Routte—my dog, no mere words can suffice. To Tiffani, for your patience and support. To Diane, for your steady faith.

To Professors Cornell West, Wahneema Lubiano, Barbara Browning, and Andrew Ross for showing me how to think about culture. To Lisa Kennedy, who jump-started my writing career, Ann Powers, Joe Levy, Greg Tate, Peter Noel, Andy Hsiao, Bob Christgau, Eric Weisbard, and everyone from the *Village Voice* of the mid-nineties; Joe Wood, may you rest in peace. To the passionate readers of *The Source* and its capable staff through the years. Adario Strange, thanks for hookin' a brother up. Paula Renfroe and Felicia Williams, if not for your efforts, insanity would have long claimed me. Bakari Kitwana, Dimitry Léger, Smokey Fontaine, Tracii McGregor, Akiba Solomon, Nigel Killikelly, Elliot Wilson, Carlito Rodriguez, Riggs Morales, Joanne Hwang, Kim Jack-Riley, and Frank Williams, every editor should be blessed to have folk like you make him look good. Bakari, special props for sharing the voyage on that long-ago Fugees trip to Haiti from which sprang "Return of Preacher Son." Dave Mays, I still got love for ya.

To the family from 360hiphop.com, God rest its soul. Stephanie Reyes, Sheena Lester, Chris Kaye, Kris Ex (you next, cat!), Yvette Russell, Andrea Duncan, Serena Kim, Nandi Dalen, Sonya Magett, Kweli Wright, Jeff Chang, Joseph Patel, Ola Kudu, Jon Caramanica, Jungwon Kim, and everyone else. Especially to Russell Simmons, Lyor Cohen, Kevin Liles, Osman Eralp, and Leyla Turkkan.

To the old-school team from *Vibe*—we fought the good fight, didn't we?—Keith Clinkscales, Len Burnette, Danyel Smith, Alan Light, Carter Harris, Mimi Valdés,

Emil Wilbekin, Bonz Malone, Karen Good. Special big-up to Rob Kenner and Vibe/Crown Books. The essay "Sweetest Thing [Rationalization]" first appeared in their book, *Hip-Hop Divas*. To my peers on both sides of the divide in the wonderfully wacky world of hip-hop journalism: publicists Miguel Baguer, Wendy Washington, and Chris Chambers (the rest of you don't kill me); and fellow writers Michael Gonzales, Chairman Mao, and Gabe Alvarez (the rest of you don't kill me).

To the talented artists, old and new, who created this hip-hop of ours, especially Grand Master Flash, coming to your home to sit among your turntables, records, and old stories was such an honor for a young writer; Kool Herc, I know it was a pain in the ass getting me on the phone some years back but you, truly, hold all of my respect; and Wyclef Jean and Jerry Wonda, one love every time, fellas, *sac passé*.

To Joni Evans, the best literary agent in the world, and the Robins to her Batman: Jen and Andy. To Graydon Carter and the folk at *Vanity Fair*. To Tracy Sherrod for buying the bloody book and shepherding it through to the end. To everyone at Atria Books, especially Demond Jarrett. To Tiffany Ward, who remembered the hip-hop-writing kid she went to school with and brought him to the William Morris Agency, and then sustained his faith in his work whenever the candle burned low. Girl, I owe you so much.

To the Roach family—Max, Raoul, Karla, Kyle and Kadar, Daryl, Maxine, Gina, and Dara—for your love, support, and warm wlecome, and to Janus Adams and Muriel Tuitt.

To my family—Hinds, Hamit, and Simon. Since there are far too many of you to note, allow me to make do with Mom, Dad, Mama, Aunt Ena, Aunt Lela, Robin, Paula, Roger, Michelle, Diane, my brothers, and my sisters, love you all. Nolan and Jeff, I don't call so much these days, but we're still the hopeful teenage crew waiting to see *Golden Child*.

To my daughter, Maxe. The look in your eyes is all the motivation I'll ever need. And to Ayo, without whom nothing makes much sense at all.

Thank you.

Selwyn Seyfu Hinds
Brooklyn, New York

Printed in the United States
By Bookmasters